Religion in Contemporary European Cinema

The religious landscape in Europe is changing dramatically. While the authority of institutional religion has weakened, a growing number of people now desire individualized religious and spiritual experiences, finding the self-complacency of secularism unfulfilling. The "crisis of religion" is itself a form of religious life. A sense of complex, subterraneous interaction between religious, heterodox, secular and atheistic experiences has thus emerged, which makes the phenomenon all the more fascinating to study, and this is what *Religion in Contemporary European Cinema* does. The book explores the mutual influences, structural analogies and shared dilemmas, as well as the historical roots of such a "post-secular constellation" as seen through the lens of European cinema. Bringing together scholars from film theory and political science, ethics and philosophy of religion, philosophy of film and theology, this volume casts new light on the relationship between the religious and secular experience after the death of the death of God.

Costica Bradatan is Associate Professor in the Honors College at Texas Tech University, US

Camil Ungureanu is Assistant Professor of Political Philosophy at Universitat Pompeu Fabra, Spain

Routledge Studies in Religion and Film

Edited by Robert Johnston and Jolyon Mitchell

1 **World Cinema, Theology, and the Human**
   Humanity in Deep Focus
   Antonio Sison

2 **American Theology, Superhero Comics, and Cinema**
   The Marvel of Stan Lee and the Revolution of a Genre
   Anthony R. Mills

3 **Religion in Contemporary European Cinema**
   The Postsecular Constellation
   Edited by Costica Bradatan and Camil Ungureanu

Religion in Contemporary European Cinema
The Postsecular Constellation

**Edited by Costica Bradatan
and Camil Ungureanu**

NEW YORK AND LONDON

First published 2014
by Routledge
711 Third Avenue, New York, NY 10017, USA

and by Routledge
2 Park Square, Milton Park, Abingdon, Oxfordshire OX14 4RN

First issued in paperback 2017

Routledge is an imprint of the Taylor & Francis Group, an informa business

© 2014 Taylor & Francis

The right of the editors to be identified as the authors of the editorial material, and of the authors for their individual chapters, has been asserted in accordance with sections 77 and 78 of the Copyright, Designs and Patents Act 1988.

All rights reserved. No part of this book may be reprinted or reproduced or utilized in any form or by any electronic, mechanical, or other means, now known or hereafter invented, including photocopying and recording, or in any information storage or retrieval system, without permission in writing from the publishers.

Trademark Notice: Product or corporate names may be trademarks or registered trademarks, and are used only for identification and explanation without intent to infringe.

Library of Congress Cataloging-in-Publication Data

Religion in contemporary European cinema : the postsecular constellation / edited by Costica Bradatan ; Camil Ungureanu.
   pages cm.—(Routledge studies in religion and film ; 3)
Includes bibliographical references and index.
1. Religion in motion pictures. 2. Motion pictures—Religious aspects.
3. Motion pictures—Europe—History and criticism. I. Bradatan, Costica, editor of compilation. II. Ungureanu, Camil, editor of compilation.
  PN1995.9.R4R3975 2014
  791.43'682—dc23
  2013040161

ISBN 13: 978-1-138-06308-2 (pbk)
ISBN 13: 978-0-415-73376-2 (hbk)

Typeset in Sabon
by Apex CoVantage, LLC

Contents

Introduction: Dealing (Visibly) in "Things Not Seen"   1
COSTICA BRADATAN

1 Deconstructing Christianity in Contemporary European Cinema: Nanni Moretti's *Habemus Papam* and Jean-Luc Nancy's *Dis-Enclosure*   11
CATHERINE WHEATLEY

2 "Casting Fire Onto the Earth": The Holy Fool in Russian Cinema   27
ALINA BIRZACHE

3 The New Aesthetics of Muslim Spirituality in Turkey: *Yusuf's Trilogy* by Semih Kaplanoğlu   44
ASUMAN SUNER

4 Pasolini: Religion and Sacrifice   61
GEOFFREY NOWELL-SMITH

5 Entangled in God's Story. A Reading of Krzysztof Kieślowski's *Blind Chance*   74
COSTICA BRADATAN

6 The Evidence of Things Not Seen: Sound and the Neighbor in Kieślowski, Haneke, Martel   91
PAUL COATES

7 Bruno Dumont's Cinema: Nihilism and the Disintegration of the Christian Imaginary   110
JOHN CARUANA

8 Religion Against Religion in Lars von Trier   126
CAMIL UNGUREANU

9 The Banalities of Evil: Polanski, Kubrick, and
   the Reinvention of Horror   145
   NATHAN ABRAMS

10 Postsecular Ethics: The Case of Iñárritu's *Biutiful*   166
   ROBERT SINNERBRINK

11 Understanding Religion and Film in "Postsecular" Russia   186
   JOLYON MITCHELL

   Final Remarks: What Is the Use of Postsecularism?
   Conceptual Clarifications and Two Illustrations   199
   CAMIL UNGUREANU

   List of Contributors   219
   Index   223

Introduction
Dealing (Visibly) in "Things Not Seen"[1]

Costica Bradatan

"Regardless of my own beliefs and my own doubts, which are unimportant in this connection, it is my opinion that art lost its basic creative drive the moment it was separated from worship. It severed an umbilical cord and now lives its own sterile life, generating and degenerating itself. In former days the artist remained unknown and his work was to the glory of God. He lived and died without being more or less important than other artisans; "eternal values," "immortality," and "masterpiece" were terms not applicable to his case. The ability to create was a gift. In such a world flourished invulnerable assurance and natural humility.... if I am asked what I would like the general purpose of my films to be, I would reply that I want to be one of the artists in the cathedral on the great plain. I want to make a dragon's head, an angel, a devil—or perhaps a saint—out of stone. It does not matter which; it is the sense of satisfaction that counts. Regardless of whether I believe or not, whether I am a Christian or not, I would play my part in the collective building of the cathedral."

(Ingmar Bergman)[2]

MATTERS OF FAITH

When *La Vie et La Passion du Christ* (Pathé, Dir. Lucien Nonguet and Ferdinand Zecca, 1903) was about to be shown in Russia, the Orthodox Church's Holy Synod objected to the screening. This was no small matter; the Russian Church's power and influence in society at the time could hardly be overestimated. A censored version of the film was eventually allowed, but police were present at the screening to make sure that those in attendance took off their hats as a sign of reverence.[3] This is a highly revealing gesture. For in their muddled way, the officials of the Russian Orthodox Church admitted that the new art form could perform a certain liturgical function. By asking viewers to take off their hats during the screening, which was exactly what people were supposed to be doing in a church during service, they granted film the religious status that arts such as painting, sculpture or music had enjoyed for millennia. Barely in existence as an art form, film was already seen as something that could be used for praising God's glory. On the other hand, from a more pragmatic standpoint, cinema could not afford not to access the enormous repertoire of myths, archetypes and symbols that came with religion; they were excellent, time-tested story-telling devices and sophisticated narrative-generating machines.

Thus, from its inception, film became intrinsically linked to the sacred. In an article published in 1951, André Bazin could say that cinema "has always been interested in God" and that the *"The Gospel* and *The Acts of the Apostles* were the first best-sellers on the screen." He refers, for example, to *Quo Vadis?* (1951; dir. Mervyn LeRoy) as an "immense catechism-in-pictures."[4] Out of a superior impulse to celebrate God in moving images or out of a more pragmatic need to appeal to large audiences, cinema emerges as an art form that engages with the sacred in complex, subtle and multifarious ways. Indeed, it is not at all surprising that such an academic subfield as "film and religion" came into existence; what is surprising is that it took it so long to happen (during the last few decades of the twentieth century).

Yet the relationship between cinema and religion is not only of a "representational" nature in the sense that film functions as a vehicle for religious topics, notions or symbols; film—in particular, of the "art house" variety— does more than "illustrate" religion in some outward, mechanical fashion. Film and religion share a set of more fundamental, ontological suppositions. For what after all makes film possible, what turns some lump of matter—the reel of celluloid—into a unique event in the life of the mind is, ultimately, an *act of faith*. To bridge the gap between the little we actually see on screen and what it stands for—the whole world that's not seen but is there somewhere— faith is needed. And I mean "faith" here not in some narrow, confessional sense but as an elementary act of the human subject that engages in a process of self-overcoming. Phenomenologically, it is only through such an act that you can transcend the sheer succession of frames you see on screen and inhabit the complex universe that it opens up. The process is echoed in the Paulinian definition of faith: Saint Paul speaks of faith as "the substance of things hoped for, the evidence of things not seen." (Heb.11:1)

The language of faith has pervaded film scholarship for quite a while. In *Qu'est-ce que le cinéma? (What is Cinema?)* (1958–1962), André Bazin frequently brings up the issue of "faith" (*croyance*); at some point he talks, for example, of a *pacte de croyance* between the film and the viewer.[5] On the other hand, a good part of the early academic writing on film, following Christian Metz, engages with another facet of faith—namely, faith redefined psychoanalytically as credulity before the image. Filmmakers haven't been shy about venturing themselves into this territory. An otherwise materialist film director and theorist, Serguei Eisenstein goes as far as to work with what seems to be a conception of filmmaking as dealing in "things not seen." For central to the montage theory is the notion that out of the juxtaposition of two shots a third element is produced, which is by definition some "thing not seen." Even though this is something unseen, Eisenstein's whole theory is based on a belief in its existence. Ingmar Bergman, to give another example, openly admits that filmmaking has something important to do with magic. The director is nothing but a sophisticated, technologically savvy magician: "since cinematography is based on deception of the human eye, I really am a conjurer," says he.[6] In a mode of disarming sincerity, Bergman even describes the mechanics of the deceiving process: "I have worked it out that if I see a film with a running-time of one hour, I sit through twenty-seven minutes of complete darkness—the blankness between frames."[7] Like in other forms of magic (politics, for example), the raw material with which the filmmaker works is nothing other than our "incredible need to believe," as Kristeva would put it. That the trick works does not have much to do with the trick itself but with *us:*

> When I show a film, I am guilty of deceit. I use an apparatus which is constructed to take advantage of a certain human weakness, an apparatus with which I can sway my audience in a highly emotional manner—make them laugh, scream with fright, smile, believe in fairy stories, become indignant, feel shocked, charmed, deeply moved.[8]

Once in the movie theater, as the screen lights up, the viewer entertains the hope of a transportation of sorts, of becoming part of another world, if only for a brief period. At the same time, however, you cannot in an important sense know what you will encounter when you cross the threshold. To deal in "things not seen" is to take risks, to be ready for leaps into the abyss; movies are usually presented in the dark, which only accentuates this sense of danger. And it is precisely here that a fissure in the fabric of your existence opens up; having left behind your ordinary existence you now enter a space of self-creation and re-invention. This is why to deal in "things not seen" is also to give yourself a chance of renewal. There is a strong sense of "conversion" in the encounter with a great art film; you come out a *different person*. In *The Faith of the Faithless* (2012), Simon Critchley describes "the true nature of faith," which is the "rigorous activity of the subject that proclaims itself into being at each instant without guarantees or security."[9] To the extent that film relies on faith for the actualization of the new world it promises to bring about, this is what happens to the film viewer as well: by leaping into the abyss, she creates herself and the world anew.

At this juncture, S. Brent Plate's considerations on the structural analogy between cinema and religion in *Religion and Film* (2008) are worth recalling. In this book Plate, undertaking a comparative analysis of film and religion, is struck by a strong sense of parallelism: the "altar and the screen are . . . structured and function in comparable fashion."[10] The inside of a temple and that of a movie theater are organized along analogous lines, just as much of what takes place in there is similar. This is because, and here's Plate's finding, at the heart of both religion and film there lies one and the same "cosmopoietic" program: "filmmaking and religion-making are bound under the general guise of *worldmaking.*"[11] The filmmaker, just like the mythmaker, *creates worlds;* out of the boundless multiplicity of the real, via a process of exclusion, selection and framing, she brings new worlds into existence. The language that Plate employs when talking about the parallel between religion and film is revealing:

They both function by recreating the known world and then presenting that alternative version of the world to their viewers/worshippers. Religions and films each create alternative worlds utilizing the raw materials of space and time and elements, bending each of them in new ways and forcing them to fit particular standards and desires. Film does this through camera angles and movements, framing devices, lightning, costume, acting, editing and other aspects of production.[12]

The traffic not only of content, but also of practices and work habits, of stylistic options and rhetorical protocols between religion and film makes the study of their interaction a fascinating scholarly enterprise. Religious scholars have important things to learn from film scholars and the other way around: "by paying attention to the ways films are constructed, we can shed light on the ways religions are constructed and vice versa."[13] Plate does not seem to pay sufficient attention to the element of *faith* that worldmaking both in religion and film presupposes, but his thesis is compelling and his analysis fascinating.

A FILMMAKER'S RELIGION

Ingmar Bergman's reflections that I used as an epigraph for this Introduction are taken from a short text, "Why I Make Movies," an artistic *credo* of sorts, which he issued separately but also as an introduction to the published version of *The Seventh Seal* script. Bergman's reflections are important for several reasons.

First of all, what is striking here is Bergman's call for grounding art (including his own) into *something else*: something deeper, grander, more ancient; to be relevant, art has to be part of a larger human project. If he is to produce something of any worth, it is crucial for the artist to transcend himself and leave behind his limited, all-too-human subjectivity—the accidents of his biography, his inherent egoism, the eccentricities to which he may have fallen prey. The filmmaker may be a worldmaker, but if she doesn't connect her work to a larger worldmaking project, the worlds she creates remain uninhabitable and her efforts are in vain. Art may be something great, yet it is equally something mysterious, fragile and precarious; when it does emerge, a work of art is due to more complex factors than the poor self of the artist, who is nothing more than a vehicle or a tool. A distinct sense of humility pervades Bergman's piece, which is utterly consistent with his view of himself as an artist; he liked to see himself as nothing more than a craftsman, a maker of objects, which people may find useful for a while and then possibly throw away.

Second, coming from the notorious religion-basher that Bergman was, the text reveals an unusually complex religiosity.[14] Bergman's is a paradoxical, agonistic faith; for him, even though God may not exist, worshipping and conceptualizing him has cast a long, positive shadow on the history of humankind. God may be dead now, but he lived long enough among humans to cause in them an important revelation: that of their own "holiness." Says Bergman elsewhere:

My feeling that God does not exist is not a terrifying feeling. It is a feeling of security. This is the earth, we are here, and the holiness that exists—because it does exist—is inside us. It is a creation of generations and generations of hope, fear, desire, creative minds, prayers—that still exists, in me, and I am happy to have it in me.[15]

An absent God shapes our history and our minds just as effectively as an overwhelmingly present one would do.

Thirdly, Bergman's text is delightfully sly and misleading. He seeks to reconnect art to its multi-millennial liturgical function, but he knew it only too well: as far as cinema was concerned, filmmakers could not be part of any cathedral building project; they simply came too late for that. As an art form, in the West at least, film was born about the same time when God was dying; film and religion should have no business together. And yet, Bergman's language is emphatically religious; this cannot be an accident—he is too good a writer for that. It is as though through such language he relates filmmaking (his own and others') to a post-theological paradigm where the artist keeps participating in the erection of the cathedral (granted, the most absurd of cathedrals), and art sings praise to a God that doesn't exist anymore. In an important sense, then, if we read him between the lines, for Bergman film is an art form that does not deal so much with God as with the aftermath of God's death, which makes it all the more fascinating.

WHERE WE STAND

In his book *Cinema, Religion and the Romantic Legacy* (2003), Paul Coates does not use the "death of God" terminology openly, yet he works with a distinction between religion and spirituality that could, implicitly, accommodate Nietzsche's insight as a distinct form of "spirituality." Religion is institutionalized, collective, "official," whereas spirituality is individual, personal, "existential" even.[16] One always needs the other—a good balance between them is crucial;[17] yet in history it often happens that we have too much religion and not enough spirituality, or the other way around. Interesting as it may be, a detailed discussion of Coates' thesis cannot be done here; however, his conception of cinema in terms of this distinction is worth dwelling on. For Coates defines cinema "as a post-Romantic form for which religion and spirituality can be unified only problematically,"[18] which, to me, is another way of saying that, philosophically, cinema as an art form works at its best when it engages a *crisis of religion* rather than religion itself. This is precisely one of the meanings of Bergman's text as I tried to decipher it in the previous section.

This is also what circumscribes thematically the present volume. A religion in crisis (which is something more complex than just secularization, agnosticism or atheism) is today more prevalent in Europe than anywhere else; thus, focusing this volume on contemporary European cinema is an obvious choice. The conventionally *religious*, "catechism-in-images" type of film that Bazin talked about had its heyday and is still relevant. Yet there is here a sense of philosophical and even theological shallowness which critics have pointed out when talking about such films. Paul Coates relates the genre (if it is indeed a genre) to large-scale film industries (mainly Hollywood) that, having to rely on sales, cannot be but "fearful to give offense."[19] We touch on, if only minimally, this type of filmmaking in our volume. More independent cinema would typically approach religious topics from *secular* positions, often in provocative, heretical or openly atheistic fashions. Such productions, philosophically and theologically complex, do not ordinarily come from Hollywood. As David Jasper expressively puts it, theology, "whether within the Judeo-Christian tradition or otherwise, emerges from more problematic and disturbing material than Hollywood dare show."[20] Our volume pays significant attention to such a type of cinema—from Serguei Eisenstein to Lars von Trier. This is an ongoing process; in Paul Coates' terminology, the "crumbling of a larger, institutionalized 'religion' into a mass of small spiritualities is still underway, and jerks forward strongly at such significant moments as World War II or the 1960s."[21] Finally, as a third dialectical movement, a significant number of recent filmmakers seem to display a certain degree of frustration with the typically secular—agnostic or atheistic—approach. Instead, they appear eager to grant the religious a new, enhanced role—a new chance, if you will. Their productions are symptomatic of a *postsecular* world where strict secularism, plain rejection of religion and traditional atheism are deemed intellectually insufficient and seen as offering existentially poor options. It is especially in this third area that the present volume seeks to make a contribution.

At the core of this project there lies the notion that religion cannot be simply dismissed from our lives as a useless remnant from the past. Often in disguised forms, the religious always returns; it keeps shaping our lives, informing our imaginary and dominating our thinking. Churches may have emptied in many parts of Europe, but religion seems to have found other, subtler outlets; behind the façade of a secularized world, a wide range of "spiritual experiences" gives people a new sense of belonging to a grander, cosmic order, as well as of personal fulfillment. Various forms of philanthropy, yoga, transhumanism and even vegetarianism or environmentalism could be considered such spiritual experiences. Religious notions or imagery still pervade our intellectual conversations; they shape the philosophical discourses (the theistic as well as the atheistic ones) and sometimes even the scientific debates (many an atheist physicist has been on a quest for "God's particle" for several decades now). Matters of life and death are commonly tackled, even by agnostics, with reference to theology and spirituality. Modern politics is saturated with religion to such an extent that a philosopher could recently suggest that "the history of political forms can best be viewed as a series of *metamorphoses of sacralization.*"[22] We make wars and call them "crusades" and then we seek peace in the name of religion.

Filmmakers, as artists often do, have long sensed the importance of this postsecular constellation. They have given it artistic expression in their works

Introduction 7

and made it part of their "cosmopoietic" projects, but a comprehensive and nuanced conceptual articulation of this new cinematic trend is yet to come. Hence this book; our project has been born precisely out of a need to facilitate and disseminate such an understanding. At its core this is a philosophical project, but to make it intellectually more relevant and ecumenical, we have invited contributors from several humanistic fields, which makes it a profoundly interdisciplinary enterprise: contributions come not only from philosophers but also film scholars, political scientists and religious scholars.

THE BOOK'S STRUCTURE

The volume is not organized chronologically, nor does it generate a systematic and exhaustive taxonomy of all the possible ways in which cinema interacts with religion in contemporary Europe; it rather presents a number of case studies, of particularly relevant "knots," where authors delve into instantiations of this relationship and specific configurations of the religious/secular/postsecular triad. The first such "knot" is Nanni Moretti's *Habemus Papam* (2011), which Catherine Wheatley reads through the interpretative lens provided by Jean-Luc Nancy's book *Dis-Enclosure* (2007). Such a pairing offers the author the opportunity to cast a fresh light on "the place of Christianity within contemporary European society." While the first chapter revolves around the Pope, the central figure in Catholicism, the second brings into focus the Eastern Orthodox version of Christianity; in it Alina Birzache traces the presence of the "holy fool" figure in Russian cinema, paying close attention to the films of Sergei Eisenstein, Andrei Tarkovsky and Pavel Lungin. A seemingly humble figure, the "holy fool" performs, in Birzache's reading, a number of important cultural, political and social functions; moreover, it comes to reveal something fundamental about the Eastern-Christian type of religiosity. The third chapter proposes yet another shift, this time from Christianity to Islam; here Asuman Suner discusses Semih Kaplanoğlu's films *Egg* (2007), *Milk* (2008) and *Honey* (2010), also known as *Yusuf's Trilogy*. Suner's chief claim is that through this trilogy Kaplanoğlu articulates a "new aesthetic form," which she relates specifically to Muslim spirituality in Turkey. This chapter, by bringing in Turkey and Islam, is also the first in the book to challenge the more conventional definition of what "Europe" is.

The next chapter marks the transition towards a class of directors who display a more "problematic" relationship to faith. One such director was certainly Pier Paolo Pasolini; while not a Catholic, Pasolini made what is considered one of the most important religious films of the twentieth century, *The Gospel According to Matthew* (1964). In his chapter, Geoffrey Nowell-Smith advances the argument that central to Pasolini's understanding of the sacred is the concept of sacrifice, which he illustrated not only through his cinematic and literary work but also biographically, through his life and especially his gruesome death. Krzysztof Kieślowski was another director with an uneasy relationship to Catholicism; a self-declared agnostic in matters religious, he made films of a distinctly "transcendent style." Thus, in Chapter Five Costica Bradatan offers a reading of Kieślowski's *Blind Chance* (1981) that revolves around a theology of God's absence, which the director seems to articulate in this film. The next chapter, contributed by Paul Coates, builds on another kind of meaningful absence: that of the "neighbor," who we can't see, but we can hear. An important "knot" within the book's economy, Coates' chapter deals with the experience of the audible in a number of films by Krzysztof Kieślowski, Michael Haneke and Lucretia Martel. By bringing in a non-European (Martel), the book yet again challenges a too-strict definition of "Europeanness."

With Chapter Seven, the volume shifts toward a new category of directors: filmmakers who, even though openly atheist, create works with a distinct religious problematique. One such director, a veritable "unorthodox atheist," is Bruno Dumont. In his chapter, John Caruana discusses Dumont's paradoxical religiosity through Julia Kristeva's notion of the "incredible need to believe," which structures human subjectivity. In the next chapter, Camil Ungureanu traces in the work of Lars von Trier, primarily *Breaking the Waves* (1996) and *Antichrist* (2009), a profoundly ambiguous attitude toward religion: at once appreciation and protest ("religion against religion").

A rather distinct type of relation to religion is revealed in those works where the religious does not show up as such but under the guise of the ethical. Two "knots" in the volume are meant to illustrate this. The first one, Chapter Nine, is contributed by Nathan Abrams, who focuses on Stanley Kubrick's *The Shining* (1980) and Roman Polanski's *Rosemary's Baby* (1968) to show how two secular, areligious Jewish directors deal with the nature of evil in a post-Holocaust world. The evil that such films depict is not relatable to God or the Devil, but it is performed, and has to be resolved, on a strictly secular plane. Abrams' chapter, dealing with an American director who made most of his films in Europe and a European director who made some of his in the US, deliberately challenges a narrow definition of "Europeanness." And so does Robert Sinnerbrink's chapter, which offers a discussion of *Biutiful* (2010) by Mexican director Alejandro Iñárittu—a film made in Europe, about Europe, and engaging a European philosophical problematique. Even though the film has a certain "transcendent" (religious) dimension, Sinnerbrink chooses to consider it primarily from the angle of "post-secular-ethics" that it illustrates. To make it part of a larger European conversation, he also compares and contrasts *Biutiful* to the Dardenne brothers' film *La promesse* (1996).

In the last chapter of this volume, Jolyon Mitchell covers the complex ways in which cinema in the Tsarist Empire, then in the Soviet Union and finally in the post-Soviet Russia, has approached religion. Dealing synthetically with the history of the film–religion relationship in the case of a significant "national cinema," this chapter in a way touches on many of the issues discussed in the previous ones. This is why, in a sense, thematically the chapter offers the volume a sense of "rounding-off." Conceptually, however, the book has its closing in Camil Ungureanu's "Final Remarks." Here a conceptual framework, centered on the notion of "postsecularism," is proposed. These theoretical remarks are meant to provide a reading tool for many of the films discussed in this book, and others still.

ACKNOWLEDGMENTS

At the origin of this project there was an international conference, "Dilemmas of Religion and Secularity in Contemporary European Cinema," organized by Camil Ungureanu and Costica Bradatan at the Universitat Pompeu Fabra in Barcelona in October 2011. Some of the chapters in this volume were initially presented at the conference, while others were invited later. The conference was funded by Universitat Pompeu Fabra (Spain) in collaboration with Texas Tech University (USA). The editors are grateful for the financial support they received from the two institutions for the organization of the conference.

NOTES

1. I am grateful to Robert Sinnerbrink, Paul Coates, Jolyon Mitchell and John Caruana for their feedback on an earlier version of this text.
2. Ingmar Bergman, "Why I Make Movies," *Horizon* 3:1 (September 1960), 8–9.
3. Jolyon Mitchell mentions the story in his chapter in this volume.
4. André Bazin, "Cinema and Theology: The Case of *Heaven Over the Marshes*." Translated by Bert Cardullo, in *Journal of Religion and Film*, 6: 2 (October 2002).
5. André Bazin, *Qu'est-ce que le cinéma?* (Paris: Cerf, 1975), 372.
6. Ingmar Bergman, "Why I Make Movies," 5.
7. Ibid.
8. Ibid.
9. Simon Critchley, *The Faith of the Faithless. Experiments in Political Theology* (London: Verso, 2012), 18.
10. S. Brent Plate, *Religion and Film. Cinema and the Re-creation of the World* (London: Wallflower 2008), vii.
11. Ibid., vii–viii
12. Ibid., 2–3.
13. Ibid., 3.
14. In his biography, Peter Cowie has insightful observations about Bergman's relation to religion. Cowie notices, for example, that "[o]rthodox religion runs in Bergman's blood. He often signs his scripts with the initials S.D.G. ('Soli Deo Gloria"—'To God alone the Glory') as J.S. Bach did at the end of every composition. He is fond of quoting Eugene O'Neill's dictum that all dramatic art is worthless unless it deals with man's relationship to God." (See Peter Cowie, *Ingmar Bergman. A Critical Biography* [New York: Charles Scribner's Sons, 1982], 137).
15. Quoted in Irving Singer, *Ingmar Bergman, Cinematic Philosopher. Reflections on His Creativity* (Cambridge, MA: The MIT Press, 2007), 117–18.
16. Paul Coates, *Cinema, Religion and the Romantic Legacy* (Aldershot: Ashgate, 2003), 4.
17. Coates writes, "just as a religion devoid of spirituality concludes in the empty communal ritual that repels individuals, so a spirituality lacking the checks and balances of religion can conclude in horror, the unaided individual's plunge into a vacuum." (Ibid., 3)
18. Ibid., 3–4.
19. Ibid., 8.

20. David Jasper, "On Systematizing the Unsystematic: A Response," in *Explorations in Theology and Film: Movies and Meaning*, eds. Clive Marsh and Gaye Ortiz (Oxford: Blackwell, 1997), 244.
21. Ibid., 4.
22. Simon Critchley, *The Faith of the Faithless*, 10.

FURTHER READINGS

The academic study of "film and religion" has flourished over the last two decades or so. The countless books that come out every year, the book series, online portals, journals, special issues and conferences dedicated to the interaction of cinema–religion are all signs that this is now an "established" field. Here are some sample book titles, out of a much longer list:

Blizek, William, L. *The Bloomsbury Companion to Religion and Film*, London: Bloomsbury Academic, 2013.
Coates, Paul *Cinema, Religion and the Romantic Legacy*. Aldershot: Ashgate, 2003.
Deacy, Christopher. *Screen Christologies: Redemption and the Meaning of Film*. Cardif: University of Wales Press, 2002.
Deacy, Christopher, and Gaye Williams Ortiz. *Theology and Film: Challenging the Sacred/Secular Divide*. Malden, MA: Blackwell, 2008.
Flesher, Paul V. M. and Robert Torry. *Film and Religion: An Introduction*. Nashville, TN: Abingdon Press, 2007.
Hamner, Gail. *Imaging Religion in Film: The Politics of Nostalgia*. New York: Palgrave Macmillan, 2011.
Johnston, Robert, K. *Reel Spirituality: Theology and Film in Dialogue*. Grand Rapids, MI: Baker Academic, 2006.
———. *Reframing Theology and Film: New Focus for an Emerging Discipline*. Grand Rapids, MI: Baker Academic, 2007.
Lyden, John C. *Film as Religion: Myths, Morals and Rituals*, New York: New York University Press, 2003.
———. *The Routledge Companion to Religion and Film*, London: Routledge, 2009.
Marsh, Clive. *Theology Goes to the Movies: An Introduction to Critical Christian Thinking*. New York: Routledge, 2007.
Marsh, Clive, and Gaye Ortiz (eds.). *Explorations in Theology and Film: Movies and Meaning*. Oxford: Blackwell, 1997.
Martin, Joel, and Conrad E. Ostwalt (eds.). *Screening the Sacred: Religion, Myth, and Ideology in Popular American Film*. Boulder, Co: Westview Press, 1995.
Mazur, Erich Michael. *Enciclopedia of Religion and Film*. Santa Barbara, CA: ABC-CLIO, 2011.
Miles, Margaret R., *Seeing and Believing: Religion and Values in the Movies*, Boston: Beacon Press, 1997.
Mitchell, Jolyon, and S. Brent Plate. *The Religion and Film Reader*. London and New York, Routledge, 2007.
Pak-Shiraz, Nacim. *Shi'i Islam in Iranian Cinema: Religion and Spirituality in Film*. London: IB Tauris, 2011.
Plate, S. Brent. *Religion and Film: Cinema and the Re-Creation of the World*. London: Wallflower Press, 2009.
Wright, Melanie. *Religion and Film: An Introduction*. London: IB Tauris, 2006.

1 Deconstructing Christianity in Contemporary European Cinema
Nanni Moretti's *Habemus Papam* and Jean-Luc Nancy's *Dis-Enclosure*

Catherine Wheatley

INTRODUCTION

In his seminal article "Cinema and Theology," André Bazin offers a rather damning account of a category of films that he labels "the priest's or nun's story."[1] Comparing the European iterations of this type (*Angels of the Streets*, 1943; *Diary of a Country Priest*, 1951—both dir. Robert Bresson) with some North American equivalents (*The Bells of St. Mary's*, 1945, dir. Leo McCarey; *Angels with Dirty Faces*, 1938, dir. Michael Curtiz), Bazin argues that the former offers a far "greater sophistication in the treatment of religious themes"[2] but that, nonetheless, these films rest "on a glamorous myth, which is to say an extrinsic one for the most part"—that is, "the mystery of priesthood."

For Bazin, these films disappoint because they focus on protagonists "whose glamor in the eyes of the public derives precisely from their *difference* from common mortals."[3] He contrasts them with another category of films in which religious sense lies not in the expression of *a priori* ideas ("not even the idea of God") but in the implication of *faith* in God. Such films take a cinematic approach to the sacred that discloses not its surface appearance but its inner strivings. Although Bazin only makes passing reference to him in this particular article, the quintessential filmmaker within this category is French director Robert Bresson. While several of Bresson's films make explicit or implicit reference to Christianity, it is not through the films' narratives alone that Christian faith is evoked, but rather through their austere style—referred to by Paul Schrader as "the transcendental style" and itself inspired by the Protestant filmmaking of Danish director Carl Theodor Dreyer. These are not films about Christianity, but *Christian films.*

Bazin's article was written in 1951. For a long while after it was published, the first kind of films he describes mostly disappeared from view.[4] Nanni Moretti's *Habemus Papam* (2011) is, however, part of a new wave of European films which features priests, monks and nuns as their protagonists. We might think here, for example, of *Hadewijch* (2009, dir. Bruno Dumont); *Into Great Silence* (2006, dir. Philip Gröning); *The Island* (2006, dir. Pavel Lungin); *Of Gods and Men* (2010, dir. Xavier Beauvois) and

Beyond the Hills (2012, dir. Cristian Mungiu). The theologically inclined critics Brett Bowles, Bert Cardullo and David Sterritt are amongst several scholars who read these films as not only variants on the "priest's story" but as continuations of Bresson's approach: as *Christian films*.[5] Sterritt and Mikita Brottman, for example, place Dumont in a line of descent which begins with the theologian Blaise Pascal and passes through Robert Bresson, arguing that the filmmaker's work is concerned with relationships between "reason, emotion and divine" and aims to "instill religion into our minds with reasoned arguments and into our hearts with grace."

In seeking to situate these films within a vertical history of Christianity and film, these readings fail, however, to take into account the horizontal context—socio-historical and cinematic—against which these films are being made. In today's pluralistic Europe, Christianity is no longer the de facto religion but is one of many choices available to us. Institutionally, today both Catholic and Protestant churches (in addition to other faiths) must operate as voluntary associations. That is, religious institutions must now recognize the right of other competing institutions, including those of Islam, to exist. The loss of taken-for-granted status in the consciousness of individuals means they are forced to make choices—that is, to exercise their "religious preference." As the sociologist Peter Berger underlines, "on the level of consciousness, this means that religion [. . .] becomes the object of reflection and decision."[6]

The depictions of the clergy, saints and martyrs within these films are likewise objects of contemplation rather than judgment. And as such they resist easy interpretation.[7] Even the most apparently pro-Christian of the films listed above, *Of Gods and Men*, offers a decidedly complex and ambivalent portrait of the religion and what it is to have faith. Certain amongst them may be concerned with Christianity, but to read these works—including those of Dumont—as "Christian films" would be reductive at best, and at worst, straight-forwardly wrong. Just so, we should also be careful not to read these films as standing in a tradition of Christian satire or critique.[8]

This chapter uses *Habemus Papam* (2011) as an indicative example of the ambiguity inherent to contemporary variants on the "priest's story," offering a close reading of the film in relation to Jean-Luc Nancy's 2007 work *Dis-Enclosure*.[9] In this work, Nancy turns his attention to what he terms "the unthought remainder" of Christianity, proposing that this remainder structures the secular, humanist and atheist traditions of modern culture, and that an interrogation of it may well help us to clarify the modernity's complexities and ambiguities. Equally important for my purposes, it will help us to understand the persistence of religion in our postsecular era, and in particular its challenging and often painful presence within the sociopolitical scene—and screen—of the twenty-first century.

In what follows, I hope to make a case for understanding this renewed cinematic interest in such "privileged" figures not as a return or revisiting of religion but rather as part of a broader concern with what remains of

Christianity in contemporary Europe. The essay aims to open up an alternative reading of the "religious film," one which shifts the agenda from the ways in which the film imparts a personal dimension (satirical or sincere) to privileged figures, raising questions of subjectivity and humanism, to a discussion of what such films suggest about the place of Christianity within contemporary European society. Motivated by a desire to excavate the remains Christianity without imposing interpretation upon them, Nancy's deconstruction—or dis-enclosure (*déclosion*), to borrow his term—of Christianity offers a useful model for this endeavor. I shall therefore first attend to the prospect of Christianity's deconstruction as it is developed by Nancy across his body of work and most fully developed in *Dis-Enclosure* before mapping it onto *Habemus Papam*. Through close analysis, I shall demonstrate how the film traces the relationship between Christianity and modernity in complex, often contradictory, ways. As a cultural product inflected by Christianity, and as a commentary on that same culture and faith, *Habemus Papam*, I argue, *turns around* the subject without coming to rest at a particular viewpoint and therefore resists seeing Christianity from a particular perspective. As such, its engagement with Christianity can be characterized in terms of opening (dis-enclosure) as opposed to more closed interpretative strategies (closure).

JEAN-LUC NANCY: THE DECONSTRUCTION OF CHRISTIANITY

Jean-Luc Nancy's engagement with Christianity begins with the essay "Of Divine Places," which is featured in his 1983 *The Inoperative Community* and is sustained in passing glances and longer treatments throughout his subsequent oeuvre, receiving increasing emphasis in later years.[10] His concerns find their fullest form in *Dis-Enclosure: The Deconstruction of Christianity* (2007), a collection of essays "that turn around" the object of Christianity, offering an extended attempt at elaborating what an engagement with Christianity might entail for Nancy. We learn here that it is not a question of reviving religion, "not even the one that Kant wanted to hold 'within the limits of reason alone'."[11] Nor is it a matter of taking an adversarial stance towards Christianity—not because it is beyond criticism but because we must acknowledge the degree to which Christianity has determined and continues to determine the philosophical and societal traditions in which we, as inhabitants of the Western world, live and work. As Nancy explains in *The Sense of the World*, the deconstruction of Christianity signifies "something other than a critique or a demolition: the bringing to light of that which will have been the agent of Christianity as the very form of the West, much more deeply than all religion and even as the self-deconstruction of religion."[12]

The transcript of a 1995 lecture, "The Deconstruction of Christianity," lays the groundwork for this project of deconstruction. Quoting the Italian philosopher Luigi Pareyson, Nancy first lays out a first principle according to which: "Only a Christianity that contemplates the present possibility of its negation can be contemporary."[13] Inverting it, he comes to a second principle, more important for his purposes: "Only an atheism that contemplates the reality of its Christian provenance can be contemporary."[14] Following these two complementary principles, he then lists three more pertaining to Christianity as we find it in Europe today:

"Christianity is inseparable from the West."

"All of Western thought is Christian through and through."

"To deconstruct Christianity is to accompany the West up to the void that is the limit and possibility of sense."[15]

These claims seem somewhat hyperbolic, to say the least, but what Nancy is gesturing at through them is the proposition that if we are living in a secular Europe, it is nonetheless a *Christian secular* Europe. One need only look to our public holidays (Easter, Christmas) for example to recognize that Christianity has been, and continues to be, the privileged faith in Western society and culture. As Richard Dyer puts it in his seminal study *White*:

> The European feeling for self and the world has been shaped by Christianity [. . .] If Christianity as observance and belief has been in decline over the past half-century, its ways of thinking and feeling are none the less still constitutive of both European culture and consciousness and the colonies and ex-colonies (notably the USA) that it has spawned. Many of the fundamentals of all levels of Western culture—the forms of parenting, especially motherhood, and sex, the value of suffering, guilt, the shock of post-enlightenment materialism—come to us from Christianity, whether or not we know the Bible story or recognize the specific items of Christian iconography.[16]

For both Dyer and Nancy, modern Europe and its culture is wrought with Christianity. It is for this reason that when writers such as Christopher Hitchens, Richard Dawkins, Sam Harris and Daniel Dennett complain about religion, it is to the Christian God and Christian traditions that they make reference. To think about Europe's religious heritage is to think about Christianity (even if Christianity is not uniquely European).

From this point it follows that any critique of Christianity born of that world (coming from within Europe) is also a product of Christianity. That is, any attempt to move beyond Christianity is by necessity a process of self-superseding embedded in its own internal logic of development, what Nancy calls self-overcoming. The shift towards secularization since the Enlightenment and the increasing suspicion toward, or critique of, abstract and metaphysical categories—as typified by the writing of Hitchens et al. or by the anti-Christian satire of filmmakers such as Luis Buñuel and Pier Paolo Pasolini—can be seen as part of the Western tradition's self-overcoming. Any deconstruction of these categories is therefore indebted to the Christian structures of meaning always already informing Western thought. To posit an end to such categories is to remain locked within a logic of providence inherited from Christian eschatology by reinforcing the binaries it proposes. That is, to move away from Christian structures of meaning is to acknowledge their original authority. We thus find ourselves victims of a circular logic since "the defined has merely been placed within the definition."[17] The extreme example of this logic is atheism. According to Nancy, atheism must be understood as another stage in Christianity's process of self-overcoming; it is Christianity which renders possible the thought of atheism in the first place. And so, he writes, "The only current atheism is one that contemplates the reality of Christian provenance."[18]

For Nancy, then, we have entered the end of Christianity and exist in it: "we are in the shadow" of Christianity.[19] Therefore, "it is precisely that shadow that we must bring to light." Overcoming is not a simple passing beyond if that means acceding to another sphere; similarly, for Nancy, overcoming and self-overcoming "do not mean that Christianity is no longer alive" (even though it "has ceased giving life"). It continues to have a hold on us; we exist in its "nervation" to the point that "all thought is Christian through and through [. . .] which is to say, all of us, all of us to the end." [20] Nancy thus issues the following imperative: "We must try to bring to light how we are still Christian."[21]

Habemus Papam

This challenge to contemporary philosophy is also, potentially, a challenge to contemporary European cinema and its study, which has largely overlooked Christianity over the last two decades in favor of other religions. In recent years, the 9/11 attacks and the resultant fear of terrorism have placed religion at the center of our collective consciousness; consequently, many European films and television series produced in the last decade have striven to understand what the place of religion in Europe might be and what it is that drives religious fundamentalism. However, it is Islamic fundamentalism in particular in which the media are interested. Works as varied as Chris Morris's contemporary British satire *Four Lions* (UK/France, 2010); Michael Haneke's opaque meditation on guilt, history and its consequences, *Caché* (*Hidden*) (France/Italy/Germany/Austria, 2005) and Rachid Bouchareb's historical study of Algerian resistance, *Hors la Loi* (*Outside the Law*) (France/Algeria/Belgium/Tunisia/Italy, 2009) have examined—implicitly or explicitly—the place of Muslims within Europe.[22] Meanwhile, the last decade has seen a flourishing of scholarly work that—via a range of approaches—raises questions about Islam and cinema. One might think here of the emergence of Iranian and other Middle Eastern cinemas as popular subjects for critical consideration, as well as of the fashionable status of trans-national directors such as the Franco-Algerian Bouchareb, Turkish-German Fatih Akin or the Franco-Tunisian Abdellatif Kechiche. Equally significant is the body of work that follows Jack Shaheen's *Reel Bad Arabs* (published in 2001) and that is concerned with the representation of Islam in Western cinema.[23] To a certain extent, Islam has become the latest in a long line of categories—women, the working classes, homosexuals, non-white people (including the ethnic category of Jews)—to be identified as groups defined, in Richard Dyer's words, as "oppressed, marginal or subordinate" and thus subject to work which exposes how media representations contribute to its oppression, marginalization or subordination.

But while Islam is consistently discussed as, to borrow Edward Said's term, the Western world's "Other," there has been almost no discussion of what it is "other" than—an omission that seems to reflect Nancy's assertion that the question of how and in what sense we are Christian that remains obscure, "because at bottom it is never confronted head on."[24] Few Film Studies scholars have made any sustained attempt at engaging with questions of Christianity and cinema. This is not to say that film theory and criticism avoids the subject entirely, of course; rather, Christianity tends to be posited as a subordinate feature or category in the study of other areas of interest. In colonial and post-colonial approaches to film, Christianity more often than not becomes synonymous with Western Imperialism. In studies of transnational cinema, it can be an implicit feature of the national psyche, and in auteur theory, a facet of the director's self-expression. For feminist critics, Christianity is another feature of the patriarchal society; for Marxists, it is configured as one of many various conservative, right-wing forces—the church being, in Althusser's terms, an ideological state apparatus. Christianity is thus present in almost all areas of cinematic criticism, yet it remains un-emphasized. It is thus contingent on us as scholars to pay attention to what these films have to say about Christianity today and to make this the central category in our readings of the works.

Can we understand the recent return to depictions of Christianity in European cinema as an attempt of sorts to enact the very confrontation that Nancy calls for? Might the variants on the "priest's story" listed serve as investigations into what remains of Christianity today, what it is to exist in its "nervation?" And if so, how might we as scholars go about responding to the challenge that they lay down? These are the questions which structure the following analysis of *Habemus Papam*. Of course, this exegesis is but a first step in what ought to be a much wider-ranging response to these questions which takes in a range of contemporary films from Europe. It should also be noted that as a modern version of the "priest's story," *Habemus Papam* is amongst the more explicit examples of contemporary European cinema's confrontation with Christianity, forcefully demanding a reading of the film that engages with the religion as a key concern. It is for precisely this reason, however, that it serves as an appropriate starting point for the proposed investigation.

Deconstructing Christianity in Contemporary European Cinema 17

The film opens in the aftermath of a pope's death. The cardinals have assembled in conclave where they must remain until a successor has been elected. Eventually a majority vote is reached, and Cardinal Melville (Michel Piccoli) is chosen as Supreme Pontiff. The white smoke rises from the chimney and the call goes out: "Habemus papam!"—"We have a pope!" The massed crowds in St. Peter's Square stare up at the balcony—but no pope appears. Letting out a scream of "I can't do it!", Melville flees into the interior of the Vatican palace. The remainder of Moretti's film is concerned with the aftermath of this (non) event. The crowds are constantly reassured (the newly elected pope, they are told, is taking some time to pray and reflect before appearing before them). In accordance with the customs of the Church, until the pope appears before the people on the balcony, the ceremony of election is not over and no one in the conclave can have contact with the outside world. The priests are therefore confined to the Vatican. A psychoanalyst (played by Moretti himself) is called in to visit Melville. Meanwhile Melville himself slips out of the Vatican palace and wanders the streets of Rome, unrecognized, interacting with various members of the public, including a theatrical troupe rehearsing Chekhov's *The Seagull*. As days pass, there is growing unrest, bewilderment and speculation in Italy and throughout the Western press.

Habemus Papam presents us with a society unsure of what the role of the contemporary Church is. That it continues to exercise a compelling presence is made clear from the opening series of wide, deep-focus shots of massed hordes assembled outside the Vatican to mourn the loss of one pope and await the announcement of another. The image is repeated—in variants—throughout the film as the wait for the new pope draws out over several days, and it finds echoes in the flickering screens and stark black-and-white headlines that announce the non-news of its perpetuity. The solemnity of the opening sequence, set to mournful choral music, stands in stark contrast with the atmosphere within the conclave, which shifts from bewildered confusion as the power momentarily fails to brisk bureaucracy as the democratic voting process begins. Outside, journalists check screens and babble meaningless speculation into microphones: meaningless because of the absolute separation between inside and outside. Later in the film, a media specialist on the Vatican will break off mid-sentence to tell his interviewer that he has no idea where his commentary is going: "I'm improvising," he admits; "I'm totally confused." This might be the motto of each and every one of the film's cast of characters.

The depiction of the cardinals themselves is riven with anachronism and incongruity, suggesting that they hide mobile phones about their cassocks and care as much about finding a decent cappuccino as they do about following their divine calling. Their paradoxical existence is neatly captured by their decision to summon a psychoanalyst, Professor Brezzi, whose practice they then go on to undermine, reminding him that the "soul and subconscious cannot possibly co-exist" and that the following topics are off-limits: sex, parents, fantasies, desires—that is, the very pillars on which psychoanalysis is founded. Dreams are best not mentioned. Childhood can be only treated "discretely." A consultation must take place in front of the assembled cardinals. Unsurprisingly, the psychoanalyst declares that he is unable to do his job. His role as he knows it sits at odds with those who seek his authority and the circumstances in which they have asked him to work. Therefore he, too, participates in the climate of (self-) doubt and uncertainty that runs throughout *Habemus Papam*. If Moretti has described the film as being about "a fragile man," one who "feels inadequate in the face of the role he's called to fill," it is not necessarily evident to which of the film's characters he is referring.[25]

Central to the depiction of Christianity throughout, and within, the film is the fear of isolation or abandonment, which unravels numerous individuals and institutions. A running joke mocks the fact that Brezzi's wife, herself a psychoanalyst, is outstanding at her job but attributes all her patients' conditions to parental deficit. Given the rhetoric of paternity and parenthood that runs through the Christian bible, the emphasis on a theory stating that distant parents generate insecure children should not be dismissed as a mere frivolity. Indeed, what happens when the bonds between parental figures and their would-be children are destabilized is one of the film's key concerns.

Nowhere are the consequences of this instability presented more clearly, albeit densely, than in the figure of Melville, the newly elected Supreme Pontiff. Since the Pope (the word comes from the Greek πάππας, "father") is God's representative on earth, Melville's abandonment of his post can be read as a manifestation of God's "abandonment" of us.[26] A beautifully calibrated sequence sees Melville on a public bus, musing out loud over what he might say in his inaugural speech. As he chatters into the silence ("recently it's been hard for the Church to understand things"), an upset-sounding voice interjects: "Why? What's changed? I can't live without you!" As the camera pans and zooms out, the voice is revealed as that of a jilted lover, crying down a mobile phone. Yet, the initial confrontation lingers, posing the question of what might remain for us if we are to be abandoned by God and the Church.

Melville's literal flight from the Vatican potentially comes to stand for the divine in flight. But one might ask whether Melville himself has not also been abandoned. In his reading of Claire Denis's 2001 *Beau Travail*, Nancy proposes that the film's protagonist, Sentain, is a Christ figure thrown into an atheistic world. Noting that the film is an adaptation of Herman Melville's *Billy Budd*, in which the battleship where the central action takes place is called the Athée (the Atheist), Nancy writes that "the tragedy of both Billy and Sentain is that of Christ in a world without God."[27] *Habemus Papam* presents a world that is similarly dense in Christic allegory (there are echoes here of the Fall and of Christ in the desert), but it is not an atheistic world. What we see here is not the *death* of God and the religion's end, which Nancy describes as "the death of death, the negation of negation, the end of the separateness of God, the divinisation of man, the making absolute of his knowledge and his history (or the affirmation of their total insignificance)."[28] At this point, Melville has not yet abdicated. Rather, it is the *thought* of God's death. For Nancy, the god does not die in that thought "since he rises again there endlessly," but "things are worse: he is abandoned there—or else, he abandons us."[29]

Are we abandoned by God or have we abandoned Him? As the voting for Pope takes place, a solitary voice entreats "Please, Lord, let it not be me." Others join, uttering variants on the same prayer, until the soundtrack is filled with a cacophony of competing pleas. The words somehow echo those spoken by Christ in the Garden of Gethsemane, "Father, if you are willing, take this cup from me," a request commonly understood as a display of human weakness in the face of the impending crucifixion. In the apostles' accounts, these words are balanced by the refrain "may your will be done": the acknowledgement that if the prayer is denied, then Christ will assume the responsibility bestowed upon him. When Melville's prayer goes unheard or ungranted, he is unable to complete the second half of the equation. Here, Melville's tragedy is that of a Christ who flees the cross.

DÉCLOSION

Where does this flight take Melville? In his introduction to *Dis-Enclosure*, entitled "Ouverture," Nancy uses the word "*déclosion*" in contrast with *closion* (closing, or closure) to indicate an un-closing or de-closing. In this sense, *déclosion* might be understood as denoting a movement akin to "tearing down the walls, opening the cloister," as Adam Kotsko glosses it.[30] Understood in this sense, we may well see Melville's escape from the enclosed spaces of the Vatican City and into the open spaces of Rome as a form of personal, spatial *déclosion*. Likewise, his move away from the restrictive practices of the priesthood and towards the street, the theater, the donut shop—might be configured as a form of existential *déclosion*.

In the final chapter of *Dis-Enclosure*, however, *déclosion* is contrasted with *éclosion*: a term which, translated literally, means "hatching." Historically, *éclosion* is used to signify breaking through a barrier to a wider world (as in, for example, Columbus's journey and, more immediately, space exploration). Understood thus, the two terms—*déclosion* on the one hand and *éclosion*, its ostensible antonym, on the other, appear to hold similar if not the same meanings. Nancy explains the difference between the two by claiming that in contemporary society we have reached a point where no further *éclosion* is possible—hence we are entering a phase of *déclosion*, "the *éclosion* of *éclosion* itself."[31]

This excess of "hatching" over itself is difficult to think about, and Nancy's explanation of it is rather dense. [32] Nonetheless, if we are to better understand the place of Christianity in contemporary Europe, it is worth unpacking the important points involved here. First amongst these is the idea that to deconstruct Christianity is to grasp it in the movement of a self-deconstruction: the gesture of deconstruction, as a gesture neither critical nor perpetuating, is only possible from within Christianity: "Indeed, it is only from within that which is in itself constituted by and setting out from the distention of an opening that there can be a sense to seek and disassemble."[33] Dis-enclosure is, therefore, constitutively implosive. That is, dis-enclosure takes place from within; it is by definition a form of self-deconstruction. To deconstruct Christianity is not a process of external intervention onto an object but simply "accompanying it [Christianity] in the movement by which it displaces, complicates and undoes its own closure."[34]

Secondly, we are part of Christianity: we are shaped by it, it constitutes us and we constitute it, willingly (wittingly) or not. As Nancy continues:

> It is important, therefore, that we not take the assemblage of Christianity en bloc, to refute or confirm it, for that would be tantamount to placing ourselves outside or alongside it. [. . .] It has been too long taken for granted that we are no longer Christian, and that is why we keep between ourselves and Christianity a distance sufficient to allow us to *take it en masse*. When we do so, it appears as an autonomous mass in relation to which we can, it is true, take all sorts of attitudes, but concerning whose point of assemblage we will remain always ignorant.[35]

Finally, and as a corollary of the second point, we can see the manner in which Nancy's understanding of deconstruction differs from that of other philosophers. The term "deconstruction" has become identified with the name and thought of Jacques Derrida; however, its provenance lies with Heidegger, and Nancy explicitly refers to this in *Dis-Enclosure*.[36] The way Nancy understands deconstruction diverges from its Heideggerian root, and it is important to make this difference explicit.

Seeking to clarify how he understands deconstruction, Nancy recalls the history of the term, the tradition to which it belongs, for as he states, deconstruction belongs to "a tradition, to our modern tradition."[37] Its name appeared as a philosophical concept in Heidegger where it took the sense of a re-appropriative dismantling of our tradition. Heidegger indeed stressed the positive intent of *Destruktion,* aiming at retrieving the original experiences of being. This is where Nancy asserts his difference. For him, this is not a question of retrieving or re-appropriating the proper human experience and original Dasein, nor a matter of returning to origins. To deconstruct means instead "to take apart, to disassemble, to loosen the assembled structure in order to give some play to the possibility from which it emerged but which [. . .] it hides."[38] Dis-enclosure, or *déclosion*, is first of all an un-closing—but an un-closing which un-closes itself. It does not reveal some hidden contents, but reveals openness itself, what it is to be open.

Returning to *Habemus Papam*, we can note the way the film takes pains to detail the structures of Christianity before it unsettles them. Although it appears in many ways to be a character study, a not insubstantial amount of time is given to capturing the rhythms, routines and rituals of life within the Vatican before the film turns to examine what happens when these structures are loosened. The result, as discussed, is insecurity and instability, confusion and improvisation, playfulness and precarity.

Even as he abdicates his responsibilities, Melville prays forgiveness of the God whom he has abandoned. This much is clear in his final abdication speech given to the assembled faithful from the Vatican balcony:

> In these days, you must have asked yourself, why doesn't our pope come to say hello. He mustn't worry. If the Lord chose him, He couldn't have made a mistake.
>
> Yes, *I was chosen*. But this instead of giving me strength, consciousness, it crushes me, confuses me.
>
> In this moment, the Church needs a guide who has the strength to bring great changes, who seeks an encounter with all. Who has, for all, love and understanding.
>
> *I ask the Lord's forgiveness for what I am about to do.*
>
> I don't know if he will forgive me.
>
> But *I must speak to Him* and you with sincerity.
>
> In these days I've thought very much about you, and I realise I am not able to bear the role entrusted to me.
>
> I feel I am amongst those who cannot lead, but must be led.
>
> I can only say, pray for me. The guide you need is not me. I can't be the one.[39]

Even as he turns his back on the role to which he was elected, Melville reaffirms, several times over, the existence of a divine God. "I was chosen," he states. "I ask the Lord's forgiveness." "I must speak to Him."

This leaves us—and Melville—in a complex position at the end of *Habemus Papam*. As he performs his speech, Moretti alternates between medium solo (head and shoulders) shots of Michel Piccoli; medium group shots of the cardinals; and long, wide shots of the assembled faithful, flag-waving and cheering the eventual appearance of the new Pope. While Melville remains calm, even beatific, throughout, the atmosphere of celebration transforms to one of uncertainty over the course of Melville's three-minute speech. His ultimate announcement of abdication sends a ripple of shock through the cardinals and crowds. Finally, three shots condense the shift in emphasis that the scene enacts, from the individual (Melville) to the society that looks towards him. Melville turns his back to the assembly. A cut shows us the horrified cardinals, shoulders hunched, heads bowed or buried in their hands. Finally, we cut to a shot taken from amongst the crowds looking out over the heads and slowly sinking flags to the stolid, solid sight of the Vatican and its empty, distant balcony. We leave them there—stunned, inert, leaderless—as the film ironically declares "Habemus Papam."

In ending on this rather somber note, Moretti's film perhaps departs from Nancy's deconstructive celebration of self-overcoming, openness and creativity. Indeed, his statement of inability—"I can't"—suggests failure, disappointment. Yet there is a courage involved in the act of abdication that undermines an interpretation of the scene, and the film as a whole, as a straightforward depiction of Christianity's falling away and society's turn towards the secular. That is, there is also a victory to be found in Melville's personal liberation: rather than bow to pressure to perform a relationship with the divine that he sees as inauthentic and stifling, Moretti, while continuing to profess a faith of sorts, escapes the hierarchies and boundaries of the Church. The spectatorial allegiances encouraged by Moretti's narrative and mise-en-scène position us to experience this escape as a relief, albeit one that leaves us in a precarious position of uncertainty. The finality of Melville's act shuts down one avenue of possibility as he turns his back on history and on the Church as it *has been*, but it opens up an endless (almost overwhelmingly so) horizon of other possible directions in which he—and his relationship with Christianity—might now turn.

THE VEINS OF CHRISTIANITY

It is particularly in this regard that *Habemus Papam* can be said to serve as indicative of a wider development within contemporary European cinema post-2001. Of course, Christianity as it appears in *Habemus Papum* is of a specific sort. It is, first and foremost, Catholicism. It is also the particular Catholicism of Italy. Moreover, it is that of the twenty-first century, at a moment in history when both the country and the Church are undergoing a particularly turbulent time. It is remarkable in this respect that the film's release was timed to coincide with the beatification of the late Pope Jean Paul II: a gesture which Geoffrey Nowell Smith understandably reads as "a political gesture on Moretti's part, analogous to the release of his Berlusconi-themed *The Caiman* (2007) with an election campaign in 2007."[40] But while it is no doubt possible—even sensible—to read the film within the context of national cinema, this should not preclude its placement within the context of European cinema more widely. Indeed, the film's tone is far less barbed than that of *The Caiman*, and its targets are far less clearly delineated. As Nowell Smith admits, "if there is satire, it is very light, and its target is as much the babble of the psychoanalysts as the Catholic Church in its pomp and glory."[41]

The film's approach to Christianity thus echoes that of Nancy's project, which refuses satire or provocation. Nancy writes that "No one can imagine being confronted today by a Voltaire-like philosopher, having at Christianity in an acerbic tone—and doubtless not in the best Nietzschean style."[42] He claims that it is no longer timely or relevant to attack or defend Christianity since Christianity has ceased to give sense, even to hold the promise of sense. His claim is backed up by sociological research. Peter Berger, Grace Davie and Effie Fokas delineate the contemporary state of religion in Europe with reference to survey data:

> Both Catholic and Protestant churches are in deep trouble in Europe. Attendance at services has declined sharply for many years, there is a shortage of clergy because of lagging recruitment, finances are in bad shape, and the churches have largely lost their former importance in public life. When people are asked about their beliefs—such as in God, life after death, the role of Jesus Christ as redeemer—the scores are low both in comparison with the past and with other parts of the world. The same is the case when people are asked whether religion is important in their lives.[43]

Berger admits that there are differences within Europe but argues that 'it is fair to say that western and central Europe is the most secularized area in the world," and this has become so much a part of European culture that the term "Eurosecularity" has been coined to describe it. He draws explicit comparisons with the situation in the US, revealing that the North American picture differs sharply from the European one. Both behavioral and opinion indicators are much more robustly religious here. At least since the middle of the twentieth century, there has been what Berger refers to as an "American intelligentsia," who are much more secular than the rest of the population. This intelligentsia is heavily associated with the Democrat party, whereas the Republican party has a strong Christian bent. Between these two poles of devotion and secularity lie the majority of North Americans, who tend to profess what Nancy Ammerman, an American sociologist, has called "golden-rule Christianity"—a somewhat vague and broadly tolerant form of religion—but who nonetheless have to ally themselves politically with one secularity or religion.

If, in the US, Christianity has come to be associated with the political right, the response of filmmakers has been to produce a politically inflected body of work that reflects this state of affairs. Since the turn of the century, there has been a surge in evangelical Christian filmmaking: ranging from big-budget productions such as Mel Gibson's notorious *The Passion of the Christ* (US, 2004) and the Christian production company Walden Media's cinematic adaptations of C.S. Lewis's Narnia series to the grassroots melodramas directed by pastor Alex Kendrick, namely *Flywheel* (US, 2003); *Fireproof* (US, 2008) and *Courageous* (US, 2011). At the same time, independent documentaries such as Rachel Ewing's *Jesus Camp* (US, 2006) and Amy Berg and Frank Donner's *Deliver Us From Evil* (US, 2006) have castigated right-wing Catholic groups and Evangelicals for their hypocrisy.

The new European variants on the "priest's or nun's story" are, quite to the contrary, not concerned with condemning Christianity any more than they are interested in celebrating it. The approaches to Christianity that they offer are, rather, like that of *Habemus Papum*: confused and confusing. It is difficult—indeed nigh-on impossible—to read these films individually or collectively as a coherent or unified perspective on religion, faith and, in particular, on Christianity. These films incorporate Christianity—in some cases they focus upon it—but they do not appropriate it.

Nancy wishes to keep his distance from such appropriation, from damning or saving Christianity. So, too, does Moretti. Instead, both men's engagement with Christianity is, as we have seen, interested in Christianity's self-surpassing, its dis-enclosure. As those reading these films, and their ambiguous engagement with Christianity, we too must strive to avoid the tendency towards appropriation. It is the task of viewers, critics and scholars to mirror the approach that Nancy proposes and that these films enact: to accompany Christianity in its movement of self-deconstruction and, in so doing, to recognize how Christianity structures our own ways of thinking and writing about film and, in doing so, to put these structures into play.

Moretti's film and Nancy's writing withhold from critiquing Catholicism as an institution or ideology. They are not interested in what we might call structural flaws. Instead, they pose as a form of postsecular theological questioning. As Nancy puts it in "The Deconstruction of Christianity," "We are in the veins of Christianity; they keep hold of us, but *how*?"[44]

NOTES

1. André Bazin, "Cinema and Theology," in *Bazin at Work: Major Essays and Reviews from the Forties and Fifties*, ed. Bert Cardullo, trans. Bert Cardullo and Alain Piette (New York: Routledge, 1997), 61–72. (Original work published in French in 1951.)
2. Bazin, "Cinema and Theology," 63.
3. Ibid., 64.
4. This is not to say that religious films, or films about religion, disappeared from screens—still less, films which were critical or satirical of religion; merely the specific variant on a theme which placed the clergy, clerics and other men and women of the cloth at the center of its narrative. And indeed, exceptions exist, including Jean-Pierre Melville's *Leon Morin, Priest* (1961), Ingmar Bergman's *Winter Light* (1962), and Andrei Tarkovsky's *Andrei Rublev* (1971), to give three examples.
5. Brett Boweles, "The Life of Jesus," *Film Quarterly* 57:3 (Spring 2004), 47–55. Bert Cardullo, "Rosetta Stone: A Consideration of the Dardenne Brothers' Rosetta," *Journal of Religion and Film* 6:1 (April 2002). Available at www.unomaha.ed/jrf/rosetta.htm. Last accessed April 23, 2012.

David Sterrit and Mikita Brottman, "L'Humanité," in *The Hidden God: Film and Faith*, eds. Mary Lea Brandy and Antonio Monda (New York: Museum of Modern Art, 2005), 229–34.
6. Peter Berger, Grace Davie, and Effie Fokas, *Religious America, Secular Europe? A Theme and Variations* (Farnham: Surrey, 2008), 13.
7. For more on the various iterations of Christianity within contemporary European Cinema, see my chapter "Do Unto Others: Christianity and European Cinema," in *The Europeanness of European Cinema*, eds. Mary Herrod and Mariana Liz (London: I.B. Tauris, 2013.). Here, I argue that this resistance continues both through other recent films which flirt with Christian myth and iconography, including Eugène Green's existential drama *A Religiosa Portuguesa (The Portuguese Nun)* (Portugal/France, 2009); Christian Alvart's horror *Antikörper (Antibodies)* (Germany, 2006); Pascale Bailly's rom-com *Dieu et grand, je suis toute petite (God is Big and I am Small)* (France, 2001) and Dumont's quiet thriller *Hors Satan (Outside Satan)* (France, 2011). There is no pattern to the surfacing of Christian myth and iconography in contemporary European cinema, nor are there any discernible trends in its use.
8. European directors who have cast a skeptical eye on religious institutions include the Italian Pier Paolo Pasolini (*La Ricotta*, Italy/France, 1963); Greek-born Costa-Gavras (*Amen*, France/Germany/Romania, 2002) and Swiss Jean-Luc Godard (*Je vous salue, Marie*, France, 1985). The most prolific member of this group is Spanish director Luis Buñuel, whose films consistently present Christianity as a rigorous system abused by the powerful to subdue the masses.
9. Jean-Luc Nancy, *Dis-Enclosure: The Deconstruction of Christianity*. Translated by Bettina Bergo, Gabriel Malefant, and Michael B. Smith (New York: Fordham University Press, 2007).
10. Jean-Luc Nancy, "Of Divine Places," in *The Inoperative Community*, ed. Peter Connor, trans. Michael Holland (Minneapolis: University of Minnesota Press, 1991), 110–50.
11. Nancy, *Dis-Enclosure*, 1.
12. Jean-Luc Nancy, *The Sense of the World*, (Minneapolis: University of Minnesota Press 2008), 183n50.
13. Nancy, *Dis-Enclosure*, 140.
14. Ibid.
15. Ibid., 142–43.
16. Richard Dyer, *White* (London and New York: Routledge, 1997), 15.
17. Nancy, *Dis-Enclosure*, 143.
18. Ibid., 140.
19. Ibid., 142.
20. Ibid., 142.
21. Ibid., 140.
22. It is worth noting that in all three of these films, the "other" is visually marked as non-white (and sonically by a difference in accent). But this is not always the case: "Muslim-ness" and "Christian-ness" are not necessarily visual terms in the same way that "blackness" and "whiteness" are.
23. Amongst other works, this list includes: Martin Barker's *A "Toxic Genre": The Iraq War Films*; Stephen Prince's *Firestorm: American Film in the Age of Terrorism*; Susan Faludi's *The Terror Dream: Fear and Fantasy in Post 9/11 America* and Shaheen's own *Guilty: Hollywood's Verdict on Arabs After 9/11*.
24. Nancy, *Dis-Enclosure*, 139.
25. Scarpa, Vittoria, "Interview with Nanni Moretti," *Cineuropa*, April 21, 2011. Available at: http://cineuropa.org/it.aspx?t=interview&lang=en&documentID=202248.

26. Nancy, "Of Divine Places," 129.
27. Jean-Luc Nancy, "A-religion," *Journal of European Studies*, 34:1/2 (2004), 14–18.
28. Nancy, "Of Divine Places," 129.
29. Ibid.
30. Adam Kotsko, "Already, Not Yet," *Journal for Cultural and Religious Theory*, 6:3 (Fall 2005), 87–95. Available at www.jcrt.org/achives/06.3/kotsko.pdf.
31. Nancy, *Dis-Enclosure*, 160.
32. Ibid., 161.
33. Ibid., 148.
34. Ibid., 10–11.
35. Ibid., 149, emphasis in original.
36. Ibid., 148.
37. Ibid.
38. Ibid.
39. All citations from the UK Soda Pictures release of *Habemus Papam* (*We Have a Pope*) (2001, dir. Nanni Moretti, Italy).
40. Geoffrey Nowell-Smith, "Turin Notebook," in *Film Quarterly* 65:2 (Fall 2011). Available at *www.filmquarterly.org/2011/10/pope-shrinking/*. It is worth noting that the resignation of Pope Benedict XVI in February 2013 adds an additional patina of prescience to Moretti's narrative.
41. Nowell Smith, "Turin Notebook."
42. Nancy, *Dis-Enclosure*, 141.
43. Berger et al., 2008: 11.
44. Nancy, *Dis-Enclosure*, 142.

2 "Casting Fire Onto the Earth"
The Holy Fool in Russian Cinema

Alina Birzache

In a disturbing scene from his 1983 film *Nostalghia*, Andrei Tarkovsky has the camera pan across the Piazza del Campidoglio on the Capitoline Hill in Rome, unfolding a gallery of misfits loitering between the imposing columns. We are then shown the face of a man speaking frenetically before the view zooms out to reveal that he is standing on the equestrian statue of Marcus Aurelius. The man, whom the viewers recognize as the recluse Domenico, concludes his diatribe with a rhetorical question: "What kind of world is this if a madman has to tell you to be ashamed of yourselves?" and proceeds to set himself on fire. The use of the madman to reveal some great truth, especially of a divine nature, is a typically Tarkovskian device, one that would have been particularly familiar to his Russian audience. But how has this Russian-like fool traveled to the symbolical heart of the Roman Empire and the spiritual center of Western Europe?

In order to answer this question, we need to journey back to the fool's home—Soviet and Russian cinema—where the holy fool has been a recurring player in a subversive visual discourse, standing as a powerful critic of the established order. For such characters, film directors have either drawn their inspiration from hagiographic writings in the Christian Orthodox tradition or have lifted the figure out of its original context and transformed it into modern cinematic variants, not necessarily within any explicitly religious setting. The translation of the holy fool from its original Christian hagiographical model into other genres has resulted in stylized variants of the figure, lacking some paradigmatic features. In order to map out these transformations, I will proceed, first, by examining two portrayals of holy fools that were directly inspired by hagiographic models before turning to the stylized variants created by the most significant innovator of the figure: Andrei Tarkovsky. I will argue that Tarkovsky distinguished himself from other Russian directors attracted by the versatility of the holy fool as a result of his unique interpretation of the figure and his translation of its function outside the Russian context. This was achieved both literally, as a result of Tarkovsky's later self-exile in Western Europe, and figuratively, with the holy fool assuming a universal mission in his artistic vision. My intention here is to show how Tarkovsky modernized the figure in such a way as to grapple with the question of faith in the contemporary world, showing in the process that socialist and capitalist societies alike were suffering from the crumbling of religious certainties.

First of all, it is worth considering the lineage and profile of the holy fool. The occurrence of the holy fool in Russian cinema is relatively recent, but we are in fact dealing with a pre-modern figure whose origin, in the Christian context, can be traced back to St Paul's explanation of the "fool-for-Christ" in the First Epistle to the Corinthians (4:9–13), as well as to Christ himself, who could not escape accusations of madness (John 10:20), and even further back to the noted eccentricities of the Hebrew prophets. Some four centuries after St. Paul gave his advice: "If any man among you seems to be wise in this world, let him become a fool" (1 Cor. 3:18), people in the Byzantine provinces of Egypt and Syria in search of spiritual advancement began to interpret the apostle's words in a rather curious way. By "renouncing their mind," they meant the adoption of a provocative behavior, which verged on madness or idiocy—a lack of reason designed to disguise their personal sanctity and challenge the social and cultural assumptions of their contemporaries. It was this Byzantine tradition of the holy fool as transgressor of social conventions for a higher purpose that was inherited by Russian ecclesiastic and folk cultures. In so doing, these cultures frequently credited the holy fool—the *yurodivyi*—with clairvoyance and prophetic powers.[1] A compensatory mechanism was at work which replaced "worldly wisdom" with "God's wisdom" or rather "God's foolishness," the ultimate example of which was often taken to be, following St Paul's explanation (1 Cor.1:25), the crucifixion of Christ. The Russian Orthodox Church canonized a significant number of native holy fools active between the eleventh and nineteenth centuries; yet, the number of practitioners of holy foolishness was much greater, the phenomenon acquiring widespread social visibility. Often the actions of these fools were invested with political significance, especially after the establishment of autocracy in Russia in the sixteenth century: a situation I will examine in my first cinematic example.

Even within a Christian context, however, various cultures and ages have found space to emphasize different aspects of holy foolishness. In his monograph on the phenomenon in Byzantium and Russia, cultural historian Sergei Ivanov observes that: "The culture which gives birth and semantic form to the concept of holy foolery notes and endows with meaning only these features of insane behaviour which are conceptually relevant to it, while ignoring the rest."[2] In Russian culture, consistent with the ideal of sanctified humility, two prominent features of the holy fool came to be established: public humiliation and clairvoyance. Often, holy fools walked around in rags or almost naked, while at other times chroniclers noted how they would don chains or other odd paraphernalia. In the eyes of their contemporaries, their mysterious words and unconventional behavior had an ominous quality, and their mere presence could disrupt not only the social order, but the order of nature as well. All these peculiarities only enhanced their apparent spiritual stature and otherworldliness. Their excruciating ascetic feats were just the visible face of their familiarity with God, while their unconventional ways reflected His impenetrable judgments. Through them God was thought to pass some kind of judgment on the world, even though the verdict was not easily or immediately understood. It is precisely this surplus of meaning invested in the holy fool figure that has helped to make it such a versatile cinematic device.

TWO CINEMATIC REPRESENTATIONS OF THE HAGIOGRAPHIC HOLY FOOL

One of the earliest appearances of the iconography of the holy fool in Russian film is found in the work of a founding father of Soviet cinema: Sergei Eisenstein. This might appear surprising at first, given the extent to which Eisenstein's artistic talents were in the service of the Soviet regime. Even more surprising, perhaps, is that the holy fool should emerge in *Ivan the Terrible* (1944): a film commissioned by Stalin during the Second World War as part of a campaign designed to legitimize, by means of recourse to an idealized past, both the centralization of power in his own hands and the terror he used to subdue his people.[3] In the figure of the holy fool, however, Eisenstein found a powerful cultural device for speaking truth to power. He drew on a well-known episode in Russian hagiographic literature when a certain *yurodivyi* called Nikolka offered Ivan a piece of raw meat to eat. The Tsar objected that he could not possibly do so because it was Lent, only for the holy fool to reply that the Tsar had eaten human flesh already: an obvious reference to his savageries.[4] In the Russian hagiographic tradition, the holy fool played an important role in relation to the Tsar and his claim to be God's representative on earth and a guarantor of the Christian Orthodox faith.[5] Yet, positioned as they are at each extreme of the social hierarchy, the fool and the Tsar nonetheless could be seen to derive their power—be it spiritual or earthly—from the same divine source of authority.

In this context, it becomes easy to decipher how the employment of the holy fool device related to Eisenstein's intentions in *Ivan the Terrible*. Recently crowned Tsar by the Metropolitan of Moscow, Ivan faces a mob riot during his wedding feast. In Eisenstein's portrayal, the Tsar only needs to exchange a few angry looks at his subjects to reestablish order. While everybody is submitting to Ivan's will, the holy fool stands out as the only figure that dares to raise his voice. Eisenstein marks out the character of the holy fool to his audience using a few characteristic insignia: nakedness, chains and a wooden scepter topped by a cross—all of which customarily signify asceticism, solidarity with the oppressed and spiritual authority in the hagiographic tradition. Challenging authority, the fool casts his own malevolent looks, and castigates the Tsar's decision to side with blood-thirsty families, all the while pulling the chains worn across his naked torso in a gesture evoking a proletarian protest as much as a divine mission. Although he cannot be deceived as easily as the mob, he is nevertheless shown slipping out of the cinematic frame, an indication that even he will be eventually silenced. Is this holy fool intended to expose the malefic side of Stalin's despotic power, contrary to the leader's propagandistic expectations, or is he a representation of the revolutionary proletariat protesting against absolute monarchy? There is no certain answer beyond noting that the film itself was designed to be ambiguous, causing contradictory readings. Eisenstein himself was deeply ambivalent about Stalin's use of power.[6] If intended and read as the embodiment of the revolutionary spirit, the holy fool offers a critique of Stalin's own vicious methods for suppressing dissent. In this interpretation, Eisenstein manipulates the symbolic function of the holy fool to serve his own artistic and political ends, and possibly subvert the encomiastic reading of the film.

In the example discussed above, the holy fool is not treated as a central character in his own right, but is rather a dramatic device taken from Russia's cultural repository and employed for a time-honored political role. The conformist Soviet cinematic landscape was rarely disrupted by films bearing ideologies at odds with that promoted by the state, and films appearing to support an overtly religious message risked being withdrawn from public viewing for years. It is not surprising therefore that the holy fools, though adorned with their religious attributes, were severed from the living faith that had given rise to them. In this example, the religious function of the holy fool is subordinate to the political function to the extent of annihilation. The major exception to this practice in the Soviet cinematic landscape was Andrei Tarkovsky, and for this reason I will examine his treatment separately later on in this chapter.

The post-Soviet era, however, heralded a renewed interest in the traditional model of the holy fool: a figure now able to be explored in all its spiritual significance. The redefinition of Russian national identity after 1991 included a desire to reconnect with the nation's Christian Orthodox heritage of the pre-Soviet era. As a result, the religious potential of holy foolishness has not only been widely explored by recent Russian directors, but often vigorously affirmed. Pavel Lungin's *The Island* (2006) is a notable case in point, being, to the best of my knowledge, the first feature film to elaborate so deeply on the hagiographic model of the holy fool that the figure becomes the film's central concern.

Lungin's film purports to offer a spiritual solution to the latest stage in Russia's ongoing search for identity and has been hugely popular. In his preface to an interview with the director, film critic Andrei Plakhov comments on the symbolic value the film holds for today's Russia: "Nowadays, more than likely it is considered more important to resolve inner problems—symbolically within the individual, as within the country".[7] The director's acknowledged ambition is to "open up new genres in film, in this case the genre of the lives of the saints."[8] Hence the whole film is intended as an alternative to a mainstream cultural and political discourse that overlooks religious hagiography in favor of secular references. Although the story is set in Soviet times—the 1970s—for most of its length, Lungin utilizes the traditional figure of the holy fool in such a fashion that he projects the figure as a new spiritual guide for the post-Soviet era.

The functions of Anatoly, the holy fool in the film, are in keeping with those of his hagiographical antecedents. He is a clairvoyant, though often a playful one. Through his irreverent behavior and metaphorical gestures, Anatoly acts out the various conflicts smoldering within people's own consciences in an attempt to ease their troubled minds and unify their torn interiority. He assumes the status of an outsider: he has the lowest position in the monastery because he has refused to take the habit and is a simple stoker. He is often shown next to the furnace or carrying coal for its maintenance—his deliberate association with fire evoking a wide range of symbolic meanings from the Holy Spirit to the fires of the Last Judgment, forces both creative and destructive. Indeed, endowed with divine awareness and discernment of spirits, he keeps alight the spiritual fire for the whole monastery, and his mysterious acts provoke others into a state of self-reflection.

Anatoly's unconventional behavior and his profound, penitential religiosity place him in stark contrast not only with the materialistic ideology of the Soviet state but also against the formalism often practiced in the monastery. A few episodes stand out as particularly revealing. The first time the viewer sees the old Anatoly after the initial sequence of his youth is when he is interacting with a young woman who comes to ask for permission to terminate her pregnancy after she has been abandoned by the father of the child. The fool knows that she is pregnant and predicts that she will never marry, and this child will be her only comfort in life. Elsewhere, in a darkly humorous episode, Lungin deliberately creates a situation where the Abbot, Filaret, realizes he is completely unprepared for death. Filaret's comfortable boots are burned in the fiery furnace, and his favorite blanket is thrown into the sea, exposing the inconsistency between such self-indulging practices and his former ascetic ideals. Moreover, the fact that the boots were a gift from a bishop alludes to the spiritual slackness of the Church at a time when it was assuming a subservient position towards the Soviet state. Filaret is not, however, the only monk Anatoly subjects to his pranks. Job, a monk charged with administrative duties, is constantly teased into an acute awareness of his human fallibility.

In another episode, this time involving lay people, Anatoly performs a miracle, pointing to contradictions in human nature. A mother brings her lame son to the island, hoping for a cure from the monks since the doctors have given up hope. She is a white-collar worker and very fond of her designing work, presumably in a factory. Anatoly cures her son, but advises her to allow the child to receive communion the following day. Fearing that she will lose her job, she decides not to wait and prepares to leave. In response, Anatoly snatches the boy from the returning boat and dismisses her anxiety using his clairvoyant abilities. The woman and the boy cannot envisage a situation that contravenes the experiences of their material world and so have difficulties believing in the miracle they have sought. While there is no explicit political criticism of the Soviet regime here, the holy fool points to something more profound: control is frequently achieved not through violence, Lungin suggests, but insidiously, through an acceptance of the norms and conventions that come to regulate the mind and negate the universe of possible impossibilities provided by faith.

The film's plot maintains a strong psychological element. In contrast with the playful episodes mentioned above, the director also takes the viewer into the private moments of Anatoly's daily torment whereby he (wrongly) believes that, in a moment of cowardice, he took the life of his commander in World War II. The holy fool model is here conflated, to great effect, with the sinner-turned-saint motif. Anatoly was a sinner like many other unremarkable sinners, yet he is now a model for both monastics and lay people. He is within the monastery but not integrated in its order, within the world but estranged from it; as such, he is the man of God in whom grace manifests itself freely and visibly. More importantly, Lungin seems to tell us, Anatoly is the embodiment of that flame of spirituality that has never been extinguished in Russia, not even by the communist authorities. It has survived untainted on isolated islands or souls, and it is now able to reconnect the present with the pre-revolutionary past, in so doing bypassing seven decades of atheism and reducing this to an unfortunate interlude. By reconnecting to the perennial source of tradition, Lungin seems to suggest, social life can return to its previous course.

The message of the importance of tradition is emphasized throughout *Island* with its frequent references to Orthodox spirituality. Modern technology is used here to produce a canonic cinematic hagiography. But the technology of the cinematic medium is almost all that is modern about this film. In a way, we should expect nothing less (or more) from a holy fool who gives up everything that ties him to this world, including his mind, in order to return to a state of primordial purity. Anatoly offers old-time solutions to old-time problems, and, for that matter, the transformations that human society and culture have undergone in the last three hundred years seem to leave him untouched. The setting of the film on the island, with its ascetic monastic location, helps to distance Anatoly and the viewer from contemporary culture. The film therefore reinforces a traditionalist mindset in which there is not much discontinuity between the present and the past.

Other directors have been much more ambitious in engaging the problem of the present. Almost certainly, the most significant was Andrei Tarkovsky (1932–1986), a director for whom the problem of modernity was a recurring theme in his output. Unlike Lungin, in his denouncement of the wrongs of modernity Tarkovsky did not use the holy fool as a clarion call for a return to tradition. Instead, Tarkovsky redefined the holy fool for a secular age and a non-Orthodox audience in such a way that his criticisms of modernity resonated well beyond the borders of the Soviet Union.

HOLY FOOLS IN TARKOVSKY'S FILMOGRAPHY

Many commentators have noticed, if only in passing, Tarkovsky's use of the holy fool in his films, pointing out that this half-dim Russian figure credited with supernatural powers accounts for some of the director's enigmatic, if not absurd, characters. Few though have examined the obvious discrepancies between the traditional Russian holy fool and that developed by Tarkovsky. The director was not the first in Russia to develop the figure out of its original hagiographic context: others before him had created stylized fools for literary purposes. A couple of clarifications about what the literary scholar Ewa Thompson called "stylized" holy fools are in order here.[9] The term was first applied to literary characters to explain the transformation that the hagiographical figure underwent once adapted to a new genre. While their depiction departs from the canonical iconography, losing some of the features that made up the paradigm, the identification of these stylized figures as holy fools is reliant on a similarity of function and literary precedents in Russian culture. Probably the most prominent and influential of such literary transformations of the holy fool is Prince Mishkin in Dostoevsky's *The Idiot* (1868).

However, the originality of Tarkovsky's experimentation with the holy fool lies primarily in the way holy foolishness is grafted onto individuals with very modern mindsets. Such an individual is aware of the rupture with the past and its traditions that modernity brought about. What distinguishes Tarkovsky from the Russian directors I have discussed so far and others who have employed the figure[10] is that he spent much of his career developing an original and modern conception of holy foolishness, which is nonetheless explicitly used for promoting a moral and religious vision. I will argue that in his rendition, holy foolishness is framed by a particular existential philosophy, which, with the passing of time, aimed toward the achievement of a universal expression. Under this philosophy, Tarkovsky used the holy fool as a figure uniquely capable of criticizing contemporary society and modernity across national boundaries. In this respect, Tarkovsky was able to criticize both the socialist modernity of the USSR and the capitalist modernity of Western Europe.

The genesis of his conceptions can be traced at an early stage in Tarkovsky's filmography. His preoccupation with the holy fool figure started with his second feature film *Andrei Rublev* (1966), was continued through *Stalker* (1979), matured in *Nostalghia* (1983), and reached its zenith in his final film *The Sacrifice* (1986).[11] Moreover, one of his unrealized projects was an adaptation of Dostoevsky's *The Idiot*: an undertaking to which he refers several times in his book *Sculpting in Time*.

The first of Tarkovsky's films to make explicit use of the versatility of the holy fool figure is *Andrei Rublev*. Only loosely based on the life of the eponymous fifteenth-century Russian icon painter, the film presents the complex situation of an artist torn between his inner vision and the religious orthodoxy, on the one hand, and the vicissitudes of history, on the other. Rublev is struggling to keep his faith in goodness and beauty, all the while confronted with a host of malign forces, including the authorities' violent suppression of unlicensed laughter and pre-Christian beliefs, the betrayals and discord within the ruling families, and the atrocities of the Tartar invasion—all of which were standing in stark contrast to the faithfulness and brotherly love of the people.

Features of holy foolishness are spread among several characters in *Andrei Rublev*. The most traditional forms follow the typology established by Peter C. Bouteneff: the blessed idiot, the scandalous prankster, and the terrifying ascetic,[12] corresponding in Russian terminology to the *durochka*—the mute female holy fool in Tarkovsky's film, to the *skomorokh*—the street performer in the film, and to Theophanes the Greek, Rublev's master. The *durochka* follows closely the traditional *yurodivyi* as a composite of idiocy and intuition, innocence and irreverence, confounding all expectation at the end of the film when, after being abducted by the Tartars, she reemerges unscathed and of sound mind. Though mostly passive, *durochka* plays a very important role in Rublev's spiritual development since she involuntarily puts to the test his artistic and ethical ideals. It is she who reacts viscerally at the sight of the cathedral's white wall smeared with dark paint by a Rublev unwilling to paint the Last Judgment, and it is to defend her that Rublev kills a soldier. At the other extreme, the *skomorokh*'s obscene provocations and pranks could be viewed as those of a holy fool deriding the vices of society. To the extent that his profession exposes him to the persecutions of officialdom, the *skomorokh* in *Andrei Rublev* has similarities with the holy fool's voluntary submission to public aggression. In this sense, it is worth noting that Tarkovsky makes the character spread his arms to mimic the crucifixion.

A more sophisticated instance of the coalescence of holy fool and artist is associated with Theophanes the Greek in the film, who was an unconventional character oscillating between terrifying ascetic feats and irreverent acts. In his first conversation with Rublev, Theophanes is shown in a forest, resting his feet on an ants' nest, presumably as a means of mortifying the flesh, while in another conversation with Kirill, Rublev's rival, he confesses he had irreverently used an icon panel to press cabbage. In one sequence, Tarkovsky has Theophanes lying on his back, glimpsing the world as an image turned upside down. This can be interpreted as a visual metaphor for the message that the fools are trying to get across: "in the kingdom of God reigns a complete inversion of our earthly values"[13]. From a divine perspective, therefore, Tarkovsky appears to be saying that it is our world which is upside-down.

This inversion of the conventional patterns, whether ethical or aesthetic, is replicated more forcefully by Rublev in both his rejection of the traditional fear-inducing way of representing the Last Judgment and in his declaration that the *durochka* is not a sinner for having failed to follow St. Paul's injunction to cover her head. Even though Andrei Rublev is not generally considered to meet enough of the attributes of holy foolishness to qualify as such a figure, the vow of silence he makes after killing a soldier can be read as a form of sharing in the silence of the holy fool: a form of penitence and "his most exasperated act of resistance" as "he withdraws from participation in human communication as a willful act of opposition to the sociality in which he is implicated."[14] Rublev's obstinate faith in the redeeming goodness of humanity places a different kind of foolishness in counterpoint to the more traditional forms. In so doing, Tarkovsky anticipates some of his significant later holy fools: modern day intellectuals caught in an existential friction with the world not because they want to return to the traditions of the Church, but because they need to rediscover faith for themselves and the world.

Tarkovsky returned to the idea of holy foolishness in his last three films—*Stalker, Nostalghia* and *The Sacrifice,* in unconventional and peculiar ways. During the 1970s, his increasing disillusionment with the Soviet regime encouraged him to develop fresh ways of criticizing it. He found in the science-fiction genre an ideal medium to express his thoughts in a way that would deflect the censors' suspicion. Yet, the metaphysical substratum of his scripts could hardly be missed. Both *Solaris* (1972), loosely based on Stanislaw Lem's science-fiction novel, and seven years later *Stalker,* based on the Strugatsky brothers' novella *A Roadside Picnic,* can be read as parables disclosing the existence of another reality beneath the crude surface of the contemporary materialistic world.

The religious undertones of *Stalker* are made explicit by Tarkovsky late in the film when we hear in a voice-over the passage from the *Book of Revelation* (6:12–17) about the sixth seal. This is followed shortly by a recitation of the first verses describing Jesus' appearance on the road to Emmaus (Lk. 24:13–18). Who are the three on the road, and what is this Emmaus that they seek? Three characters, allegorically called Scientist, Writer, and Stalker, set off on a journey through the Zone in search of the Room where one's desires are fulfilled. The Zone itself is a mysterious land, supposedly created by an alien civilization and governed by its own natural laws, which the authorities are striving to keep off limits. Only the "stalkers" can guide someone there and back unharmed since the partly apocalyptic, partly paradisiacal landscape is allegedly rife with dangerous traps. In spite of the lack of direct reference to a particular regime, the ban on entering the Zone and the Scientist's self-assigned mission to plant a bomb to destroy it allude to nuclear practices familiar in the Soviet Union.

The character Stalker is fashioned by Tarkovsky in the spirit of the traditional holy fool by way of an emphasis on his humility and simplicity. Even the film's text contains an explicit reference to Stalker as a holy fool: his wife calls him "not of this world" while Writer concludes: "You are just a God's fool (*yurodivyi*)." Tarkovsky directs the camera to scrutinize his appearance in order to reveal the characteristics of an individual on the fringes of society: his head is shaven with discolored patches, his face wrinkled by the hardships of life, and his clothes worn out. He looks vulnerable and ineffective, in keeping with his creed that "weakness is a great thing and strength is nothing": a clear reversal of worldly values. Tarkovsky himself confessed a particular attraction towards the human weakness that discloses a different kind of strength, different from the affirmation of the self at the expense of others, and which he thought was evident in "the capacity of a human being to make a stand against the forces which drive his fellows into the rat race, into the rut of practicalities."[15] It was this moral ideal that he followed throughout his work[16] and which, I suggest, lends the quality of holy foolishness to his characters. Although sharing in weakness and simplicity, Stalker is far from the opaque idiocy of *durochka*. The twist comes towards the end of the film when this broken man, an outcast with no social ambitions, is discovered to be a voracious reader and, presumably, a major intellectual as the camera reveals the books covering an entire wall of his decrepit house. This type of intellectual could not provide a starker departure from the "self-assured, integrated and infallible" model of the hero promoted in Soviet socialist realism.[17]

But why is this powerless man deemed so dangerous that he needed to be restrained in a prison? Let us consider the threat that the mysterious Zone is posing. Once inside the Zone, the first thing the travelers are warned about is its alleged flaunting of any natural rules. The Zone is dangerous since it can turn even the distance between two points into a labyrinth replete with traps. However, this illusory quality of the place is compensated by its truth-revealing function. According to Stalker, not only are objective certainties tested but, more importantly, personal assumptions are challenged as well. Stalker's troubling revelation is that the secret Room unmasks people's hidden evil desires as somewhat more real than their apparently good intentions.

Visually, the strangeness of the place is rendered though unusual juxtapositions. The Zone is not something completely new, replete as it is with vestiges of heavy industrialization in a state of dereliction and engulfed by wilderness. Disused industrial sites provided Tarkovsky with the ideal settings for the issues he wished to raise. Here, these concrete symbols of Soviet modernization are subject to what De Baecque calls "degradation through mysticism"[18]: their decay is necessary in order to release their spiritual potencies. There is, however, more than a critique of Soviet industrialization at play here. The desolate space appears as a morgue for the whole of modern human civilization, be it socialist or capitalist: scattered around we see tanks in advanced stage of degradation, rotting in the tall grass, while guns and syringes rust under the water. The landscape looks apocalyptic. Everything that suggests the materialism of contemporary worldviews lies unredeemed and yet, as on the road to Emmaus, there are also redeeming possibilities lurking unrecognized for those who do not know how to look.

Stalker is deemed dangerous by the authorities because by taking people into the Zone he is trying to activate the transcendent-seeking potential of the human being. Tarkovsky intentionally construes the Zone in such an ambiguous way so that it is not clear whether it is an objective reality or Stalker's fantasy.[19] Let us take the example of a sequence that can support both readings. In one attempt to access the entrails of the Zone, the character Scientist leaves his rucksack behind. Worried, he returns to retrieve it in spite of Stalker's warning that he will never be able to find its location because the Zone changes continuously. In what appears to be one of the "traps," Stalker and Writer continue their journey only to arrive and find Scientist at the starting point. This raises questions in the viewer's mind about the reliability of Stalker's words. However, right before encountering Scientist, Writer spots some embers burning by themselves in the immediate vicinity of water, suggesting that something unusual is at work in the Zone. To explain these unusual phenomena, we are invited to assume that Stalker might either be a link with a space that exists outside the laws of everyday experience, or he is recreating the Zone himself, transforming the wasteland through "his faith in its power and beauty, into a receptacle of the sacred."[20] In either case, Stalker can be seen as an eschatological holy fool. In a world that has lost the religious legitimations of order, he is trying to recall the memory of the sacred, both scriptural and natural. In two dream-sequences, we hear voice-over readings from Scripture describing the sixth seal of the Apocalypse and Jesus's disciples on the road to Emmaus—standing for the sacred embodied in the text. Stalker's moments of tactile communion with the earth and the way the camera captures the spiritual potentiality of matter hint at the sacred embodied in nature. In this reading, Stalker recreates the sacred for a post-apocalyptic and post-"death of God" era, an impression emphasized by seeing the discarded reproduction of St. John the Baptist from Jan van Eyck's Ghent Altarpiece lying under the water.

If in *Stalker* the socialist socio-political context is immediately recognizable, in Tarkovsky's final two films, *Nostalghia* and *Sacrifice,* his critique of contemporary society extends more widely, and it is here that he transforms the holy fool into an opponent of what he sees as the wrongs of modernity, regardless of their national or political context. Since Tarkovsky had in 1982 made the decision never to return to the Soviet Union, these two films (his last) were made in Western Europe. Escaping a totalitarian regime, he was also quickly disappointed with the state of affairs in the West and ultimately came to deplore the way that the materialism imposed by the state in his country was embraced freely in democratic Europe.[21]

In *Nostalghia,* a new idea, that of sacrifice, comes to the fore, working in a tandem with holy foolishness. The protagonist, the Russian poet Andrei Gorchakov, visits Italy on a research trip. Like Tarkovsky himself, Gorchakov suffers from nostalgia for his mother country and also for his wife and son. But what appears to be the natural result of a geographic dislocation acquires a higher significance when he meets the native recluse Domenico: a figure that everybody considers mad. Yet, it is this madman who holds the key to understanding the critical power of the film. In one of his interviews, Tarkovsky explicitly ascribes to Domenico's madness a spiritual significance and conceives him in the terms that define holy foolishness: possessing an inner freedom, irrationality, child-likeness, marginality, self-sacrifice and a provocative function. In his words, Domenico's role is "to force us to act, to change the 'now'."[22] He demands from Gorchakov an act of faith:

to carry a candle across a pool, accomplishing what he is not allowed to do on grounds of insanity. Later, Domenico startles the viewer with an act of self-immolation, wanting to shock into spiritual awareness his lethargic audience in Rome's Piazza del Campidoglio.

Tarkovsky writes in *Sculpting in Time* that nostalgia overcomes Gorchakov because he remains unable "to find a balance between reality and the harmony for which he longs, in a state of nostalgia provoked not only by his remoteness from his country but also by a global yearning for the wholeness of existence."[23] This "wholeness of existence" is manifested in Gorchakov's inner struggle to "abolish borders" and in his attempt to unify three levels of existence: the moral—including the dream-like memories of Russia and his wife, belonging to the past; the aesthetical—the Italian ancient cultural heritage and Eugenia (his beautiful Italian translator); and the spiritual, manifested in Domenico's world.[24] Gorchakov is the only one who doubts that Domenico is mad and even argues that the mad are somehow closer to the truth. And indeed, Domenico's mysterious $1+1=1$ demonstration is not only the expression of the revolt against instrumental rationality but the mathematical formulation for what Andrei is experiencing and the solution for his existential crisis. In this respect, the Italian Domenico seems to manifest the clairvoyant powers of the Russian holy fools and the enigmatic language in which they hid their prophecies. For Gorchakov, the unity he has longed for in life is achieved only by his death and the absorption of his aesthetic and moral values into the religious. It is this accomplishment of the act of faith demanded by Domenico that is presented in the stasis of the final scene of the film. In a space beyond death, Gorchakov is shown sitting on the grass with Domenico's dog on his left-hand side and a Russian *dacha* (house) and trees in the background. As the camera tracks back, the whole landscape is revealed surrounded by the walls of a ruined Italian cathedral. Tarkovsky seems to suggest that his soul has finally managed to redeem his fragmented experiences through an act of faith.

What kind of faith is this though? It is one discovered outside Gorchakov's native country and seemingly outside the boundaries of official churches, and it is enacted in a ritual laid down by someone generally thought to be insane. Domenico's reputation for madness proceeds from a time when he kept his wife and child locked up in his house for seven years, awaiting the end of the world. In a tracking shot, we see his child venturing into the world outside their home. A priest standing on some church steps momentarily enters the frame, but there is no significant interaction with Domenico, who passes past him following his child. Years later, when Korchakov visits Domenico, the same church is shown in a state of desertion and dilapidation, while the madman's decaying house seems to have become so integrated with nature that the landscape is shown as thrusting forward from one of his rooms. At the same time, the fool's activity gravitates around St. Catherine's pool, and he offers Gorchakov wine and bread, unambiguous references to the Christian Eucharistic tradition. The figure of the fool is evidently used here to signify religion beyond the institutional boundaries of the official Church. Domenico is represented as a lay person who takes upon himself a divine mission prompted by what he considers to be apocalyptical signs.

Domenico's mission is not, however, restricted to single individuals. As he confesses to Gorchakov, he was wrong when he sequestered his family for seven years in a desperate attempt to save them: "My motives were egotistical when I tried to save my family. You should save everyone." Still, if he entrusts Andrei with the mission to cross St Catherine's pool with a lit candle, he reserves for himself a much more difficult task: the need to awaken consciences. He attempts to do this first through a speech from on top of the equestrian statue of Marcus Aurelius in Piazza del Campidoglio. He not only urges the return to the great ideals but also addresses ecological concerns and stands up for the disempowered of the world in the name of fraternity. His aim is a reversal of modern values and the social order if not a total transformation of the world as we know it: "It must be sunny at night and snowy in August" he declares.

The location he chooses for staging his protest is Rome: the city most charged with historical and religious significance for the European civilization. Moreover, set atop the Capitoline Hill, the Piazza del Campidoglio, he faces the Vatican Hill, underlying his uneasy relationship with one of the great religious institutions. In order to call the world's attention to his message, he proceeds with an act of self-immolation. At first sight this solution seems irrational in its radicalism. And yet, it would not be something totally alien to Russian religious dissenters[25] and certainly was a means of political protest familiar to late twentieth-century audiences, both within and without the Soviet Bloc.[26] Remaining within a Christian ethos though, the fire triggers a number of connections: the purifying fire of God (Zech. 13:9); Jesus Christ, who has come to cast the eschatological fire onto earth (Lk. 12:49); the Holy Spirit in the form of tongues of fire at Pentecost (Acts 2:3) and God as consuming fire (Heb. 12:29). Domenico turns himself into a human candle—his self-sacrifice being envisioned as an eschatological renewal of the world through his aim of rekindling the divine spark in human souls.

Tarkovsky revisited this network of connections between madness, self-sacrifice, apocalyptic destruction and regeneration by fire in his subsequent and last film. In *The Sacrifice* (1986), the supreme sacrifice Domenico offered of his life is matched by that of the character Alexander, who renounces everything he possesses, including his family and beloved son, in order that the world is spared from a nuclear disaster. Alexander is an intellectual whose moral aspirations have been stifled by the lack of spirituality around him. A former actor, whose most successful roles were impersonating two extremes of humanity—Prince Myshkin, the personification of goodness, and Richard III, the embodiment of evil—Alexander strives for an authenticity and meaning of life that he can only find in sacrificing himself for the salvation of others. When the occasion presents itself, he not only rises to the challenge, but warmly welcomes it: "I have waited my whole life for this." Turning to God for salvation, he offers everything he has in order to avert a nuclear holocaust. His immolation echoes Domenico's. The burning of his wooden house is a symbolic act; the building is reminiscent of the *dacha,* the Russian country house that is a recurrent image in Tarkovsky's films. It can be used metaphorically to represent the human body, in which case Alexander's final act can be interpreted not only as a renunciation of the materialistic concerns but also as a denial of his self.[27] In this interpretation, his descent into madness is just the result of this total surrender into God's hands and marks the beginning of his spiritual regeneration as well as the salvation of the world. In other words, it is a passage from the sphere of the aesthetic, represented by his artistic interests, into the sphere of the religious. Through the character of Alexander, Tarkovsky offers us the moment of transformation when an ordinary person becomes a holy fool.

In *Stalker, Nostalghia* and *The Sacrifice,* holy foolishness abstracts the hero from the usual order of things and places him in a position from which he can launch a critique of the fundamentals of the modern world. Stalker, Domenico and Alexander are all existentialist characters who take upon themselves the responsibility for the entire world, and each wants to save humanity from the perceived domination of materialism, spiritual bankruptcy and looming disaster. All have a sense of the imminence of the end of this world, which Tarkovsky also shared.[28] This moment of crisis is at the same time a moment of judgment in which the solution for salvation is given. The eschatological dimension Tarkovsky incorporates into his fools is connected to the idea of salvation, both physical and spiritual. As a result, the image of the holy fool becomes conflated with that of a savior. Stalker believes that he alone can save people from despair and unhappiness, which have become their second nature. Domenico thinks he is called upon not only to save his own family from spiritual death but also the whole of humanity. In *The Sacrifice,* the fate of the whole world seems dependent on Alexander's actions. For Tarkovsky, this emphasis upon the individual was not in contradiction with the communal since each human person bears responsibility for the whole community.[29] In a way not so dissimilar to Christ's sacrifice for the purpose of universal salvation, in Tarkovsky's films the sacrifice of the holy fool takes on a universal significance.

I would like to argue that this universality takes on various guises. In his final films, Tarkovsky moves beyond the boundaries of his own culture in an attempt to reach out to a world in an advanced state of desacralization. His characters are not pious ascetics but rather people who live ordinary lives in a secularized world. Through Tarkovsky's films, we witness a conscious move towards a translation of "things Russian" into a universal language: one that would be widely intelligible for a Western audience as well.

In his final films, after his exile from Russia, and especially in *Nostalghia,* the problem of cultural translation came into particularly sharp focus, prompted by the necessity of making himself understood by a primarily non-Russian audience. The last part of Tarkovsky's artistic career can therefore be seen as evolving a transformation of the holy fool into a universal, less traditional figure, with *Nostalghia* trying to reconcile East and West while still offering a nod to the Russian utopia. For this purpose, the cultural model of the holy fool, with its non-dogmatic, anti-structural component was an ideal form of expression. Domenico is not a Russian in spite of embodying much of the maximalism of the Russian spirit. Neither is Alexander, but he appreciates the art of both Leonardo and the Orthodox iconographers, and his kimono bears the yin and yang signs, a symbol for the complementarity of opposites, while *Sacrifice* itself is particularly marked by cultural eclecticism.[30] We witness, therefore, a progression towards a religiosity which transcends the boundaries of national ideologies and institutionalized Christianity.

Tarkovsky's achievement illustrates the manner in which some Russian directors have managed to elevate the figure of the holy fool beyond its historical and cultural context and explore the universal significance of its religious function. In so doing, they have proved the versatility of the holy fool as a mechanism for responding to a wide range of concerns in a pluralistic modernity. It is in a Russian context that the traditional religious role of the holy fool is most intelligible, and it is no surprise that the adoption of the hagiographic formula in cinema has offered us Anatoly, a holy fool who, under divine inspiration, reclaims from the fringes of the Christian Orthodox religion a return to the living God of faith. It is when the holy fool has been translated out of this context, however, by more ambitious directors, that the figure has been best able to grapple with issues of universal significance across faith boundaries. As we have seen, the work of Andrei Tarkovsky comprehensively revised the image of the holy fool, adapting its functions to launch a damning critique of what he saw as the wrongs of modern society brought about by a destructive rationality. With Tarkovsky, holy fools are no longer easily circumscribed by a single religious tradition. They are latter-day holy fools whose hypersensitivity places a contemporary spiritual void under a magnifying glass. If Nietzsche's madman was heralding the "death of God" already underway, a century later Tarkovsky's madmen can be considered post –"death-of-God" holy fools. In an apocalyptic atmosphere, which yokes together the catastrophic event with the void of spirituality, they are trying to keep the memory of faith alive and to recreate religion from scattered fragments of modern culture. Theirs is a *de profundis* cry to a God, both known and unknown, to save humanity from itself.

NOTES

1. Sergei A. Ivanov, *Holy Fools in Byzantium and Beyond* (Oxford: Oxford University Press, 2006), 24.
2. Ibid., 399.
3. Joan Neuberger, *Ivan the Terrible* (London, New York: I. B. Tauris, 2003), 28.

4. Ivanov, *Holy Fools in Byzantium and Beyond*, 297.
5. Aleksander Yanov, *The Origins of Autocracy: Ivan the Terrible in Russian History* (Berkeley and Los Angeles, California: University of California Press, 1981), 176.
6. Joan Neuberger, 'The Politics of Bewilderment: Eisenstein's *Ivan the Terrible* in 1945," in *Eisenstein at 100: A Reconsideration*, eds. Al La Valley and Barry P. Scherr (New Brunswick, NJ: Rutgers University Press, 2001), 247.
7. The press kit for "Around the World in 14 Films—The Berlin Independent Film Festival at Babylon, 2006." Available at www.berlinbabylon14.de/ger/presse/pr_russland.pdf. Last accessed October 1, 2008.
8. Ibid.
9. Ewa M. Thompson, *Understanding Russia: The Holy Fool in Russian Culture* (Lanham and London: University Press of America, 1987), 133.
10. Russian cinema offers a gallery of stylized holy fool figures put to various uses in films such as Pyotr Todorovsky's *Wartime Romance* (1983), Alexander Kaidanovsky's *Kerosene Seller's Wife* (1989) and Andrei Konchalovsky's *Dom Durakov/The House of Fools* (2002). However, for the purpose of this chapter, I will only refer to stylized holy fools whose function is overtly religious.
11. It is also worth noting the existence of a non-cinematic holy fool in Tarkovsky's artistic career. When directing Mussorgsky's *Boris Godunov* in 1984 for the Royal Opera House, Covent Garden, he made a striking portrayal of a historical holy fool by adding to Nikolka's iron chains a hood reminiscent of those condemned to death, an idea that he used in his last two films.
12. Peter C. Bouteneff, " 'What kind of Fool Am I?', Further Gleanings from Holy Folly," in *Abba: the tradition of Orthodoxy in the West*, festschrift for Bishop Kallistos (Ware) of Diokleia, eds. John Behr, Andrew Louth, and Dimitri Conomos (Crestwood, NY: St Vladimir's Seminary Press, 2003).
13. George P. Fedotov, *The Russian Religious Mind, vol. 2, The Middle Age: The Thirteenth to the Fifteenth Centuries* (Cambridge, MA: Harvard University Press, 1966), 322.
14. Paul Johnson, "Subjectivity and Sociality in the Films of Andrei Tarkovsky," in *Through the Mirror: Reflections on the Films of Andrei Tarkovsky*, eds. Gunnlaugur A. Jónsson and Thorkell Á. Óttarsson (Newcastle upon Tyne: Cambridge Scholars Press, 2006), 70.
15. Tarkovsky, *Sculpting in Time: Reflections on the Cinema*, trans. Kitty Hunter-Blair (London: Bodley Head, 1986), 209.
16. Andrei Tarkovsky, "Tarkovsky at the Mirror," interview by Tonino Guerra, *Panorama*, 676 (1979), 160–70. Available at www.ucalgary.ca/tstronds/nostalghia.com/TheTopics/Tarkovsky_Guerra-1979.html. Last accessed 5 January 5, 2009.
17. Rufus W. Mathewson, "The Soviet Hero and the Literary Heritage," *American Slavic and East European Review*, 12 (1953), 508.
18. Antoine De Baecque, *Camera Historica: The Century in Cinema* (New York: Columbia University Press, 2012), 256.
19. Andrei Tarkovsky, "Interview with Andrei Tarkovsky (on Stalker), by Aldo Tassone (1980)," in *Andrei Tarkovsky: Interviews*, ed. John Gianvito (Jackson: University Press of Mississippi, 2006), 55.
20. De Baecque, *Camera Historica: The Century in Cinema*, 258.
21. Andrei Tarkovsky, "A propos du *Sacrifice*," interview by Annie Epelboin, *Positif* (May 1986), 3–5.
22. Andrei Tarkovsky, "To Journey Within," interview by Gideon Bachmann. Available at www.ucalgary.ca/tstronds/nostalghia.com/TheTopics/Gideon_Bachmann.html. Last accessed January 20, 2009.
23. Tarkovsky, *Sculpting in Time*, 204–05.

24. Balint Andras Kovacs and Akos Szilagyi, *Les Mondes d'Andrei Tarkovski* (Lausanne: L'age d'homme, 1987), 154.
25. Sergei Nikolaevich Bulgakov, *The Orthodox Church* (Crestwood: St Vladimir's Seminary Press, 1988), 177.
26. Famous cases that raised self-immolation to international awareness are Thích Quảng Đúc in Saigon in 1963 and Jan Palach in Prague in 1969.
27. Vida T. Johnson and Graham Petrie, *The Films of Andrei Tarkovsky: A Visual Fugue* (Bloomington and Indianapolis: Indiana University Press, 1994), 225.
28. Andrei Tarkovsky, "Red Tape," interview by Angus MacKinnon (1984), in *Andrei Tarkovsky: Interviews,* ed. John Gianvito (Jackson: University Press of Mississippi, 2006), 160.
29. Andrei Tarkovsky, *Time within Time: The Diaries, 1970–1986* (Calcutta: Seagull, 1991), 16.
30. Vida T. Johnson and Graham Petrie, *The Films of Andrei Tarkovsky,* 182.

3 The New Aesthetics of Muslim Spirituality in Turkey
Yusuf's Trilogy by Semih Kaplanoğlu

Asuman Suner

Turkish director Semih Kaplanoğlu's film *Honey* (*Bal*) (2010) won the Golden Bear at the 60th International Berlin Film Festival in 2010.[1] *Honey* is the last installment of Kaplanoğlu's trilogy *Egg* (*Yumurta*) (2007), *Milk* (*Süt*) (2008) and *Honey* (2010), also known as *Yusuf's Trilogy*, named after its main character. The trilogy narrates three stages (adulthood, youth and childhood, in that order) of a man's life.

Over the last two decades, Turkey's new wave cinema has gained considerable visibility and recognition, particularly in Europe. Today, it is quite common for films from Turkey to compete at international film festivals. What is new about Kaplanoğlu's award is that for the first time a director who emphasizes his Muslim identity and associates himself with the Islamic cultural field in Turkey has received a major European award.

The Golden Bear that *Honey* won was intriguing in terms of the cultural resonances it generated in Turkey. While the religious standing of Kaplanoğlu's film has seen a positive reception from viewers in Europe (apart from the Golden Bear, *Honey* also received the Prize of the Ecumenical Jury, an award created by Christian filmmakers and film critics to honor works of artistic quality that give witness to the power of film to reveal the mysterious depths of human beings), its religious connotations have been largely ignored by the secularist cultural establishment and intellectual circles in Turkey. Praising the film for its artistic accomplishments, Turkish cultural critics, who often come from a secular and leftist background, did not exactly know what to make of its religious orientation and turned a blind eye to this aspect. Contrary to the ambivalent reception in secular circles, *Honey*'s victory in Berlin was largely celebrated by Turkey's Islamic circles and perceived as an accomplishment of rising Islamic culture in Turkey.

As a Turkish film exploring Muslim spirituality, *Honey* occupies an ambiguous cultural space in terms of its reception in Turkey. This chapter seeks to make sense of *Yusuf's Trilogy* with reference to the competing discourses and frames of reference surrounding it. The first part of the chapter offers a glimpse into the historical roots of the secularist cultural establishment and the growing Islamic cultural field in Turkey. The second part presents a brief assessment of the conventional works of Islamic cinema in Turkey

The New Aesthetics of Muslim Spirituality in Turkey 45

and their disparity with Kaplanoğlu's films. The third section is based on a close reading of *Yusuf's Trilogy* through the concept of "spiritual realism." Finally, the concluding part suggests that the kind of Muslim spirituality and aesthetics that Kaplanoğlu's films articulate does not point to institutional and dogmatic aspects of Islam but that it directs attention to the ways that Islam is perceived and lived by ordinary people in Turkey. I contend that the making of this new aesthetic form is informed by the competing social and political discourses surrounding it.

THE SECULARIST ESTABLISHMENT AND THE ISLAMIC CULTURAL FIELD IN TURKEY

As a constitutionally secular state with a majority Muslim population, the Republic of Turkey was established in 1923 on the ruins of the Ottoman Empire. Throughout the 1920s and 1930s, the Turkish state implemented rigid secularist policies to regulate and control the presence of Islam in public life.[2] Under the leadership of Mustafa Kemal Atatürk, the founders of the Republic abolished the Caliphate and religious orders. They secularized the legal system, educational institutions and culture. This particular form of top-down modernization and secularism has shaped the worldview of the educated elites and the military in Turkey ever since.[3] Secularism, Yael Navaro-Yashin suggests, has never been a "neutral paradigm" in Turkey; rather, it has been a "state ideology" as well as a "hegemonic public discourse."[4]

In the Kemalist ideology, Islam has often been associated with backwardness. In the discourse of the Republican elites, Reşat Kasaba states, "Islam became an all-purpose bogey representing everything that reform, progress, and civilization were not."[5] Consequently, Islamists were harassed, persecuted and shunned as reactionary during the early decades of the Republic.[6] Yet, Islamic movements have managed to survive the state-imposed secularism.[7] In 1950, Turkey moved away from a single-party to a multi-party regime, which increased the presence of Islam in public life and relaxed the state's hold on religion.[8] During this period, new ideas that promoted the revival of Turkey's Islamic inheritance began to be expressed in Parliament.[9] As of the mid-1960s, the rising wave of political Islam in the Muslim world began to affect the ideas of Turkish Islamists.[10] By the late 1960s, efforts to represent the Islamist movement in the form of an independent political party became visible.[11] Following the economic and political turmoil of the 1970s,[12] the 1980s began with the September 12, 1980, military coup, which brought about a restructuring of the social and political institutions in line with the anti-democratic 1982 Constitution. In economic terms, the first half of the 1980s saw the introduction of a series of neo-liberal reforms as well as a number of ground-breaking legal and technological reforms, particularly in the information and communication sectors that paved the way for Turkey's full integration into the global capitalist system.[13]

Although the policy of systematic de-politicization pursued by the military regime was still effective, the mid-1980s witnessed the emergence of new social movements, including those of feminists, gay communities, environmentalists, religious and ethnic minorities and Islamists. The key common motive behind these diverse movements was their opposition to the Kemalist project of creating a uniform national identity.[14] This was the context in which a new generation of "Islamic intellectuals" and Islamic cultural actors emerged.[15] The new generation of Islamic intellectuals contributed to the social and cultural debates of the 1980s and 1990s by adding an Islamic perspective to the critique of the Kemalist modernization project.[16] It was also during this period that a powerful Islamic media and culture industry emerged in Turkey.[17] Constituting a discursive space outside the hegemony of both the state and the traditional hierarchy of Islam, these cultural outlets allowed new Islamic actors to construct their own version of Islam. The 2002 general elections represent a turning point in Turkey's recent history, in the sense that for the first time an "Islam-sensitive" political party, the Justice and Development Party (AKP),[18] came to power alone.[19] Under the rule of a pro-Islamic party, the Islamic cultural field has significantly expanded in Turkey since the 2000s.[20] During this period, Islamic groups, rather than the Kemalist elite, have begun to shape the norms of everyday life and define Turkish mainstream culture.[21]

ISLAMIC CINEMA IN TURKEY

Popular cinema in Turkey, which is generally called "Yeşilçam Cinema" (literally, pine tree cinema) after the street in Istanbul where the film production companies were located, had its heyday in the 1960s and early 1970s when the country was among the top film producers in the world. The project of building an Islamic cinema had first been discussed in the same years by the conservative right-leaning youth rallying around the National Turkish Student Union (*Milli Türk Talebe Birliği*).[22] The Islamic "National Cinema" movement was critical of the commercial Yeşilçam Cinema for its uncritical appropriation of a modern Westernized life-style. It aimed at creating, according to Hilmi Maktav, a new vision of the Turkish "nation" constituted on the basis of a shared Islamic identity and culture.[23] The first significant example of the Islamic "National Cinema" movement was Yücel Çakmaklı's 1971 film *Crossing Roads* (*Birleşen Yollar*),[24] an adaptation of Şule Yüksel Şenler's 1970 bestselling Islamic novel *Serenity Street* (*Huzur Sokağı*).[25] Revolving around the love story between a girl from a wealthy, secular, modern family and a pious boy from a traditional, low-income neighborhood, the film advocates Islamic values and a traditional conservative life-style against the "degenerating" and "corrupting" influences of modern society. Ironically, with its melodramatic structure, simple plot-line and exaggerated mise-en-scène, the narrative and visual style of Yücel Çakmaklı's film has a lot in common with the popular narratives of 1960s' Yeşilçam Cinema. The typical Yeşilçam love story involving a rich girl and a poor boy (or the other way around) was now reconceived with an emphasis on Muslim identity.[26] In the following years, young directors emerging from the National Turkish Student Union, such as Salih Diriklik and Mesut Uçakan, made Islamic films addressing issues such as disintegrating families, moral degeneration, alienation and anomy among youth, destructive influences of communist ideology and so forth.[27] These social problems, in their understanding, arose from the weakening of Islamic thinking and way of life in Turkish society. The shared concern of these films, according to Ayşe Saktanber, was to "fill the moral void created by the denial of a place for Islam in society in general and in Turkish cinema in particular."[28]

Despite their attempt at ideological critique, Islamic films did not succeed in articulating a distinct intellectual and aesthetic cinematic vision. Instead, they tended to reproduce the conventional cinematic codes of Yeşilçam Cinema based on clichés and stereotypes. In line with the popular Islamic salvation novels of the 1980s, popular Islamic films tended to reflect the relation between the good, modest and authentic traditional Muslim person and the degenerate, alienated and bad modern one.[29] Just like Yeşilçam Cinema's stereotypes, the characters in Islamic films were either "good" or "bad." They did not retain a complex subjectivity torn between moral, personal and social dilemmas.

After its two-decade-long successful commercial growth, popular Turkish cinema started to decline in the late 1970s.[30] The crisis in the film industry deepened throughout the 1980s and early 1990s, a period when the number of both domestically produced films and of their viewers drastically decreased. The mid-1990s witnessed a revival of Turkish cinema with the emergence of a new generation of young directors. By the 2000s, art-house films from Turkey were featured extensively in competitions and showcase programs of all major international film festivals.[31] While some of the internationally acclaimed auteur directors of the new wave cinema tend to make personal films exploring the human soul, a growing number of them address political issues in their films, such as the periods of martial law or the discriminatory policies against religious and ethnic minorities in the history of the Republic.[32]

Islamic cinema could not synchronize itself with the rise of Turkey's new wave cinema. This is partly because Islamic films could not reach the degree of intellectual and aesthetic sophistication that new wave art films have offered. More significantly, however, Islamic films were primarily preoccupied with the idea of conveying a religious message rather than engaging in in-depth and critical investigation of Muslim subjectivity.[33]

YUSUF'S TRILOGY BY SEMİH KAPLANOĞLU

In a period when Islamic cinema was on the wane in Turkey, the critical acclaim that *Yusuf's Trilogy* by Semih Kaplanoğlu received in the international arena has created excitement and celebration in Islamic circles. While Kaplanoğlu publicly emphasizes his Muslim identity and relates himself to the Islamic cultural revival, his films are in no way continuous with the Islamic cinema tradition in Turkey. For one thing, Kaplanoğlu's trilogy invokes a sense of Muslim spirituality without addressing contemporary religious issues. Kaplanoğlu's films do not try to convey an "Islamic message"; they do not even entail "Islamic" characters. Rather than taking issue with the highly politicized questions of secularism and religion in Turkey, Kaplanoğlu's films display Muslim faith as it is experienced in the everyday life by ordinary Turks. They seek to offer a spiritual aesthetic experience. Given the intellectual and aesthetic sophistication of his style, we can suggest that Kaplanoğlu's trilogy has more in common with Turkey's new wave art cinema than with Islamic films.

Semih Kaplanoğlu does not come from a religious background. He was raised in a modern secular, middle-class family in İzmir during the 1960s. He was educated in secular institutions. Apart from his closeness to his elderly grandparents—as a child he enjoyed observing them performing Islamic religious rituals—there was nothing in his childhood and youth connecting him to religious life. The discovery of what he calls a sphere of "spirituality" and of a profound meaning of Muslim faith came much later in his life. After studying film and arts at the university, he took up several jobs as a screenwriter and director in the television and advertisement sectors throughout the 1990s. He made two feature films during the first half of the 2000s, *Away From Home (Herkes Kendi Evinde,* 2001) and *Angel's Fall (Meleğin Düşüşü,* 2005). Neither of these films fully reflects his gradual religious awakening. Kaplanoğlu's search for spirituality materialized in the mid-2000s as he grew increasingly uneasy with the conventional rational, secular and materialist worldview he had internalized. In this period, he began to discover how the process of radical Westernization and secularization in Turkey had created a shallow intellectual environment alienated from its own cultural roots. It was during this time that Kaplanoğlu came to define himself as a faithful Muslim and chose to lead a life in accordance with Islamic rules.[34] From then on, he embraced Muslim faith to find a deeper meaning in life and in cinema.

Kaplanoğlu conceives cinema as a "spiritual" domain. He describes his cinematic style as "spiritual realism" in the sense that he attempts to balance spirituality and realism without falling into either an extreme realism leaning toward rigid naturalism or into a fantasmatic spirituality devoid of reality.[35] He rather seeks to capture the spiritual dimension in reality. The balance that he tries to reach in his films, he states, reflects God's preaching of the kind of life that devout people should lead. The life of a faithful Muslim, Kaplanoğlu indicates, should not be about isolating oneself from the world and living in abstract spirituality. It should be about living spirituality within the reality of everyday life.[36] The vision of "spiritual realism," which comes in full view in *Yusuf's Trilogy,* has been influenced by the earlier generation of European auteur directors who explored spiritual and religious subjects in their films, such as Robert Bresson, Ingmar Bergman, and most notably Andrei Tarkovsky. Kaplanoğlu cites Tarkovsky's *Mirror* (1975) as a film that shaped his approach to cinema.[37] Seeing *Mirror* as a film addressing the central issues of life and human existence, Kaplanoğlu particularly admires the sense of "time" that the film invokes through merging its non-linear narrative with historical footage.[38] He describes the effect of the film as "the heart's (not the mind's) witnessing of the passage of time."[39] *Yusuf's Trilogy* resonates with *Mirror* in terms of the centrality of remembrance in the organization of the narrative as well as its preoccupation with the motifs of childhood, poetry and dreams.

The trilogy narrates the life of a man, Yusuf, in reverse order. It begins with Yusuf's adulthood in the first film (*Egg*), goes back to his adolescent years in the second (*Milk*) and concludes with his childhood in the last one (*Honey*). At the beginning of *Egg*, we see Yusuf (Nejat İşler) as a man on the threshold of middle age, running a second-hand bookstore in Istanbul. He seems lonely and depressed, finding refuge in alcohol. The film narrates Yusuf's journey back to his native Tire, a provincial town in western Turkey, for his mother's funeral. In *Milk*, we see Yusuf (Melih Selçuk) as a young man aspiring to become a poet while working in his mother's rural dairy business. *Honey* takes the viewer back to Yusuf's childhood. Now, Yusuf (Bora Altas) is a first-grader, keeping his father, a beekeeper, company during his trips to the deep corners of the forest in search for honey.

While *Yusuf's Trilogy* represents three stages of a man's life, Kaplanoğlu is not interested in offering a sociologically accurate representation of reality. *Honey* and *Milk* were not shot as period films that represent the historical reality of the social context when Yusuf's childhood and youth presumably took place. Instead, the different stages of Yusuf's life are all set in the present. Focusing on the character's inner journey, the trilogy aims to create a "cosmic time"—that is, a time conceived of in its entireness and permanence.[40] The trilogy's visual style, in this regard, recalls Gilles Deleuze's notion of "time-image" cinema, particularly the way in which it appears in films by new wave Iranian directors (most notably Abbas Kiarostami) where the camera makes us witness mainly the passing of time.[41] Different from the model of the "movement-image," where there is a tightly structured narrative and where objects and settings have a functional reality, "time-image" cinema tends to describe open-ended situations where things do not necessarily serve a narrative purpose. The visual style of *Yusuf's Trilogy* is closer to the "time-image" cinema because of its preference for long shots and long takes that present situations in their spatial and temporal entirety, without any interruption. Time is not divided into fragments through heavy editing. Events are de-dramatized. No musical soundtrack is used. Like new wave Iranian films, "open images" are preferred particularly in film endings.[42] These images do not "close down a narrative but rather open it out to the viewer's consideration."[43] The cinematic style of the trilogy conveys a sense of "cosmic time" mirroring the pace of nature. Close-up shots are reserved, particularly in *Honey*, for the detailed examination of the internal rhythm of natural elements, such as insects and birds, leaves and flowers. In many scenes, time unfolds all by itself without serving any narrative purpose.

Kaplanoğlu's preference for "time-image" cinema is closely related to his interest in spirituality and religion. He emphasizes that he perceives cinema as a "spiritual realm."[44] The type of film language that divides time into fragments through fast editing, he states, takes the viewer away from the realm of spirituality.[45] Cinema, Kaplanoğlu contends, should instead create an experience of "spiritual transcendence," an experience which is not necessarily based on any specific religious doctrine.[46] This should be possible by conveying time in its entireness and permanence. In *Yusuf's Trilogy*, the narrative centers on a perpetual present. The present contains the traces of the past and signs of the future; it embraces life and death at once.

Taking us back to Yusuf's childhood, *Honey*, the third installment of the trilogy, tells the story about the loss of the father. After the epilogue, the film begins with the disembodied voice of the father coming from somewhere in the dark. The voice commands: "Read." Then, we see Yusuf reading slowly and with some difficulty the date of the day from the calendar on the wall. In this way, as Senem Aytaç indicates, the film places Yusuf in its opening sequence at the "threshold of the symbolic order" by emphasizing the process of the "acquisition of language."[47] With his authoritative voice commanding to read, the father compels the entrance of the child into the domain of language. Yet, in *Honey* the father does not turn into a figure representing "symbolic authority." On the contrary, he is someone who for the child opens up the domain of transcendence, imagination and spirituality.

Later in the film, we discover that Yusuf, struggling with a stutter, is having a hard time learning to read. Reading aloud in class is an ordeal for him. He feels so depressed in school that he remains indoors during recess. The only subject that intrigues him is poetry. An overheard passage of Arthur Rimbaud's "Sensation" read aloud by a little girl deeply impresses him. Not enjoying school, Yusuf likes accompanying his father during his daily trips into the forest to cultivate honey, a work that sometimes requires the suspension of hives from tree branches at dangerous heights. During these trips, Yakup, the father, teaches the child how to listen to the voices of nature. He helps his son understand that there may be ways of connecting to the world other than language. Yakup never challenges his son about his stuttering or difficulty with reading. He seems totally disinterested in the boy's success in school. Rather, he lures Yusuf into an imaginary world they both enjoy sharing. Yakup tells his son that when he does not want to talk he can whisper. Whispering turns into a secret ritual between the two. Likewise, Yakup tells his son not to reveal his dreams to others because they possess a secret meaning. In this way, he directs the child's attention to the domains of imagination and spirituality.

The special bond between father and son becomes manifest also through the epilepsy they share. In *Honey*, Yusuf witnesses his father having an epileptic seizure. From the first two parts of the trilogy, we know that Yusuf will suffer from the same disease in his adult life. The theme of epilepsy is linked to the imaginary realm that father and son share in the sense that this neurological condition creates a different experience of reality by altering the perception of the world.[48] As opposed to the strong bond between Yusuf and his father, the mother appears as a rather shallow figure in *Honey*. She is a gentle and caring young woman worried about her husband's business, which is threatened by the encroaching environmental pollution that kills bees and requires him to seek better terrain far away from home. Indeed, eventually Yakup does not return from one of his trips. The young woman embarks on a journey to find her husband, only to learn that he has died in an accident while trying to reach high tree branches. *Honey* ends with the loss of the father. In the final sequence of the film, we see Yusuf in the darkness of the night, lying down motionless in the fetal position between the large roots of a massive tree as though trying to hide from the world.

While *Honey*'s story centers on the loss of the father, *Milk,* the second installment, tells the story of separation from the mother. Here, Yusuf appears as a young man at the end of his adolescence living with his mother in Tire. Mother and son try to keep up their rural dairy business, which is about to die in a modernizing country where food production is increasingly industrialized. Unlike his teenage friends who hang out with girls, Yusuf prefers to spend his time alone, reading and writing poetry. He gets excited when one of his poems is published by a small independent literary journal. At this stage of his life, Yusuf seems ready to build an independent existence for himself. If he were to leave everything behind, a separation from his mother and hometown would be a welcome change. But things do not turn out this way. Yusuf's original plan is to leave Tire to fulfill his compulsory military service—the conventional rite of passage for young men in Turkey. Yet, because of his epilepsy, he is found unfit for military service. This means that his entrance into the social and symbolic order is once again interrupted by a physical handicap.[49] Just like the stutter that prevented him from learning to read properly, his epilepsy prevents him from military service. Perceiving this situation as a humiliating failure, he falls prey to frustration, which turns into anger when he learns that his mother is considering marriage to a widower. As it were, while Yusuf is preparing to leave his mother, it is the mother who is leaving him. At the end of *Milk*, Yusuf appears as a disillusioned young man, working in a quarry—a far cry from his poetic dreams.

Opposed to the theme of loss that prevails in *Honey* and *Milk,* the first installment, *Egg,* tells a story of recovery and reunion. At the beginning of the film, we see Yusuf as a man in his early forties. Reaching the bottom of a wine bottle, he gets ready to sleep in his small living area inside the second-hand bookstore. He seems lonely, alienated and depressed when he receives a phone call from Tire notifying him that his mother has died. Next, we watch him returning to Tire for the funeral of his mother, from whom he seems to have long been alienated. Yusuf's original plan is to spend the shortest-possible time in his hometown, which he has not visited for years, and to return to Istanbul right after the funeral. Yet, Ayla (Saadet Işıl Atasoy), a distant relative in her twenties, who had been living with Yusuf's mother for the last couple of years, tells him that he has to perform the sacrifice that his mother, due to her death, had been prevented from fulfilling. Trying to shirk the responsibility at first, at the insistence of the young woman Yusuf eventually agrees to honor his mother's vow. The two together set off on a short trip to a saint's tomb for the traditional sacrifice ceremony that Yusuf's mother had pledged. During this trip, Yusuf begins to become aware of his attraction to Ayla. Yet, he does not make any moves despite the young woman's obvious mutual interest. When they return to Tire, he drops Ayla with a plain goodbye and hits the road to Istanbul. On his way back, he pulls the car into a deserted gas station to have a rest. He takes a short walk in the vast landscape. Suddenly, a large wild dog appears from the dark and hits him with its front legs. Falling down, Yusuf remains still out of fear and sits on his knees next to the dog throughout the night. He eventually falls asleep. When he wakes up early in the morning, the dog has disappeared. This strange encounter induces a catharsis of sorts in Yusuf, making him cry for the first time after his mother's death. Upon this incident, instead of returning to Istanbul, he drives back to Ayla, who is waiting for him in his mother's house.

Honey, milk and egg are key motifs characterizing different stages of Yusuf's life in the trilogy. Honey defines Yusuf's strong emotional connection with his father and the realm of imagination and spirituality they share. In several scenes, we watch Yusuf with great pleasure tasting the honey that his father brings down from the heights of the trees. In Yusuf's childhood memory, honey signifies pure happiness, delight and a sense of wholeness. Later in life, Yusuf will try to capture this in the imaginary world of poetry. In *Egg* we learn that the title of his poetry book is "Honey." In contrast to honey, Yusuf does not like milk. As a child, he does not want to drink the glass of milk that his mother offers him; the father drinks his milk instead, thus forming a secret alliance. In his early youth, Yusuf does not enjoy the rural dairy business where he helps his mother. He is interested in reading and writing poetry. A worldly woman preoccupied with earning a livelihood for herself and her son after having been widowed at a young age, Yusuf's mother never fully appreciates his interest in poetry. She sees it superficially, as a youthful pastime, having to do with Yusuf's secret romantic feelings for the young girls around him. Yusuf is maddened by his mother's lack of intellectual depth. The motif of milk, in this regard, seems to signify Yusuf's alienation from his mother.

While honey and milk are motifs that dominate the entire narrative in the last two installments of the trilogy, the motif of the egg is foregrounded only in the final sequence of the first installment. After his encounter with the wild dog on the road, Yusuf, instead of continuing his trip to Istanbul, unexpectedly returns to Tire. He sits at the old-style kitchen table in his deceased mother's house. After a short while, Ayla appears at the door, holding in her palm an egg that she has taken from the henhouse in the garden. She seems to be pleased to see Yusuf. Without a word, she passes the egg on to him. Then, the two begin to eat breakfast silently. The film has an ambivalent ending; we do not know exactly what will happen next to the main character. We can speculate that he will start a new life with Ayla, and possibly the two will raise a family. The egg, as a motif appearing in the final sequence of the film, has an enclosed form. We do not know what it contains. Yet, its meaning is linked to the idea of reproduction and the continuity of life. In this regard, we can conceive of the egg as a motif taking the story back to the beginning of life, to the mother's womb. We can even suggest a parallel between the endings of the first and the last installments of the trilogy. In *Honey*, we see Yusuf as a child in agony, isolating himself from the world and finding refuge in nature after the loss of his father. In the final scene of the film, we see Yusuf hiding from the world in the fetal position between the roots of a massive tree, as though yearning to return to the mother's womb and the sense of wholeness that it embodies. At the end of *Egg*, we see Yusuf as a middle-aged man on the threshold of forming a family of his own, reuniting with his past and making a commitment to the continuity of life. Symmetrically, the recovery of the lonely child hiding from the world in the fetal position at the end of *Honey* seems to come in the form of an egg that retains the potential of containing new life within.

Kaplanoğlu's style of "spiritual realism" emerges in *Yusuf's Trilogy* also through subtle allusions to Muslim faith and spirituality. The opening sequence of *Honey* in which we hear the father's disembodied voice coming from somewhere in the dark and commanding "read" contains a reference to the Quran. The father's voice in *Honey* echoes the first revelation that the Prophet Muhammad received (which takes place in the sura Al-Alaq) as he was praying in a cave on Mount Hira, near Mecca, and the angel Gabriel commanded him to recite the following verse: "Read! [Or proclaim!] In the name of thy Lord and Cherished, who created man, out of a [mere] clot of congealed blood." Kaplanoğlu suggests that not only does the beginning of *Honey* echo the Quran, but that the film's overall rhythm is like that of prayer.[50] He wanted his film "to convey a sense of beauty and generate a gratefulness for the creator."[51] Another reference to the Muslim faith in the trilogy comes as allusions to the story of the Prophet Joseph (Yusuf), after whom the main character is named. While the Prophet Joseph's story is based on the loss of the son and the father's yearning for him, in *Honey* Kaplanoğlu reverses this story, centering the narrative on the loss of the father and the son's longing for him. In the Quranic story, Yusuf, the beloved son of the Prophet Yakup (Jacob), is thrown into a well by his envious brothers, later saved by some caravan travelers and then sold as slave in the slave-market in Egypt. Thereafter, he encounters a series of life-threatening incidents, which he survives through his abilities of interpreting dreams and foreseeing the future. There are several allusions to Yusuf's story in the trilogy. Echoing the Prophet Yakup, for example, the father in *Honey* warns Yusuf not to tell his dreams to others. In *Egg*, Yusuf has a dream in which he sees himself stuck in an empty well from which he desperately seeks to escape.[52]

The representation of nature in *Yusuf's Trilogy* is another key element of the style of "spiritual realism" Kaplanoğlu seeks to articulate. The enchanted shots of nature do not simply constitute a beautiful backdrop for the events depicted. Nature retains an active and independent presence in the films, one that intervenes in the narrative flow and becomes a determining force in Yusuf's fate. At several turning points in the story, the intrusion of nature is critical. In *Honey*, a bee landing on his notebook alerts Yusuf to his father's death. In *Milk*, a huge carp fish that Yusuf comes across on the shore of a lake awakens him from his rage and possibly keeps him from killing the man who wants to marry his mother. In *Egg*, a wild dog makes Yusuf change his mind about going back to his lonely life in Istanbul. Nature retains an active role in all these instances and makes the character see the events from a new perspective.[53]

As I indicated above, the notion of "spiritual realism" is conveyed in *Yusuf's Trilogy* also through the idea of a "cosmic time." Time is represented in the trilogy as the experience of a perpetual present that includes life and death, past and future. Death, in this regard, is not seen as nothingness but as giving birth to a new existence. The past penetrates the future. In the first two installments of the trilogy, Yusuf feels the presence of his deceased father through mysterious signs, such as the bees appearing around him in critical moments. More interesting, however, is how in *Egg* Yusuf's mother forms a new relationship with her son after her death by attempting to correct what had gone wrong between them in the past. Yusuf's dead mother penetrates his life by making him fulfill her sacrifice. Because of this obligation, the time Yusuf spends in Tire is prolonged against his will. Feeling depressed and bored at first, he slowly discovers that he is forming a new connection with his past, his hometown and his mother. Ayla, the young woman who at first appears to him unsophisticated and naïve, slowly turns into someone who possesses a different kind of wisdom and determination. Yusuf is impressed by her plain beauty, deep spirituality and strong connection with life. Establishing a connection between Yusuf and Ayla through her vow, the mother takes the son from his lonely and alienated existence in Istanbul and reconciles him with the idea of making a commitment to the continuity of life.[54]

The idea of "cosmic time" in *Yusuf's Trilogy* is also suggested through the peculiar organization of the narrative that creates a sense of permanent present in which the past and the future exist together. The same actors appear in different parts of the trilogy in different roles. The actress playing Yusuf's humble mother in *Honey* (Tülün Özen), for example, appears at the beginning of *Egg* as a seductive modern young woman who shows up in Yusuf's bookstore in Istanbul just before he gets the phone call from Tire about his mother's death. Similarly, the actress playing Ayla in *Honey* (Saadet Işıl Atasoy) appears in *Milk* as an intellectual young woman interested in poetry. Despite his interest in her, Yusuf fails to show up on their first date after learning that he had been found unfit for military service. The recurrence of the same actors in different roles in the trilogy seems to point to the mysteries of life, the twists and turns of fate that cannot be captured through rational thinking. It seems to imply the existence of a cosmic order, beyond our recognition and control.

The use of epilogues in the narrative is also noteworthy in relation to this idea of cosmic order. Each film opens with an epilogue, the meaning of which may or may not be directly connected to the events in the story. *Egg* opens with an old woman walking slowly out of a foggy backdrop in a vast landscape towards the camera. When she approaches the camera, she pauses for a moment as though she has arrived at a crossroads, then turns left and keeps on walking until she disappears from view. The epilogue appears to describe Yusuf's mother's journey into death. With this opening, the ghostly presence of the mother is established as a spiritual element framing the following events. Opening with the mother's death and narrating Yusuf's life in reverse chronological order from adulthood to childhood, the trilogy comes full circle in the end by connecting the past and the future, life and death in a "cosmic time."

A CINEMA "LEADING TO GOODNESS"?

Şerif Mardin has talked about the "impoverishment of Turkish culture" that resulted from the Republican reform.[55] There has been a renewed critical awareness about this "impoverishment" since the 1980s with the emergence of a new generation of Islamic intellectuals. The last decade has been a critical turning point in the history of Turkey in the sense that the Islamic cultural field has expanded significantly under the rule of a pro-Islamic party. During this period, secularism as a hegemonic public discourse has received critical scrutiny. Today, although the secularist cultural establishment in Turkey is still strong, it is increasingly challenged by Islamic voices. Yet, while Islamic actors have produced a critical discourse on how the suppression of Islam by the secularist Republic has resulted in an impoverishment of culture in Turkey, there is a scarcity of alternative works to offer an aesthetic response to this situation from within the Islamic field. Semih Kaplanoğlu's work is significant in this context. Like other contemporary Islamic intellectuals, Kaplanoğlu problematizes the process of radical Westernization and secularization in Turkey, which, he believes, has created a shallow intellectual environment by alienating Turkish people from their own cultural roots. With *Yusuf's Trilogy*, Kaplanoğlu responds to the cultural impoverishment with a new cinematic aesthetic informed by Muslim spirituality.

Commenting on *Honey*'s success, Semih Kaplanoğlu in an interview talks about his aspirations using an Islamic idiom: "I wish," he says, "my film will lead to goodness."[56] At one level, one may suggest that, although this statement might sound naïve and out of place in an art world where competitiveness and cynicism are commonplace, the idea of "goodness" is precisely what endows *Yusuf's Trilogy* with a peculiar position in today's new wave cinema of Turkey. Bejan Matur, a well-known Kurdish poet and critic in Turkey, indicates that—being different from other prominent new wave auteur directors who seem to be fascinated with the themes of malice, wickedness and the dark side of the human soul—Kaplanoğlu's films begin with the presumption that the world and humanity are inherently good.[57] Kaplanoğlu's highly subjective take on Muslim faith and spirituality is closely linked to the idea of goodness. His films point to the merciful and inclusive dimension of religion. They cultivate a sense of compassion for their characters and offer an elevating aesthetic experience that reflects the perfect harmony and rhythm of nature. Instead of "preaching" an Islamic way of life, his films encourage viewers to develop gratefulness for the perfection of the world they inhabit and to its creator.[58]

Yet, at another level, when we attempt to make sense of Kaplanoğlu's statement in relation to the social context from which it emerges, we encounter a complex cultural terrain where his words might as well be articulated into a renewed form of cultural conservatism. Shortly after *Honey* won the Golden Bear, Islamic pundits in Turkey started debating the standards of "conservative arts." İhsan Kabil, an Islamic film critic who praised *Honey* as an exemplary case for its remarkable articulation of Muslim spirituality and aesthetics,[59] revealed his discomfort with the "Rainbow Section" of the Istanbul Independent Film Festival, which features queer films.[60] Kabil questioned the extent to which such a section is justifiable for a festival receiving public funding to feature films that are "in conflict with the moral values and social structure of [Turkish] society."[61] Kabil's comments sparked a debate over "conservative arts" in Turkey. Mustafa Esen, the Secretary to President Abdullah Gül and a professor of literature, indicated that it is necessary to define the "norms of conservative arts and aesthetics."[62] Writing a manifesto of the arts from a conservative point of view, İskender Pala defined "conservative arts" as the aesthetic dimension of the efforts of a society that has experienced a traumatic rupture from its past to recover its true consciousness.[63] As such, among other things, conservative arts "respect religious sensitivities" and "refuse accounts of degeneration, banality and discrimination under the pretense of arts."[64] While Islamic social actors have been talking about re-ordering the domain of arts and culture in Turkey in accordance with the so-called "moral and religious sensitivities of society," the aesthetics of Muslim spirituality in Kaplanoğlu's cinema, in their view, provide an emblematic illustration for their project of "conservative arts."

The idea of "goodness" in Kaplanoğlu's statement might mean different things to different groups. While for some it signifies the transforming power and elevating nature of spiritual aesthetic experience, for others it suggests new modes of suppression, silencing and censorship. In the conflict-ridden cultural terrain of Turkey, the reception of Kaplanoğlu's films is inevitably shaped by competing discourses on Islam and secularism, conservatism and pluralism, and majoritarian democracy and liberal democracy.

NOTES

1. *Honey* has become the second Turkish film that won the Golden Bear after Metin Erksan's 1964 film *Dry Summer (Susuz Yaz)*.
2. Yeşim Arat, "Religion, Politics and Gender Equality in Turkey: Implications of a Democratic Paradox," *Third World Quarterly* 31:6 (2010), 871.
3. Arat, "Religion, Politics and Gender Equality in Turkey," 871.
4. Yael-Navaro Yashin, *Faces of the State: Secularism and Public Life in Turkey* (Princeton and Oxford: Princeton University Press, 2002), 6.
5. Reşat Kasaba, "Kemalist Certainties and Modern Ambiguities," in *Rethinking Modernity and National Identity in Modern Turkey*, eds. Sibel Bozdoğan and Reşat Kasaba (Seattle: University of Washington Press, 1997), 28.
6. Ibid., 28.
7. Hakan Yavuz, *Islamic Political Identity in Turkey* (Oxford: Oxford University Press, 2005), 128.
8. Arat, "Religion, Politics and Gender Equality in Turkey," 869.
9. Şerif Mardin, "Islam in Mass Society: Harmony versus Polarization," in *Politics in The Third Turkish Republic*, eds. Metin Heper and Ahmet Evin (San Francisco: Westview Press, 1993), 162.
10. In the 1960s, the intellectual basis of the National Outlook Movement (*Milli Görüş Hareketi*), the most significant independent Islamic movement in Turkey, was formed. The project of the National Outlook Movement was to integrate Islamic thought into modernity, rather than reviving a traditional mode of Islamic practice. Banu Eligür, *The Mobilization of Political Islam in Turkey* (London: Cambridge University Press, 2010), 61.
11. The first political party that came out from the National Outlook Movement, the National Order Party (*Milli Nizam Partisi*), was established in 1970. A series of Islamic parties have emerged since then. Yet, until the foundation of the Justice and Development Party (*Adalet ve Kalkınma Partisi*, AKP) in 2001, all Islamic parties in Turkey had been shut down by the Constitutional Court on charges of undermining secularism. Ibid., 66.
12. The 1970s was characterized by economic recession and a strong polarization between right-wing ultra-nationalists and radical leftists.
13. Çağlar Keyder, "The Setting," in *Istanbul Between the Global and the Local*, ed. Çağlar Keyder (Lanham, MD.: Rowman and Littlefield, 1999), 18.
14. Kasaba, "Kemalist Certainties and Modern Ambiguities," 16–17.
15. Kenan Çayır talks about the distinction made in Turkey between having an Islamic identity and simply being a Muslim. While being a Muslim refers to a subject position in which one is born a Muslim and learns about religion through traditional channels (from older generations), in the case of Islamism, one re-appropriates and revises the given Muslim identity in their engagement with worldly affairs by endowing it with a new political will to apply Islam

in private and public life. Kenan Çayır, *Islamic Literature in Contemporary Turkey: From Epic to Novel* (New York: Palgrave, 2007), 54–55.
16. The 1980s and 90s witnessed also the rise of an Islamic bourgeoisie based in the Anatolian capital. As the members of the new Islamic middle class took modern professions in emerging Islamic corporations, their participation in public life increased. Çayır, *Islamic Literature in Contemporary Turkey*, 163.
17. Ibid., 119.
18. According to Fuat Keyman, The AKP has differentiated itself from previous Islamic parties as a conservative-democratic political structure that articulates liberal market values with community/tradition-based norms. Through market-oriented and reform-based politics, the AKP presents itself to the global world as an actor that establishes a coexistence, not a clash, between Islam, parliamentary democracy, modernity and market economy. Fuat Keyman, "Modernization, Globalization, and Democratization in Turkey: The AKP Experience and its Limits," *Constellations*, 17:2 (2010), 316.
19. Founded in 2001 by the younger generation of the pro-Islamic Virtue Party (*Fazilet Partisi*, FP), the AKP has won successive electoral victories since then. In the 2002, 2007 and 2011 parliamentary elections, the AKP received, 34.3, 47 and 50 percent of the total votes, respectively. Ümit Cizre, "The Justice and Development Party and the Military: Recreating the Past After Reforming It?" in *Secularism and Islamic Politics in Turkey: The Making of the Justice and Development Party*, ed. Ümit Cizre (New York: Routledge, 2008), 132.
20. For more discussion on the expansion of the Islamic cultural field in Turkey since the 2000s, see Devran Koray Öcal, "The Development and Transformation of the Islamic Publishing Field: The Cases of Nesil and Timaş" (master's thesis submitted to the Institute of Social Sciences at Istanbul Technical University, Istanbul, Turkey, 2013).
21. Yavuz, *Islamic Political Identity in Turkey*, 121.
22. Ayşe Saktanber, "We Pray Like You Have Fun: New Islamic Youth in Turkey Between Intellectualism and Popular Culture," in *Fragments of Culture: The Everyday of Modern Turkey* eds. Deniz Kandiyoti and Ayşe Saktanber (New Brunswick NJ: Rutgers University Press, 2002), 263.
23. Hilmi Maktav, "Kuran'dan Kurama İslami Sinema," in *Modern Türkiye'de İslami Düşünce: İslamcılık*, ed. Yasin Aktay (Istanbul: İletişim, 2011), 991.
24. Previously, the films exploring religious themes in Turkish cinema had been mainly narrating the lives of the key religious figures from the early history of Islam. Maktav, "Kuran'dan Kurama İslami Sinema," 990.
25. Şule Yüksel Şenler's novel *The Serenity Street* (*Huzur Sokağı*) was adopted to a television drama series in 2012. Broadcast by a mainstream national channel, the series has immediately become a rating champion.
26. Maktav, "Kuran'dan Kurama İslami Sinema," 996.
27. The next major blockbuster of Islamic cinema was *Minyeli Abdullah*, adapted from Hekimoğlu İsmail's 1968 best-selling Islamic novel and directed by Yücel Çakmaklı in two separate parts in 1989 and 1990. Engaging in a critique of the Kemalist modernization project in Turkey through the story of Egyptian Muslims, *Minyeli Abdullah* explores the theme of suffering to maintain one's Muslim faith. Saktanber, "We Pray Like You Have Fun," 263.
28. Ibid., 264.
29. Ibid., 263.
30. The increasing production costs incurred through the transition to color cinematography, the political turmoil of the period and the nationwide expansion of television broadcasting were among the key reasons behind the crisis of Turkish film industry after the mid-1970s.
31. The second half of the 2000s has also witnessed an increase not only in the number of films produced in Turkey, but also in their box-office success. Asuman

Suner, "Between Magnificence and Monstrosity: Turkishness in Recent Popular Cinema," *New Perspectives on Turkey* 45 (2011), 123–54.
32. For more discussion on the new wave auteur directors of Turkish cinema, see Asuman Suner, *New Turkish Cinema: Belonging, Identity, and Memory* (London: I.B. Tauris, 2009).
33. In 2011, two Islamic bio-pics based on the life story and Islamic teachings of Said Nursi (the founder of the Nur community) have appealed to viewers: *Barla: God's Faithful Servant (Barla: Allah'ın Sadık Kulu)* (Esin Orhan, 2011), a feature length animation and *Free Man: Bediuzzaman Said Nursi (Hür Adam: Bediuzzaman Said Nursi)* (Mehmet Tanrısever, 2011), a historical drama. Despite their popular appeal, the films received considerable criticism even from Islamic circles on the grounds that they present a superficial and over-idealized portrayal of Said Nursi. For a critique of *Free Man* coming from Islamic circles, see, for example, Celil Civan, "*Hür Adam:* İdealle Karikatür Arasında," *Hayal Perdesi* (January 16, 2011). Available at www.hayalperdesi.net/vizyon-kritik/40-idealle-karikatur-arasinda.aspx.
34. Uygar Şirin, *Semih Kaplanoğlu: Yusuf'un Rüyası* (Istanbul: Timaş, 2010), 98–100.
35. Ibid., 185.
36. Ibid., 186.
37. Ibid., 14.
38. Ibid., 242.
39. Ibid., 244.
40. Ibid., 128.
41. Gilles Deleuze, *Cinema 2: The Time-Image*. Translated by Hugh Tomlinson and Robert Galeta (Minneapolis: University of Minnesota Press, 1989). For a discussion of "time-image cinema" in relation to Iranian director Abbas Kiarostiami's films, see Laura Mulvey, "Abbas Kiarostami: Cinema of Uncertainty, Cinema of Delay," in *Death 24x a Second: Stillness and the Moving Image* (London: Reaktion Books, 2006).
42. Shohini Chaudhuri and Howard Finn "The Open Image: Poetic Realism and the New Iranian Cinema," *Screen* 44:1 (2003), 52–53.
43. Ibid., 53.
44. Şirin, *Semih Kaplanoğlu*, 95.
45. Ibid., 129.
46. Ibid., 129.
47. Senem Aytaç, "Rüyalarını Kimseye Anlatma: *Bal*," *Altyazı* 94 (2010), 22.
48. Ayça Çiftçi, "Sütten Hayaller," *Altyazı* 80 (2009), 18.
49. Ibid., 18.
50. Tuba Deniz and Ayşe Pay, "Sinemayı Görüntüye Hapsetmemek Gerek (Interview with Semih Kaplanoğlu)," *Hayal Perdesi* (July 10, 2010). Available at www.hayalperdesi.net/soylesi/6-sinemayi-goruntuye-hapsetmemek-gerek.aspx.
51. Ibid.
52. For a discussion of other references in Kaplanoğlu's trilogy to Quran and Muslim spirituality, see Murat Gürsoy, "*Bal:* Sanatçının Kadim Dildeki Tarifi," Gece Blogspot (May 12, 2010). Available at www.602gece.blogspot.com.
53. Tuba Deniz and Ayşe Pay, "Sinemayı Görüntüye Hapsetmemek Gerek."
54. For a discussion of *Yusuf's Trilogy* from the standpoint of the mother, see Asuman Suner, "Yusuf'u Yanlış Anlamak: Semih Kaplanoğlu'nun *Yumurta-Süt-Bal* Üçlemesi Üzerine," in *Bir Kapıdan Gireceksin: Türkiye Sineması Üzerine Denemeler*, ed. Umut Tümay Arslan (Istanbul: Metis, 2011).
55. Şerif Mardin, "Religion in Modern Turkey," in *Religion, Society, and Modernity in Turkey* (New York: Syracuse University Press, 2006), 226.
56. Tuba Deniz and Ayşe Pay, "Sinemayı Görüntüye Hapsetmemek Gerek."

57. Bejan Matur, "Balın Hakikati," *Zaman* (April 11, 2010). Available at www.zaman.com.tr/yorum/balin-hakikati_971726.html.
58. The way that Kaplanoğlu draws upon Muslim spirituality in his films is different from the way that Christianity is invoked in the films by contemporary directors like Krzysztof Kieślowski, Lars von Trier and Terrence Malick in some key respects. Kaplanoğlu's emphasis on "goodness" in relation to religion and spirituality is one major difference between him and these directors. For example, in stark contrast to Lars von Trier, who is concerned with the elements of suffering and pain in Christianity, Kaplanoğlu persistently emphasizes the merciful and compassionate side of the Muslim faith. Rather than expressing the sublime through a grandiose vision of creation and the primordial life (like in Terrence Malick's *The Tree of Life*, for example), Kaplanoğlu traces the miracle of creation in minor elements of life, fate and nature. Among these directors, Kaplanoğlu's vision probably comes closest to Kieślowski in his engagement with the interconnectedness of lives and paradoxes of chance and fate. The references to the Quran, for example, recall Kieslowski's use of the Biblical theme of the Ten Commandments in his 1989 *Dekalog* series. Yet, instead of Kieślowski's fascination with modernity and the moral paradoxes that it creates, Kaplanoğlu openly expresses his distaste for modern life, and his films represent a flight from the city to nature. For a more systematic analysis of Kieślowski, see Slavoj Žižek, *The Fright of Real Tears: Krzysztof Kieślowski Between Theory and Post-Theory* (London: BFI, 2001).
59. İhsan Kabil, "Sinemada Yeni Bir Rüzgar Estiren *Bal*," TIMETURK (February 27, 2010). Available at www.timeturk.com/tr/makale/ihsan-kabil/sinemada-yeni-bir-ruzgar-estiren-bal.html.
60. İhsan Kabil, "Tartışmaya Açık Filmler," *Star* (February 21, 2012). Available at www.siyahbant.org/?p=1343.
61. Ibid.
62. "Muhafazakar Sanatın Yapısını Oluşturmalıyız," *Vatan* (March 25, 2012). Available at http://haber.gazetevatan.com/muhafazakar-sanatin-yapisini-olusturmaliyiz/439012/1/gundem.
63. İskender Pala, "Muhafazakarın Sanat Manifestosu," *Zaman* (April 10, 2012). Available at http://t24.com.tr/haber/iskender-paladan-muhafazakar-sanat-protestosu/201406.
64. Ibid.

4 Pasolini
Religion and Sacrifice
Geoffrey Nowell-Smith

Pier Paolo Pasolini, poet, novelist, filmmaker, essayist, and general intellectual gadfly, died in 1975 at the hands of a young male prostitute who may or may not have had accomplices. Much vilified in his lifetime, after his death he has been commonly sanctified as some kind of secular martyr, a heroic victim to the forces of obscurantism and reaction. That he made many enemies in the course of his life, and that his death can be viewed as in some sense sacrificial, is unquestionable. Highly questionable, however, are subsequent attempts to cleanse his memory of the contradiction and sheer contrariety that were the hallmarks of his life. A consummate modern man and modern artist, he nevertheless hated most aspects of modernity, including artistic modernism. A lifelong communist with a small c, he never attempted to rejoin the Communist Party after being expelled from it in 1949, and he regularly quarreled with it even when he was a regular contributor to the Party press. Assertively and proudly homosexual, he found his sexuality a burden and was deeply suspicious of contemporary "gayness" (though he might have found the reclamation of "queer" that emerged after his death more to his liking). An atheist and secularist, his sensibility was in many ways deeply religious, and for a short period in his life he was in amicable dialogue not just with Christianity but with the Catholic Church itself.

In an attempt to smooth over some of these contradictions, Pasolini has sometimes been described as a Catholic Marxist. But his Marxism was never orthodox. It certainly did not include any notion of historical progress and the inevitable triumph of the proletariat. He was skeptical, particularly towards the end of his life, about political causes normally described as progressive (such as the reform of Italy's abortion laws) and indeed about progress as an ideal. He came increasingly to feel that the proletariat as traditionally conceived was no longer a revolutionary force able or willing to oppose the all-encompassing forward march of capitalism. He was also never a Catholic. Although he was brought up in one of the most Catholic parts of Italy—Friuli in the far north-east of the country—his parents were not religious and he claimed to have no recollection of ever being confirmed into the Church.[1] But after his move to Rome in 1950, he retained a nostalgia for many aspects of the peasant society of his upbringing, including its religious faith on the one hand and its spirit of resistance during the Nazi occupation at the end of the War on the other.

The Resistance in 1943–5 had been a broad alliance of all forces, Catholic as well as secular, opposed to German occupation and the remnants of Fascism. The political alignment which emerged at the end of the War involved all the Resistance parties, including for a while the Monarchists. But from 1947, with the onset of the Cold War, this "unity of the Resistance" began to break up. In the general election of 1948, the Christian Democrats emerged as the largest single party; they were to remain in power, though never with an overall majority, for the next forty years. The "Popular Bloc" of Pietro Nenni's Socialist Party and Palmiro Togliatti's Communists formed a more or less permanent opposition until 1963, when the Socialists entered government as a minority party in a so-called Centre Left alliance.

The issues dividing the country—the people as a whole as well as their political representatives—were many and various, cultural and ideological as well as social and economic, and were never to be satisfactorily resolved. But in the Cold War context they were compacted in such a way as to divide the country fair and square into two blocs, a Right led by the Christian Democrats, and a Left of which the Communists were the major component. The right-wing bloc was pro-capitalist, pro-American, Catholic, even clericalist, and generally conservative in its social attitudes. Its left-wing opponents were socialist, neutralist if not actively pro-Soviet, secularist, and assertively republican and anti-Fascist. Not everybody fit comfortably into the blocs into which they had been relegated. The right-wing camp contained liberals of various kinds, including numerous Catholics who were unhappy both with the Christian Democrats' embrace of capitalism and with the conservative, not to say reactionary, attitudes of the Church itself under the leadership of Pope Pius XII.

But in general the alliances held. In the backward South in particular, parish priests regularly denounced the Communists from the pulpit and were rumored to use the confessional to counsel women parishioners to refuse sexual intercourse with husbands who voted for the left-wing bloc. The post-war Constitution, inaugurated in 1947, was liberal in many respects but respected the Concordat signed under Fascism that made Catholicism the state religion. In the world of culture, the Left was strongly implanted in the cinema, but the Christian Democrat government exercised an active monopoly over radio and (later) television. In sexual matters, the Constitution established an age of consent of sixteen that applied to homosexual as well as heterosexual activity, but abortion was illegal and female contraception unobtainable. Under the circumstances, someone of Pasolini's background and temperament could not fail in the 1950s to align himself with the left-wing bloc, including in its anti-clericalism.

There were, it should be said, already contradictions in the way he presented himself as a public figure. His novel *Ragazzi di vita,* published in 1955, was a celebration of the anarchic energy of life in the shanty towns on the outskirts of Rome. Within two years, in his long poem *Le ceneri di Gramsci*, his attitude had shifted to one of lament, taking issue with the progressive narrative propounded by the Left and seeing around him a world that had been desacralized and that in the loss of the sacred had also lost its life force. Later, in his collection *La religione del mio tempo* (1961), the "religion of his own time" evokes a spiritual emptiness, a prevailing irreligion for which the Catholic civilization of the past exists merely in the form of a series of references, name-checking the churches that remain a presence in the landscape of the modern city. By the time these poems came out, however, two significant events had taken place in the world outside that forced a radical change in the complexion of political and cultural life in Italy and Pasolini's relationship to it.

The first event was the Hungarian uprising of 1956, whose suppression by Soviet military forces precipitated an ideological crisis in the left-wing secular bloc. In Italy, as elsewhere in Western Europe, this crisis led to a rejection of the hegemony of the Communist Party and the formation of a dissident "new left." The second, and in many ways even more important, was the death of Pope Pius XII in 1958 and the unexpected election of the little-known Cardinal Giuseppe Roncalli as his successor under the name John XXIII. The Italian Communist Party, thanks to the political skills of its leader Palmiro Togliatti, soon recovered from the shocks administered by the Hungarian events. But the Church as a whole and Catholic culture in Italy in particular were profoundly changed by John's brief pontificate and its aftermath. Not only that: the attitudes of many people who were not Catholic or even Christian were also transformed, leading to increasing dialogue in Italy across the traditional ideological and confessional divide.

Pasolini's left-wing allegiance was always dictated by a strong personal identification with the poor and the outcast, the "umiliati e offesi,"—a phrase borrowed from Gramsci (and ultimately Dostoyevsky), which he also applied to himself.[2] For a while, however, he remained suspicious of John's message of solidarity with the poor, and the Vatican II promise of a Catholic renewal. An epigram of his from 1960 dedicated to John is scathing in its conclusion:

> The Church is ugly, even behind your [John's] lovely face
> it will remain: and of your smile every trace will be lost.[3]

Gradually, however, he became convinced that what John was doing was indeed revolutionary. Early in 1963 he put together a short film called *La rabbia* ("Anger"), in which John is identified as a force for good in helping to align the Church with the struggles of the Third World and in contesting the hegemony of the rich world over the poor. But for various reasons he then did his best to disassociate himself from his own film, which received only a limited release in April of that year. By that time, however, he was already starting work on two projects of far greater interest.

The larger and more important of these two projects was for a film on the life of Christ, textually based on Matthew's Gospel. Pasolini originally planned to shoot the film at the actual sites where the events recounted in the Gospel took place, and went on an extended location search in the Holy Land, taking both a camera and a priestly advisor. The short film *Sopralluoghi in Palestina* ("Location-scouting in Palestine"), which he put together on his return to Italy, records his conclusion: 1960s Palestine (Israel and Jordan) was either too modern or too abject to be usable as a representation of the Gospel story. Instead he shot the film in southern Italy, and it premiered to great acclaim at the Venice Film Festival in September 1964 under the title *Il Vangelo secondo Matteo*.[4]

All in all, from conception to release, the gestation of the Gospel film took eighteen months. During this long gestation period, however, he made another film, also on a biblical theme but very different in character and which got him into all sorts of trouble. According to Tomaso Subini, whose book on the film is the principal source for much of what follows,[5] the idea for the film, which eventually received the title *La ricotta* ("*Curd-cheese*"), originated in a newspaper report of a mishap that occurred during the shooting at Cinecittà of the Crucifixion scene in Richard Fleischer's biblical epic *Barabbas*. Pasolini planned it as a possible sketch in a compilation film, but the intended producers didn't like it and the proposed compilation never materialized. Still attached to the idea, Pasolini pitched a revised version to Alfredo Bini, the producer of his earlier features *Accattone* (1961) and *Mamma Roma* (1962). Bini then put together a package of four episodes, flanking Pasolini's idea with contributions by Roberto Rossellini, Jean-Luc Godard, and Ugo Gregoretti. The four surnames were fused in the film's eventual title *RoGoPaG*—*Ro* for Rossellini, *Go* for Godard, *Pa* for Pasolini, and the final *G* for Gregoretti.

From the outset, Pasolini's episode was the centerpiece of the package. It is the only one that is really memorable. Godard's episode is probably the most insipid thing that revolutionary filmmaker ever shot, Rossellini's has some interesting formal features, Gregoretti's has some amusing satire, but that is about it. Pasolini's episode *La ricotta* ("*Curd-cheese*"), however, was both brilliant and instantly scandalous. Shooting took place in October and November of 1962, and the whole film was released in Italy on February 21, 1963, with an "18" certificate. Even before its release, however, steps were being taken by prosecutors in Rome to have Pasolini's episode banned on grounds of offense to religion, which the censors proper had not thought fit to take into account.

La ricotta is a film about the making of a film. The film being shot is a biblical epic, and the location where it is being shot is on the outskirts of Rome. The role of the director is played by Orson Welles, but Welles does not really play himself. He is only there to provide the imposing aura attached to his name and physical presence, and he is dubbed into Italian. The voice is that of a friend of Pasolini's, the novelist Giorgio Bassani. The words that the voice utters include a poem of Pasolini's recently published as an addendum to the script of his second feature film *Mamma Roma*, in which the poet describes himself as "a voice of the past" and "a stray dog" in an alienating environment.

The main narrative action of *La ricotta*, shot in black and white, concerns the adventures of an extra called Stracci ("rags"), whose preoccupation is getting either enough food to eat or enough money to pay for it. He steals and sells an actress's pet lapdog and allows or organizes the prostitution of his sons and daughters to better-heeled members of the cast. Having finally managed to eat his fill of the curd-cheese of the title, he dies of indigestion, strapped to a cross in the role of the Good Thief crucified alongside Jesus. "Poor Stracci," quips the Orson Welles figure. "He had to die in order to prove he was alive." In parallel, and in color, the actors in the film-within-the-film are shown taking up poses in *tableaux vivants* mimicking two Mannerist paintings—"The Crucifixion" by Pontormo and "Deposition from the Cross" by Rosso Fiorentino. The actors find it difficult to hold their poses or to assume suitably pious expressions. When a crown of thorns needs to be fetched, the message passes along various minions who shout "*'a coronaa*" in increasingly strong working-class Roman accents, and when accompanying music is called for, another assistant puts on the Twist that some film extras had been dancing to earlier, rather than the more decorous Scarlatti specified for the purpose.

The targets of the film's satire are many and various, but the principal one is the film industry and the disjunction between its pious pretensions and its vulgar reality. For some people, however, notably in the magistracy, its seeming mockery of the crucifixion story was hard to bear. Pasolini knew he was treading on dangerous ground and had taken care to preface the film with an opening title which read:

> It is not difficult to foresee that my story will encounter criticism dictated by pure bad faith. Those who feel themselves targeted [by the film] will try to maintain that the object of my polemic is the Story and Texts of which they hypocritically claim to be defenders. Far from it: to avoid any possible misunderstanding, I wish to declare here that the Story of the Passion is the greatest that I know and the Texts that recount it the most sublime ever written.

This was not enough to satisfy Pasolini's enemies as to the filmmaker's own good faith. It is hard to say how much of it was genuine outrage and how much the seizure of an opportunity to go after that dangerous subversive Pasolini; whatever the combination, they went at it with a will. Copies of the newly released film were seized and the trial started on March 5, 1963. The role of prosecutor was assigned to an ambitious young Christian Democrat lawyer called Giuseppe Di Gennaro, whose speech to the court was a brilliant display of moral indignation spiced with lurid and salacious detail. The result of this performance, combined with a certain complacency on the part of the defense, was that judgment was given against the film. The director and producer were given suspended sentences of six months in prison for "vilipendio della religione dello stato," or "insulting the religion of the state"—"the religion of the state" being a status that Catholicism had enjoyed since the Concordat signed between Pope Pius XI and Mussolini in 1929. The judgment was eventually reversed on appeal and the film's re-release approved, but only after cuts and changes had been made to protect it from the risk of further prosecution.

The first of these changes is in the opening title, which in the re-released version was revised to read:

> It is not difficult to foresee the prejudiced, ambiguous and scandalized judgements that my story will provoke. So I wish to state here that, however *La ricotta* is understood, the story of the Passion—which the film indirectly evokes—is for me the greatest that ever took place and the Texts that recount it the most sublime ever.

The substance of this change is that in the revised version—the only one known to audiences since 1963—Pasolini now appears to be asserting a belief in the historicity of the Gospel story. But this should not necessarily be taken at face value. In the circumstances, it clearly needs to be read as a diplomatic move to stave off criticism and, given what we know of his other beliefs and interests, it is more likely that he continued to consider the Gospel as, in the richest sense, a myth—that is to say, a story which does not require to be factual in order to contain a profound truth about humanity. But concessions had to be made, and this was one he was prepared to make.

The other changes seem mainly to have had to do with the usual thing that censors worry about, which is sexual display. Any shots cut from the film seem not to have survived, and we are therefore reliant on differences in versions of the script to know precisely what potentially offensive material had to be removed. There is therefore no way of knowing how accurate Di Gennaro's more lurid descriptions were of the offending passages in the film. For example, Di Gennaro claimed that during the scene in which the actress playing Mary Magdalene entertained cast and crew with an impromptu strip-tease, the watching Stracci visibly had an erection and even ejaculated under his loincloth. Since the official censors had already demanded cuts in that scene, it is unlikely that the event Di Gennaro pinpoints would have escaped their expert eyes. If Di Gennaro did see what he claimed to see, however, it raises an interesting point about the scope of the trial—and about the interpretation of Pasolini's work in general. Stracci was playing a thief, not Jesus. For him to be seen to be sexually excited would therefore be indecent (at least by the standards prevailing at the time), but it cannot really be called blasphemous or an insult to the Catholic religion.

At a deeper level, though, Di Gennaro could have been right. In *La ricotta*, the focus is not on Our Lord but on Stracci, and it is Stracci who dies on the cross, a sub-proletarian sacrifice for the sins of the world—or at any rate those of the Italian bourgeoisie. Stracci, if not Christ, is the film's Christ-figure, albeit one much given to the appetites of the flesh. Metonymically, therefore, the obscene figuration of the figure of Stracci—erection or no erection—arises as a challenge to a religion with such an emphasis on chastity.

La ricotta is a complex and multi-layered film, and the possible status of Stracci as a stand-in for Christ is only one of many ambiguities which make its interpretation difficult. The principal of these ambiguities concerns the *tableaux vivants*. What exactly was Pasolini making fun of in these comic sequences in which the actors fool about while playing the roles of figures in a late Renaissance painting? Pasolini was clearly aware that some people— "hypocritically," he says—would take the scenes to be mocking the Passion story itself: hence the prefatory title to the film.

Such people, however, were not in the majority. There was little public outrage and most Catholic commentators, as well as ordinary Catholics, seem to have taken the possibly blasphemous overtones of the scenes in their stride. Italy is, after all, a country with a long history of off-color jokes about the Passion story.[6] In context, however, the most obvious reading of the scenes is the one already hinted at earlier in this chapter, which is that Pasolini was using them as an object lesson in how *not* to make a film with a biblical subject.

The other point to be made about the trial is that it was a diversion. *La ricotta* may have been the ostensible target, but almost certainly its underlying purpose was to discredit in advance the film Pasolini was about to make. Though a deeply serious and even reverential film, it was still one that, in the eyes of many, that notorious Marxist, homosexual, and blaspheming atheist was surely not an appropriate person to be allowed to make.

The Gospel According to Matthew opens, like *La ricotta,* with a prefatory title: "Alla cara, lieta, e familiare memoria di Giovanni XXIII"—"to the dear, joyful, and familiar memory of John XXIII." This too was something of a hostage to fortune. If it was bad enough for Pasolini to be making the film at all, it was worse that he should be claiming familiarity with the recently deceased and saintly Pope ("familiare" in Italian conveys overtones of "member of the family" as well as well-known). In the event, the possible provocation was not taken badly in mainstream Catholic circles. Among the many awards won by the film, three were from Catholic organizations, including two from the Office Catholique International du Cinéma. In fact there is little, if anything, in the film to which objection could be taken on theological grounds other than the fact that its maker was not a believer.

The first and most important thing to note about Pasolini's Gospel film is that it is a film of a text, not a bio-pic of Jesus. The text is that of Matthew's Gospel, the rendering almost pedantically literal. For this purpose,

Pasolini did not need a screenplay other than that provided by the Evangelist himself. There are a few cuts and transpositions from one place in the Gospel to another, but basically if something is not in Matthew it is not in the film. The famous version of the Annunciation, where the Angel appears to a virgin in a dream bearing a lily and saying, "Blessed art thou among women,"[7] is not there. Instead, you get a very literal rendering (one verse, one shot) of Matthew's version, with a visibly pregnant woman and a puzzled, angry man being told by an angel not to reject her. But this literalness towards the text is not replicated in the settings, which have no historical specificity but are generically archaic (and therefore, in Pasolini's sense, mythical) being simply locations that happened to still exist in southern Italy. Meanwhile the historic status of Christianity as the world religion that it was to become is present in a few iconographic references (the pregnant Mary is modeled on Piero della Francesca's "Madonna del Parto") but above all in the music, which covers the range from the Protestant pietism of Bach to the baroque Catholicism of Mozart to the Congolese "Missa Luba" to Negro spirituals.

Inevitably, when the film came out, questions were raised about the slant it put on the Gospel story. Was it a Marxist reading of the text? A skeptical, even atheistic one? Perhaps a Protestant one? (Perhaps mercifully, there were no attempts at the time to find a queer reading of the Gospel in the film.) The most relevant of these questions, in 1964, at a time of developing Christian–Marxist dialogue, concerned the social inflection of the film. Here it has to be said that Pasolini, while remaining faithful to the Gospel text, definitely plays up the contrast between Jesus and his followers on the one side and his various opponents and persecutors on the other. The former are poor and simply dressed, while the latter without exception wear elaborate costumes and are represented as members of a ruling class as well as defenders of religious orthodoxy against this upstart preacher. In itself, of course, the stress on the Gospel being addressed to the poor was not only traditional but, in the context of the Second Vatican Council which John had inaugurated and which continued after his death, highly contemporary.

What is perhaps more significant is the fact that Matthew's is the only Gospel addressed in the first instance to the Jews. Matthew's Jesus is cast in the mould of an Old Testament prophet, castigating his errant people for their failure to live up to their calling. This was an attitude with which Pasolini found it all too easy to identify, just as he also identified with the Jews as outcasts who had themselves been abandoned by the people they lived among.[8] It was furthermore something that was to be taken up by certain strains of Protestantism. Indeed the very invitation to attend to the actual text of either the Old or New Testament has its roots in the Lutheran Reformation, while at the same time—as with the stress on the poor—fitting closely with the evangelical spirit of John and Vatican II. (Pasolini was later to give the title *Lettere luterane,* or "Lutheran Letters," to his "heretical" journalism written shortly before his death.)

The question of Pasolini's atheism is more complex. He never made a secret of the fact that he approached the Gospel film from the point of view of a non-believer, but he issued typically confusing statements about what exactly he did believe. For example in a letter to a Catholic priest, Dr Lucio Caruso of the organization Pro Civitate Christiana, he declared:

> I don't believe Christ is the son of God, because I'm not religious—at least consciously. But I do believe that Christ is divine: I believe, that is, that his humanity is so elevated, so rigorous and ideal, as to surpass the common definitions of humanity.[9]

The film itself, however, takes the Gospel at its word, without necessarily endorsing it as historical truth. Christ performs miracles and after his crucifixion rises from the dead, exactly as in the Gospel. It has recently been claimed that Pasolini never intended either the miracles or the Resurrection to be included but was persuaded by Monsignor Luigi Angelicchio, founder of the Centro Cattolico Cinematografico, to add them to the film at a late stage in production.[10] This claim is not easy to verify. It is true that Pasolini did not like the way the miracles came out in the film, and they may even have been a reluctant inclusion, but there is no evidence—and is indeed highly unlikely—that he had a late change of heart leading to the need to reassemble cast and crew to add additional scenes after the rest of the film had been completed. All in all, it seems best to take the film completely at face value and, if one looks below the surface, to see Pasolini as, for the purposes of the film, identifying with the central character, his message, and his destiny. As to its historicity, one could do worse than to return to the opening title of *La ricotta* in its original version, where the author declares that to him, "the Story of the Passion is the greatest that I know and the Texts that recount it the most sublime ever written."

After the Gospel film, Pasolini turned his attention away from questions of religion. In his next feature, *Hawks and Sparrows* (1966), there is a charming vignette in which the central characters, played by Ninetto Davoli and the famous comic actor Totò, enact the role of two followers of St. Francis who unsuccessfully try to persuade the different species to live in peace and harmony with each other, but the main avian figure in the film is neither a hawk nor a sparrow but a talking crow, which tries to teach the central characters something about Marxism, to no avail. God also appears, off screen, in a short, "The Paper-Flower Sequence," which Pasolini contributed to the compilation film *Amore e rabbia* ("Love and Anger") in 1969. In this short, Pasolini's beloved Ninetto Davoli skips gaily down the via Nazionale in Rome clutching a giant paper flower. Intercut with his progress are shots of politicians talking, bombs falling, and the war in Vietnam. God calls to Ninetto out of a cloud. "Curlyhead," says God, "can't you see what is happening all around you?" But of course Curlyhead can't. So God invokes the parable of the barren fig tree, cut down for failing to bear fruit even if it was not yet the season. Ninetto, still oblivious, is punished for his innocence and run over by a bus—a victim, as so often in Pasolini, of a justice which is not just. But that's just about it in Pasolini's completed film work, though religious questions did continue to simmer away in the background, to appear in a script for a film based on the life of St. Paul but set in the modern world, which he did not live to make.

The only thing that can be said with confidence about this unmade film is that, if it had been made, it would have been quite difficult to watch and even more difficult to interpret since it gives the impression of being a kind of "summa" of everything that had preoccupied him throughout his career, laid out with all its contradictoriness exposed. But the central theme running through it seems, from a reading of the published script, to have been a kind of doubleness such as one also finds in the novel *Petrolio*, on which Pasolini was working at the same time and also never brought to completion. Paul in Pasolini's script is alternately saint and monster, charity and Law, otherworldly transcendence and earthly institution and in the end undone by his inability to live out all his (and the author's) contradictions.[11]

If there is a key thread connecting Pasolini's ruminations on religion, however, it is the theme of sacrifice. This is a theme that emerges tentatively, almost by accident, and having arrived takes numerous different forms. At first it is barely distinguishable from victimhood, but as Pasolini's interest in the theme develops, it becomes more explicit. At the beginning, it takes the form of a sense that the social order—in Pasolini's terms, class society— demands victims, mostly drawn from the poor, and that the death of a poor outcast can be seen as in some sense sacrificial. In *Accattone*, the death of the central character is an arbitrary and in itself meaningless accident, but Pasolini dignifies it iconographically with echoes of Christian symbolism (and a Bach Chorale on the soundtrack). Then, at the end of *Mamma Roma*, the body of Ettore, a boy whose only sin was to have been born the son of a prostitute, is framed in a manner suggestive of Andrea Mantegna's Dead Christ. Pasolini himself denied that the resemblance, widely noticed by critics at the time, was intended as a direct reference,[12] but the artifice of the framing and (as with *Accattone*) the solemn music clearly indicate a wish to treat Ettore's death as a tribute paid by the innocent to an unjust order, to which, however unwittingly, the victim has been sacrificed.

The death of Stracci in *La ricotta* is another case of unwitting sacrifice, since yet again neither victim nor perpetrators are aware of any sacrificial function being performed when he is left out in the sun to die on his cross. Christ-figure Stracci may be, but his death is no atonement nor does it propitiate any god except (possibly) Mammon.

Accattone, *Mamma Roma*, and *La ricotta* are all set in Pasolini's modern world, where all connection with the sacred has been lost and where all sacrifices are denied their inherent significance by the same society that demands them. Accattone, Ettore, and Stracci die with only the filmmaker there to mourn their death and endow it with dignity, if not purpose. *The*

Gospel According to Matthew introduced the need to confront the meaning of sacrifice in the Christian tradition. Pasolini began subsequently to take a serious interest in anthropological approaches to sacrifice in pre-modern societies and to build them into his own work. Characteristically, Pasolini's sacrificial victims are all innocent, and if they have expiation to perform, it is not for sins they have wittingly committed. His version of the Oedipus story (*Oedipus Rex, 1967*) follows Sophocles rather than Freud, its hero unaware that the man he kills is his father and the woman he marries his mother. Its chronological telling takes Oedipus' obliviousness even further from blame than does Sophocles. Whereas Sophocles' focus is on the arrogant king who refuses to recognize that he might be the cause of the curse afflicting Thebes, Pasolini's Oedipus (played by Franco Citti, who had previously played Accattone) is a youth beset by events. It is his instinctual nature that makes him violent towards an older man who stands in his way and sexually desiring of the still nubile woman offered to him. Ignorance, rather than arrogance, makes him blind to the possibility of his guilt—but he is still guilty and must still be blinded.

In *Medea,* the most didactic of Pasolini's films, there is a ritual sacrifice almost straight out of an anthropology textbook. Other films take up the motif in less obvious ways, such as the killing and eating of the pesky crow in *Hawks and Sparrows.* In these later films, we find Pasolini eclectically, but at the same almost obsessively, circling around the idea of the need for acts of sacrifice demanded of the innocent by a God or gods or, in a post-sacred world, by human society. The most condensed expression of this multi-faceted need comes in "The Paper-Flower Sequence." Curlyhead's death is on the one hand a banal traffic accident but at the same time decreed by God—except that, "God" being for Pasolini a fiction, the real blame for what happens clearly lies with a human order that has lost its humanity.

The perversion of the human order is most clearly expressed in Pasolini's last completed film, *Salò, or the 120 Days of Sodom* (1975), in which the representatives of Church, State, Law, and Capital perform horrible acts of torture and degradation upon their innocent victims. The film is notionally set in the puppet republic set up by the Fascists with Nazi support in 1943, but the "fascism" that Pasolini is denouncing is not just that defunct political regime. It is an all-encompassing order of which actual, historical, mid-twentieth-century Fascism was a symptom, one whose monstrosity has not been, and probably never will be, expiated.

This recurrence of sacrificial motifs in so many forms, pagan and Christian, social and symbolic, suggests that the theme had very powerful resonances for Pasolini, not only intellectual. Indeed, it can and has been argued that throughout his life, part of Pasolini's self-recognition was of himself as a sacrificial victim, destined to bear witness and to suffer for his destiny. It may even offer a clue to his death, the exact circumstances of which have remained obscure. Could the young rent-boy, acting alone, really have battered to death a much stronger man? There have been widespread suspicions of a right-wing plot to lure Pasolini to a spot where he could be set upon by hired assassins, but no concrete evidence of this has been produced. An alternative, admittedly speculative hypothesis was put forward in 1989 by Pasolini's longstanding friend Giuseppe Zigaina to the effect that what happened on that wasteground outside the town of Ostia was a death similar to the sacrifice in *Medea*, but with a victim who was not merely complicit but actively provoked his fate.[13] That is, the miserable rent-boy who left to himself would not have hurt a fly was made to enact the role of executioner, though not before the victim had scattered his seed on the ground to metaphorically fertilize it. As if there was no longer any realistic hope of changing the world by political means, but symbolically ancient magic could be enlisted to promote a rebirth. In the nature of things, such a hypothesis cannot be proved, but given the often perverse complexity of Pasolini's make-up, it has a frightening plausibility. As he wrote in 1967 in an essay on the long take, "It is [. . .] absolutely necessary to die, *because, as long as we are alive, our life has no meaning.* [. . .] *Only thanks to death can our life enable us to express ourselves.*"[14]

NOTES

1. Pier Paolo Pasolini, *Vie nuove* (October 22, 1964). Reprinted in Pier Paolo Pasolini, *Le belle bandiere* (Rome: Editori Riuniti, 1977), 222.
2. See Antonio Gramsci, "The Humble," in *Selections from the Cultural Writings,* edited by David Forgacs and Geoffrey Nowell-Smith (London: Lawrence and Wishart, 1985), 293. Gramsci is discussing Fyodor Dostoyevsky's 1862 novel generally known in English as *Humiliated and Insulted,* and it was Dostoyevsky as much as Gramsci who Pasolini had in mind in composing his epigrams under the title *Umiliato e offeso* in 1958.
3. Pier Paolo Pasolini, "A Giovanni XXIII," published as an Appendix to *La Religione del mio tempo* in Pier Paolo Pasolini, *Tutte le Poesie,* vol. 1 (Milan: Mondadori, 2003), 1074.
4. On its English-language release, the film was titled "*The Gospel According to Saint Matthew*," but Pasolini, on sound theological grounds, objected to the inclusion of the word "Saint"; the recently re-issued DVD has obligingly dropped it.
5. Tomaso Subini, *Pier Paolo Pasolini: La ricotta* (Turin: Lindau, 2009).
6. These date back at least as far as Lorenzo de'Medici's poem *I beoni* ("The drunkards," ca. 1480) where one of the drunks declares that "the greatest punishment / our Saviour had on earth / was when upon the cross he cried 'I thirst'."
7. Luke 1: 28.
8. For Pasolini's identification with the Jews, see Robert Gordon, "Pasolini as Jew, Between Israel and Europe," in *The Scandal of Self-Contradiction. Pasolini's Multistable Subjectivities, Traditions, Geographies,* eds. Luca di Blasi, Manuele Gragnolati, and Christoph Holzhey (Vienna and Berlin: Turia & Kant / ICI, 2012), 37–58.
9. Letter written in February 1963 and published in the script of the Gospel film, *Il Vangelo secondo Matteo* (Milan: Garzanti, 1964). Quoted in Pier Paolo Pasolini, *My Cinema,* edited by Graziella Chiarcossi and Roberto Chiesi (Bologna: Cineteca di Bologna, 2013), 71.

10. See, for example, http://trovacinema.repubblica.it/news/dettaglio/pasolini-svelato-retroscena-de-il-vangelo-secondo-matteo/413339.
11. See Robert Gordon, *Pasolini: Forms of Subjectivity* (Oxford: The Clarendon Press, 1996), 201–3. The script itself was published as *San Paolo* (Turin: Einaudi, 1977).
12. Pier Paolo Pasolini, *Vie nuove* (October 4, 1962). Reprinted in *Le belle bandiere*, 200.
13. Giuseppe Zigaina, *Pasolini tra enigma e profezia* (Venice: Marsilio, 1989).
14. Pier Paolo Pasolini, "Osservazioni sul piano-sequenza" (1967), in *Empirismo eretico* (Milan: Garzanti, 1972), 245. English edition, *Heretical Empiricism*, translated by Louise K. Barnett and Ben Lawton (Bloomington: Indiana University Press, 1988), 236, 237.

5 Entangled in God's Story
A Reading of Krzysztof Kieślowski's *Blind Chance*[1]

Costica Bradatan

> "I turn the camera on myself in all my films. Not all the time, perhaps, but often. But I do it in a way so nobody can see it."
>
> (Krzysztof Kieślowski)

NOTHING MAKES ANY SENSE

The first thing we see in *Blind Chance* is a male face, shot in close-up, first at rest, then suddenly overwhelmed by terror: "a terrified male face looks into the camera and utters a cry of pure horror."[2] It is the face of someone only seconds shy from dying in a plane crash. When we watch the film for the second time we already know that the terror we read on this man's face has to do with more than his imminent death. For this terror is caused not by one death, but by several, by a succession of deaths and failed lives. What we discern in Witek's terrified scream (Figure 5.1) is not just the sheer animal fear of annihilation, but the unbearable realization that *everything* has been wrong: his current life, his two other lives in the alternative narratives of the film, his actual and his possible existences alike, his *condition humaine* altogether. Witek's visceral scream at the beginning of *Blind Chance* is the deafening confession of a man condemned to living and dying meaninglessly, no matter the circumstances in which he lives or dies; it is the savage expression of a metaphysical protest against a historical world that does not make any sense—no matter the ethical choices he makes in life.

The three life stories that the film is about are triggered precisely by Witek's desire to lead a "good life." This is what moves the narrative(s) forward. In all his three lives Witek (played exquisitely by Boguslaw Linda), tries to make the best ethical choices he can. What characterizes Witek in all his life stories is above all his awareness that to live meaningfully, he has to structure his existence ethically: "What interests Kieślowski in the motif of alternative histories is the notion of *ethical choice*, ultimately the choice between 'calm life' and 'mission'," says Žižek in his book on Kieślowski.[3] Significantly, this is an entirely secular quest; the ethics Witek seeks are not grounded in religion. When

Entangled in God's Story 75

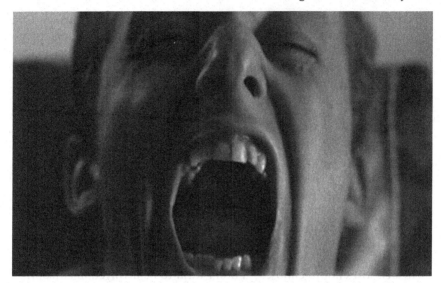

Figure 5.1 Boguslaw Linda in Krzysztof Kieślowski's *Blind Chance*

God, briefly and reluctantly, enters his life in the second narrative of the film, the event has only metaphysical, not ethical implications.

As such, a distinct ethical alertness permeates Witek's three biographies: if he cannot change the corrupted historical world in which he finds himself, he at least does his best not to let that world change him—which under totalitarian circumstances is already a significant ethical achievement. That he fails each time, despite always doing his best, becomes one of the sources of the authentic tragedy we see unfolding in this film. As each story starts out, it looks as if Witek is in a position to choose, as though he can be the author of his own life story. At the outset, each one of his lives seems rich in possibilities, full of promise and hope. In this self-sufficient universe, Witek seems to be the master of his own destiny, as it were: who he will eventually become and what will happen to him is up to him only to decide. However, as the narrative unfolds, he becomes gradually entangled in a web of chance events, accidents and misfortunes, which in the end determine what he does and what he does not do, who he is and who he is not; the mechanics of an implacable destiny gradually takes over any autonomy.

In each story, we witness an unstoppable process of existential exhaustion: the rich virtualities, hopes and promises of the beginning gradually dry out, just as the inner horizons of Witek's life become narrower and narrower; what is left in the end is only a spectacle of damnation. Regardless of what Witek chooses (to be a Communist, to be an anti-Communist, to be neither), his life fails just the same. In the first story, he joins the Communists (the "Communist reformers," more exactly), and the process of existential exhaustion takes place in the space of an official Poland. In the second, he joins the dissident camp and forces himself into becoming a Catholic: "despairingly praying to a God in whom he does not believe: O Lord, be there!"[4] The same process takes place now in an underground Poland. As Kieślowski himself (who is both the director and the script writer of the film) assures us, Witek "behaves decently in each situation."[5] Nevertheless, decency doesn't pay off and Witek's first two (political) lives end badly. Tadeusz Sobolewski puts it poignantly: "In each incarnation, an accusation of treachery awaits him—something no one in Poland can avoid."[6] There is a distinct sense of failure in both these biographies; Witek dies morally in both, even though, in the literal sense of the word, he remains alive. The failure is clearly conveyed at the end of each life story, where existential exhaustion translates into a sense of cosmic claustrophobia; we feel, along with Witek, that the world has suddenly become too narrow a place. It is as though we are kicked out.

Finally, having in some obscure way learned from his "previous" experiences that any form of political involvement is bad, in the third narrative Witek chooses not to choose:[7] "I don't want to be involved in either. [. . .] I don't want to belong to anything."[8] Needless to say, in a totalitarian system where nothing is more extraordinary than being able to live an ordinary life, choosing not to choose is in itself a significant political choice—and a rather courageous one at that: "The Witek of the third part of *Blind Chance* will be bolder—which does not mean that he revolts. He simply knows that one must not get involved."[9] This is the closest Witek could get, under the given circumstance, to living an authentic life.[10]

In many respects, the third choice, the healthiest, should also have been the safest. Witek chooses to stay away from any form of politics (whether Communist or anti-Communist) and to go into some form of inner exile; he must have hoped that the corrupted world of politics could not penetrate his inner universe. There is serenity, perfection and "calm" in this inner world; this is a space of freedom and authenticity and of self-realization. What you attain here nobody can take away from you: the joy of parenthood; the sense of solidarity with your fellow-humans; the compassion for the suffering, the weak and the poor; and a deeper understanding of the human condition[11]. It seemed as though it was at last possible for Witek to evade the all-pervading system. The scene where he watches in awe the two jugglers perform—a scene whose immediate significance and role within the economy of the film narrative are otherwise not very easy to grasp—must have evoked in him something of a superior form of freedom. The jugglers' play transpires a perfection one can only reach when one truly dedicates oneself to pursuing one's own dreams: "They've been practicing for at least ten years. . . . Seems no one in the world can juggle like that."[12]

In a sense, then, the two jugglers function as an illustration that one can still be free even in an un-free world: nobody can interfere in their play, nothing from what happens in the world around affects them in any consequential way. Undisturbed, dedicated, completely absorbed by what they are doing, they could "juggle like that" forever—a rare instance of self-sufficiency and autonomy in the middle of a world where such things seem hardly attainable. The two jugglers surround themselves with an aura of perfection and excellence, which no intruders can break; it is as though by doing what they are doing they build up a wall separating them from the unworthy outside world. Watching them, Witek must have somehow realized that the path he had chosen in his third life story—being a good doctor, practicing his profession as well as possible, in other words, pursuing a form of excellence not unlike the one displayed by the two jugglers—might have been indeed the right path.

At home, still under the two jugglers' spell, Witek tries to imitate their act. He does not come even close; the apples he plays with fall in disarray. He is obviously not meant for such performance; he could have taken that as a sign: soon enough Witek, too, will literally fall, when he will die in a plane crash, the film's most violent expression of "blind chance." While the two previous life stories were only possible, this one is actual. Kieślowski assures us that this ending is also the most important one for him:

> The third ending is the one which means the most to me—the one where the airplane explodes—because one way or another, that's going to be our fate. It's all the same whether this happens in an airplane or in bed, it doesn't matter.[13]

At the end of the film, watching the airplane explode, the viewer is left totally perplexed, her mind paralyzed; as the credits start rolling, an overwhelming silence starts settling in. If there is a key to understanding *Blind Chance,* this key should be able to help us make sense of this silence. Yet, before going any further, a short detour, an intermezzo on the issue of interpretation is in order—just to buy time, if not for something more consequential.

A MATTER OF INTERPRETATION

In a certain sense, *Blind Chance* is a film about interpretation: about the difficulty of interpretation, over-interpretation, and misinterpretation; it may not be completely wrong to say that, ultimately, the whole film is about nothing but dying to find the right interpretation.

As a leitmotif in his first two life stories, Witek makes repeated reference to what his father wanted from him shortly before his death:

WITEK'S FATHER: "They are taking me to the hospital. You mustn't . . .
WITEK:　　　　　"Mustn't what?"
WITEK'S FATHER: "Nothing."[14]

The viewer senses right away that there must be something important here, yet it is something that throughout the film remains unuttered. This something constitutes the zero-degree of Witek's first two life stories: they articulate themselves as attempts at giving meaning to his father's final silence. In a certain sense, here Witek does not have a life of his own; or, if he does, he does not know very much about it ("I want to be baptized. [...] To know why I am alive," he says in the second story[15]). He embarks on two different political projects just to forget about the identity crisis he is going through, somehow nurturing the hope that by finding out what his father might have wanted him to do—or not do—he would be able to fill this existential emptiness. That's why his first two life stories are experimental biographies, "trial lives" we may call them. He does not live for the sake of living, but to decipher a message—and an unuttered message at that. As such, each one of his first two lives is a *lived hermeneutics,* an existential project built around painful attempts at interpreting emptiness. It is as though he lives only to give meaning to his father's silence:

> He wanted to tell me something, but he waited until the last moment. I called him whenever I had a chance. He took several months to die. When he'd answer, I'd hang up. I couldn't bring myself to speak to him. He knew each time it was me.[16]

Witek knows that his father wanted something from him, although he does not know what exactly; what he is certain of is that he has to change his life and re-design it so that it will be in harmony with his father's mysterious last wish. He decides to do the impossible: to live two altogether different lives, in the (almost crazy) hope that at least one of them will match his father's wish. Without his father, Witek amounts to nothing; without his father's last wish, his life cannot mean anything.

Whether we know it or not, we always live to decipher a message. The last word that Witek heard from his father is "nothing," but this nothing is more than enough to fill one's life—in Witek's case it filled two lives. Whatever we do, we always seek to give this nothing a positive meaning. Our fathers, or our Father, terrorize us with their (real or only imagined) legacies, putting us on the wrong track, setting traps for us, making us follow empty dreams and poisonous visions—sometimes, in the process, annihilating us altogether. Although long dead, they still have a tremendous authority over us (in *I am so-so,* Kieślowski confesses: "Father talked to me often. I was afraid of him. Not because he would hit me, but because he was an authority"[17]). Ironically, much of our lives is shaped and controlled by something we don't see. Even in our most solitary moments, we are not alone: an unseen—but all-seeing—eye watches us all the time.

The third of Witek's lives is designed in such a way that he never mentions his father's legacy of silence; he lives this life as if there was never an interrupted conversation between him and his father. Having missed the train, he does not bother to understand his father's final message, and does not change his life; it never crosses his mind that he should redesign his biography in order to align it with who knows what legacy. And he is, as a perceptive critic said, "rewarded with eternal silence."[18] It is here, in the third narrative of Witek's life, that we come across that humiliating final silence, which we still have to decipher, or at least make some sense of.

DECIPHERING SILENCE

In an interview with Paul Coates, Kieślowski confesses that, of all his films, *Blind Chance* offers the most intensely religious scene he has ever shot:

> perhaps the most religious scene in all the films I've made occurs in *Blind Chance*, when the hero kneels during baptism and prays: "O God, I have been baptized, I ask only one thing of you: be there. I ask only that: be there." This is perhaps the most religious scene in all my films and I wrote its script myself.[19]

Witek prays ardently to a God of whose existence he is not at all certain. He invokes not God, but the necessity of his existence: God is not yet there, but Witek, with his unheard-of prayer, invites his existence. Read between the lines, such a prayer may suggest that, even if God has not showed up yet, there is a vacant place waiting for him; it is a place that only he can occupy and nobody else. If for some reason God decides not to show up, the place will remain vacant forever.

The existence of a transcendent vacancy that only God can fill is one of the key elements of *Blind Chance*; it is so important that it dominates even the aesthetics of the film. For from a formal standpoint, what is striking about the film's narrative construction is that, without making any explicit theological statements, the very organization of the material presupposes the existence of a transcendent point of view. Just like in Witek's theology, where God does not actually exist but has a place of his own that nobody else can occupy, in the economy of the film the narrative is articulated in such a manner that what we get in the end does not make much sense unless we accept that everything is told from a transcendent point of view. The sheer existence of the threefold narrative; the two alternative story lines that are only *possible*, not actual—the detailed unfolding of which only an omniscient narrator would know; the mysterious role played by apparently chance events (an old woman happening to be in someone's way, a dropped coin, a drunkard buying beer)—a role of which the narrating gaze seems to be not only aware but somehow in control; the entire network of odd coincidences, strange encounters and symmetries that interconnect the three story lines in some obscure yet indubitable way; the visual or only textual hints playfully scattered across the three stories (e.g., "you have a mustache"), betraying a scope of consciousness of which humans are normally incapable; the perfectly objective, imperturbable tone that characterizes the narrative; the highly puzzling role that the absurd and chance play throughout the work, which would remain utterly incomprehensible if considered exclusively from an immanent point of view—all of these can be read as indications that the generating matrix of the film is "out of this world." The narrative simply *points to* the necessity of a non-human subject from whose point of view Witek's life stories are being told: only such a broad perspective would do justice to the complexity of the film. As the "plot" progresses, an invisible niche is gradually being created (both in the conditions of possibility of the narrative itself and in the mind of the viewer), a niche that can only be filled by an "out-of-this-world" narrator. Even though Kieślowski does not mention explicitly the existence of a transcendent consciousness, *Blind Chance* would not make much sense without it.

On the other hand, this transcendent presupposition on which the film narrative is based fits quite well with what the film is about: the experience of Witek's death and its possible significance. The seeming senselessness of the third ending is one of the most disturbing aspects of *Blind Chance*: it goes totally against the viewer's sense of justice, fairness and moral life. *Especially* in the third story Witek should *not* die—this is the direction in which the sympathy of the morally minded viewer goes. Ethically, as I hinted earlier, there is something attractive about this Witek who, by choosing not to choose, worries Communists and anti-Communists alike; this Witek who understands that, beyond any artificial (ideological, political, social) divisions between people, one thing always unites them—*suffering*—and who dedicates his life to alleviating it; this Witek who is sensibly wiser than the Witeks of the other two stories and who carefully avoids their mistakes. That *this* Witek is rewarded with an absurd, violent death, is ethically scandalous. By immanent standards, such a death remains incomprehensible. The only way to avoid nihilism is to assume that *there must be* some transcendent standpoint, some superior angle from where earthly things (dying in a plane crash, for example) are understood better and measured by different standards. As Kieślowski himself puts it somewhere: "I don't think we've got perfect justice here, on earth, and we never will have. It's justice on our own scale and our scale is minute. We're tiny and imperfect."[20]

As such, apart from the device of a transcendent narrator presupposed by the film's story-telling techniques, the event of Witek's death is what opens *Blind Chance* up decisively toward the experience of the transcendent. Death is substantially, thickly present in the economy of the film; the whole of it unfolds in the shadow of death, as it were. As Slavoj Žižek noticed, what we see on screen might be nothing other than what Witek remembers during the few seconds preceding his death.[21] Just like in the Scheherazade legend, *Blind Chance* transpires a desperate effort to stick to life and resist death through story-telling. The opening scene (which, in visual-formal terms, as well as in terms of the intense emotions evoked, is clearly reminiscent of Edward Munch's *Scream*) is a prolonged, screamed "No!" The whole film then "unfolds under the aegis of this "No!," which concerns more than a political system."[22] It certainly concerns the overwhelming importance of death in our lives, its insidious proximity, its eating at us, the painful awareness that nothing can be done to stop it.

On the other hand, thanks to the many "premonitions" scattered throughout the film, there is a sense that what we see unfolding on screen is a process of familiarization with death, of "taming" it and eventually accepting it as a "gift" of sorts. It all depends on perspective; death can be indeed terrible, but it can also be the mark of a fundamental metaphysical event, the most transcendent-oriented experience we humans can have access to. Dying is ultimately transcending; in death we experience that which limits us forever, the radically different other, the source of higher meaning. Václav Havel asks

> What does death . . . awaken within us? Precisely what makes human existence a miracle or re-creation: that special belief that breathes significance, i.e., a sense of meaning, into our lives . . . the belief that despite everything, human life has a meaning and therefore every authentic human act of "transcendence" has meaning as well.[23]

A THEOLOGY OF THE SHY

At this juncture, an unavoidable discussion opens up about Krzysztof Kieślowski's theology. What complicates (and has postponed) such a discussion is, on the one hand, Kieślowski's own agnostic comments, and, on the other, his conflict with the Catholic Church in Poland,[24] especially after the release of *No End* (*Bez końca*, 1985), which was received rather critically in Catholic circles.

A theological Kieślowski, problematic as he may seem to some, should not take us completely by surprise, however. Agnieszka Holland, who knew Kieślowski quite well, comments on this issue:

> Krzysztof is somebody who had an incredibly deep need to believe in something transcendental. He did believe, but at the same time he wasn't really a member of any church, and his relationships toward the religious were less theological than ethical and metaphysical.[25]

In light of such considerations, it is tempting to see Kieślowski as a theologian, if one eternally heretic, without a god, without a church—a "religious thinker" (for lack of a better word) incapable of belonging to any particular confession or religion, yet one genuinely interested in what opens us up toward the experience of a higher reality. Kieślowski raises fundamental questions about the human condition and the humans' quest for meaning, without at the same time giving us any definite "recipes" for salvation. In this regard, we can call him a "postsecular" cinematic philosopher. And, like all good philosophers, he is at his best when he comes up with questions, old and new; the answers are not necessarily important—he leaves them to his commentators anyway.

One author who convincingly explores Kieślowski's *oeuvre* from this perspective is Joseph Kickasola. In his book *The Films of Krzysztof Kieślowski* (2004), Kickasola embarks on an ample phenomenological reading of Kieślowski's films, of their imagery and of his use of archetypes and symbols as well as of the various visual protocols his films employ in an effort to gain access to a meaning of his work deeper than what a strictly aesthetic reading normally offers. What Kickasola discovers is a Kieślowski who "charts the liminal spaces, demarcating the apparent thresholds of metaphysical and physical, transcendent and immanent, eternal and temporal."[26] It is a Kieślowski who speculates in images and visualizes fundamental philosophical issues, in the process helping us gain a deeper insight into who we are, what we care about, and how the ontology of the human condition is constituted. For this Kieślowski, says Kickasola:

> our desire for meaning makes us human and is worthy of exploration. This metaphysical quest runs consistently through Kieślowski's films. They almost never give us concrete answers to those questions, but functions best as a sort of map, charting the tortuous, often bewildering topography of human experience.[27]

In Kickasola's reading of Kieślowski, the issues of chance, choice and circumstance are never indifferent; they should always be considered in relation to "a religious dimension" implied by his work. Within such a religious perspective, the relevant question to be asked is "whether an event is caused by 'blind chance' or is a part of a preordained plan."[28] Under ordinary circumstances, we may or may not come across the "synchronies of life"; in his films, however, Kieślowski incessantly highlights them for us. Moreover, the inner logic of these synchronies and coincidences gradually asks for a resolution, which cannot be satisfactorily reached unless we adopt a transcendent viewpoint. For Kickasola, *Blind Chance* is one of the best illustrations of this tendency in Kieślowski's works.

Thus, *Blind Chance* is not just a philosophical film,[29] but also a theological one, if in a rather discreet and unorthodox way. The theology of the film is a "postsecular" one; it is a theology of the shy. Kieślowski, just like Witek,[30] is not bold enough (or just not irresponsible enough) to assert the actual existence of something transcendent, but he points to its necessity. The world is so messed-up, human beings are so weak and unwise that unless we place things in a trans-historical perspective, history does not make much sense. In strictly immanent terms, history is bound to be a succession of chaotic facts and events, "blind chances," transpiring no meaning whatsoever. Down here we are condemned to an essentially limited understanding; we cannot have access to the bigger picture, to how things really are—that is the ultimate message of *Blind Chance*. As Kieślowski himself says in his conversation with Danusia Stok, in the process employing—perhaps against his best intentions—a strikingly religious language: "given the limitation of our knowledge and the imperfection of our intelligence, there's no way we can gauge the reality or the gravity of sin, the extent of guilt."[31]

The only way we can escape the nihilism that this realization brings about is to accept, at least hypothetically, the existence of a transcendent standpoint from where our lives may make better sense. Otherwise, we will never be able to get out of the suffocating framework delineated by such poor descriptors as "chance," "luck," "bad luck," "fortune," "misfortune," etc. This does not necessarily mean to believe in God; it only means that in the absence of any transcendent system of reference, life in this world can be, philosophically, a very claustrophobic experience.

Properly speaking, however, we do *not* have access to a transcendent perspective—only to the notion of its necessity; we cannot assert it positively—we can only feel that we lack it. In virtue of our ontological make-up, we do not, and cannot, have positive means to see things from that perspective; all we can do is *hope* that such a perspective does indeed exist and that our tribulations and misery are not in vain. That's our ultimate condition: left in between, always already departed, but never yet there. Like Witek, we pray to a God who is nowhere to be found, although absolutely necessary; nowhere to be seen, but highly desirable. And yet Witek's prayer may be closer to what true faith is than even Kieślowski himself would be ready to admit. "For faith is the substance of things hoped for, the evidence of things not seen" (Heb. 11:1).

HISTORY AS GEOGRAPHY

Blind Chance could be read as a film about a set of universal themes such as the quest for higher meaning and personal autonomy, the need for a transcendent system of reference, or the confrontation with the absurdity of existence. On the other hand, behind this first—and probably the most important—layer of meaning, there is also in this film something local, a Polish ingredient, which gives it the specific flavor of an East-European masterpiece. This has to do, more exactly, with a certain philosophy of history, a specific understanding of the historical process that the film illustrates. To discuss this feature of *Blind Chance,* a brief overview of Kieślowski's "philosophy of history" (as revealed especially in Danusia Stok's *Kieślowski on Kieślowski*) is necessary.

Kieślowski tends to see historical events as being pre-determined by rules of spatial situation. In history events do not just occur, they occur in a specific location, they "take place," and are, therefore, subject to a certain geographical conditioning—which is, for Kieślowski, geographical determinism. This is true especially about his native Poland: "I really bear a grudge against history, or perhaps against the geography which treated this country the way it did. No doubt, that's how it has to be—that we'll get thrashed, that we will try to tear ourselves away from where we are and will never succeed. That's our fate."[32] Kieślowski saw himself as a man born in a wrongly placed place, so to speak. The fact left a deep imprint on his way of thinking and marked his understanding of a number of fundamental issues such as freedom of choice, self-realization (both individual and collective), autonomy, destiny and history.

Poland's curse comes, for Kieślowski, from its geography. The geographical situation of Poland is responsible for the "terror of history" Poles have had to suffer for centuries: "We, as Poles, have tried to negate our historical location several times; that is, our position between the Russians and the Germans, a place through which all new roads always pass. We always lost."[33] One can change many things about one's country; one can try to improve its government, reform its morals and better educate its youth, but one can hardly change its geography. Geography is out there, and it will not go anywhere; it cannot be changed. Moreover: geography *happens* to be there; a certain community of people, at some point in time, happens to inhabit a certain area. Thus, for Kieślowski, geography is a "blind chance" factor that has something to say about the birth and history of a nation as well as the culture and the character of its people. There is in Kieślowski, then, a deep sense of geo-political fatality, which surfaces in both his philosophical views and in some of his films, especially in *Blind Chance*: "I don't know what free Poland means. A free Poland is completely impossible simply because the country is badly situated geographically."[34]

One important characteristic of the wrongly placed places is that the rhythms of the historical processes are dictated there by the dialectics of hope—by the movement from the very possibility/naissance of hope to its gradual flourishing and maturation, and then unavoidably to the complete exhaustion thereof. For Kieślowski, living historically in these places means going all the way from complete self-deception through utter despair, and then repeating everything, endlessly, *ad nauseam*. Like in the myth of Sisyphus, a forgetting process is always under way: we never learn anything and always make the same mistakes. History is not a progression toward more and more truth, as a naïve philosophy of history would have it; it is, on the contrary, a painful process through which more and more "un-truth" is revealed. To live is to always experience disenchantment:

> Each time, a naïve, vital longing for order, for decency, for a reasonable life is motivated by hope. [. . .] but the hope is getting smaller and smaller. It gets smaller with every disappointment. It is the same whether the hope's been inspired by the Communists in 1956 or 1970, or the workers in 1981 or our new government in 1990 and 1991—it doesn't matter who inspires the hope. Every time we see that this hope was just another illusion, another untruth; another dream and not a real hope.[35]

It is worth noting that Kieślowski does not expect history to be the actualization of grand ideals such as collective happiness, a greater good, or general well-being. His expectations are much more modest: what he seeks is above all genuine, lasting *hope*. Of course, sheer hope does not solve anything, but it would be a tremendous start. For hope is after all what makes life possible by causing in us the fundamental expectation that things (the world, airplanes, the government, etc.) make sense and do not just "happen." When hope is killed repeatedly, life itself is seriously undermined.

Kieślowski might have not been surprised to learn—let it be said in passing—that in another East-European wrongly placed place, someone by the name of Václav Havel was thinking along similar lines around the same time. For Havel, hope is a fundamental pre-condition of living in the world. Just like in the case of Kieślowski, for him hope is ultimately a promise of meaning: "Hope is definitely not the same thing as optimism. It is not the conviction that something will turn out well, but the certainty that something makes sense, regardless of how it turns out."[36]

Witek's three life stories could be seen as illustrations of the process of disenchantment that, according to Kieślowski, characterizes life in a wrongly placed place: "Each time, a naïve, vital longing for order, for decency, for a reasonable life."[37] Each one of his lives starts out enthusiastically, in an enchanted mood, but it gradually turns into a movement toward more and more "untruth," to use Kieślowski's own term. The unmerciful narrator shows us a Witek who, every time, is going all the way from maximum enchantment to maximum lucidity, with the supreme lucidity of death, which is given to him as an ironical gift, in the third, and last, version of his life. It is basically the same process of existential exhaustion, of diminishing one's ability to dream and entertain hopes; in the end, one's ability to live. In a certain sense, then, the film is ultimately not about events in the social-political world but about the inner transformations that a self has to go through as a result of its encounter with a cursed historical world. As Kieślowski himself remarks, *Blind Chance* "is no longer a description of the outside world but rather of the inner world. It's a description of the powers which meddle with our fate, which push us one way or another."[38]

Witek's three life stories end badly, each in its own way. What they have in common, however, is precisely the fact that they unfold following the same logic of disenchantment and exhaustion. Interestingly, early in the film we come across a rather well articulated version of this notion of the exhaustion of hope; it is Werner, the old Communist, who brings it forth in the first of Witek's lives:

> Every generation has need of light. It needs to know, or to believe, that the world can be a better place. This need . . . is like a drug. Early in life, it brings joy, as light seems near, within reach. At life's end, it brings bitterness, as the light has grown distant. During those 40 years, I lived through many things, and today I see it more distant than before. [. . .] But . . . life without this hope, without this bitterness, wouldn't be worth living.[39]

THE "TERROR OF HISTORY"

I used the phrase "terror of history," somehow anticipatorily, a couple of times in the above considerations to describe a perception of the historical time marked by anxiety, disenchantment and chronic pessimism. The phrase expresses, accurately enough, the oppressive manner in which history appears to someone unable to find any redeeming meaning in it. One scholar who talks of the "terror of history" in this sense is Mircea Eliade (1907–1986). A Romanian-born historian and philosopher of religion, Eliade emigrated after the WWII, first to France, then to the US, where he held the Chair of History of Religions at the University of Chicago until his death. While still in France, Eliade published a little book that was to become one of his most influential: *Le Mythe de l'éternel retour* (1949); the English edition would come out some five years later: *The Myth of the Eternal Return or, Cosmos and History* (1954). Toward the end of his book, Eliade touches on the issue of historicism from the point of view of the history of religions. For him, historicism, beyond the intrinsic scholarly problems it may cause, also raises a major "existential problem." In Eliade's own wording:

> How can the "terror of history" be tolerated from the viewpoint of historicism? Justification of a historical event by the simple fact that it is a historical event . . . by the simple fact that it "happened that way," will not go far toward freeing humanity from the terror that the event inspires.[40]

If we are to make some sense of the historical event, we have to go beyond its sheer factuality and account for it in trans-historical terms. It is not difficult to find auto-biographical traces in Eliade's text. Just like Kieślowski, Eliade was coming from a place where historical events usually "happened that way," a place that for centuries had been under foreign occupations, divided and re-divided among the great powers, and deprived of independence. For those who (have to) live in such places, the historicist explanation is unacceptable.

Moreover, at the time of writing, Eliade must have been profoundly distressed by the fresh Soviet occupation of Eastern Europe (including of his native Romania) and by the accompanying process of Sovietization of life there. Further still, in the spirit of the book, he attempts to place the post-war geopolitical reconfiguration of Europe within a larger theological-historical scenario. It is within this scenario that historicism, as a theory of pure historical immanence, leads to nihilism, even though Eliade does not use the word:

> How justify, for example, the fact that southeastern Europe had to suffer for centuries—and hence to renounce any impulse toward a higher historical existence, toward spiritual creation on the universal plane—for

the sole reason that it happened to be on the road of the Asiatic invaders and later the neighbor of the Ottoman Empire? And in our day, when historical pressure no longer allows any escape, how can man tolerate the catastrophes and horrors of history—from collective deportations and massacres to atomic bombings—if beyond them he can glimpse no sign, no trans-historical meaning?[41]

This state of hopelessness, the painful anxiety that overwhelms the one who has to face the "terror of history" empty-handedly are exactly what we find in Kieślowski. It is what we sense right away in Witek's haunting "Noooo!" at the beginning of the film, but also what the director himself suggests in *Kieślowski on Kieślowski,* for example, when he talks about "all this mess which surrounds us, . . . all this dirt, powerlessness, human impotence, this inability to finish anything, to do anything well."[42]

The oppressive, if not overtly catastrophic, influence that geography can have on a given people's historical destiny, which bothered Kieślowski so much, appears several times in Eliade's argument: some peoples just *happen* to be in the way of some other peoples, at a given time in history, and that is enough for them to be, and feel, doomed. In an uncharacteristic polemical mood, Eliade deconstructs historicism biographically, finding it specific to those scholars and "thinkers belonging to nations for which history has never been a continuous terror." Such thinkers can afford to practice historicism because they enjoy the luxury of having been born in places that, in general, have not been confronted with major historical disruptions such as prolonged foreign invasions and occupations, repressions of civil liberties, and deprivations of national autonomy. However, Eliade says, they

> would perhaps have adopted another viewpoint had they belonged to nations marked by the "fatality of history." It would certainly be interesting, in any case, to know if the theory according to which everything that happens is "good," simply *because* it has happened, would have been accepted without qualms by the thinkers of the Baltic countries, of the Balkans, or of colonial territories.[43]

In other words, as a theory, historicism is wrong anyway and anywhere, but in some parts of the world, such as Eastern Europe, historicism would be not only a flawed theory, but also—morally speaking—a form of cynicism.

What is to be done? Whereas people in archaic societies could in principle escape from the "terror of history" through myths, mythical narratives and ritual "reconstructions" of the world, Eliade finds the modern man completely unprepared to cope with the atrocities of history. We moderns are in a perpetual state of anxiety, and historicism is incapable of showing us a way out. And yet living perpetually in anxiety is not an option; there must be means whereby humanity can pull itself together, some self-therapy, new ways of living meaningfully. For Eliade, this can still be done through the experience of the sacred and an understanding of life as theophany. Interestingly, Kieślowski, even though his is a more complex case, comes close to Eliade's solution. As I showed earlier on in this chapter, for him, one cannot solve the mysteries of historical existence unless one tries to place oneself outside history itself. *Blind Chance* is a brilliant illustration of such a dramatic shift of perspective. The story of Witek's life is told in such a fashion that it does not make much sense unless we decide to read it as an indirectly theological story—a tale, as it were, that only an angel could tell.

NOTES

1. This chapter represents the rewritten version of a paper originally published as a journal article: "Transcendence and History in Krzysztof Kieślowski's *Blind Chance*" in *East-European Politics and Societies,* 22: 2 (May 2008), 425–46. In turn, a shorter draft of that article was presented at the international conference *Rediscovering Polish Cinema: History—Ideology—Politics* held at the University of Lodz (Poland) from September, 23–25, 2006. I am grateful to Konrad Klejsa, the conference organizer, for inviting me to give the paper, as well as to those members of the audience who provided me with valuable feedback. A Polish version of the paper presented in Lodz appeared in *Kino Polskie: Reinterpretacje. Historia—Ideologia—Polityka,* edited by Ewelina Nurczynska-Fidelska and Konrad Klejsa (Lodz: Wydawnictwo Uniwersytetu Lodzkiego), 177–96. I owe special thanks to Tomasz Kłys for his excellent translation.
2. Slavoj Žižek, *The Fright of Real Tears. Krzysztof Kieślowski between Theory and Post-Theory* (London, UK: BFI Publishing, 2001), 80.
3. Ibid., 79.
4. Tadeusz Sobolewski, "Ultimate Concerns," in *Lucid Dreams. The Films of Krzysztof Kieślowski, ed.* Paul Coates (Trowbridge, UK: Flicks Books, 1999), 22.
5. Danusia Stok, *Kieślowski on Kieślowski* (London, UK: Faber and Faber, 1993), 113. Film critics tend to see Witek as being an essentially good person. This is how Marek Haltof, for example, sees Witek:

   > In all three parts of *Blind Chance,* regardless of his political stance, Witek is basically the same: sincere, honest, decent, passionate, eager to act and trying to do his best in given circumstances. [. . .] Although fate meddles in Witek's affairs and alters (or ends) his life, he remains good by nature. (Marek Haltof, *The Cinema of Krzysztof Kieślowski* [London, UK: Wallflower Press, 2004], 61)

6. Tadeusz Sobolewski, "Ultimate Concerns," 22.
7. "The first two variants of Witek's life are recounted in the conditional tense. Only the third variant, which ends in death, is real. Witek misses the train, avoids internal division and abandons the social race. He becomes a doctor—joins no Party, signs no oppositional protest letter. He seems to be happy and fulfilled, or as much so as is possible in life." (Ibid.)
8. *Blind Chance,* Dir. Krzysztof Kieślowski; Written by Krzysztof Kieślowski; Perfs. Boguslaw Linda, Tadeusz Lomnicki, Zbigniew Zapasiewicz, Boguslawa Pawelec, Marzena Trybala, Monika Gozdzik, Irena Burska and Jacek Borkowski; DVD; Prod. 1981 P.P. Film Polski (Poland), Dist. 2005 Kino Video (USA). All references are made to this release.

9. Tadeusz Sobolewski, "Ultimate Concerns," 26.
10. On the other hand, it should be noted here that Kieślowski, somehow paradoxically for someone living under totalitarian (or quasi-totalitarian) conditions, considered that after all politics is "not in a position to do anything about or to answer any of our essential, fundamental, human and humanistic questions." For him, whether one lives in a Communist country or Western democracy does not make any difference when it comes to answering fundamental questions such as "What is the true meaning of life? Why get up in the morning? Politics don't answer that." (Danusia Stok, *Kieślowski on Kieślowski*, 144)
11. "The fullness of his experience lies in his openness to the world of human suffering, which is no longer veiled from him by politics." (Tadeusz Sobolewski, "Ultimate Concerns," 22).
12. Krzysztof Kieślowski, *Blind Chance*.
13. Danusia Stok, *Kieślowski on Kieślowski*, 113. This post- or trans-political concern is what makes *Blind Chance*, in the view of many scholars, a truly philosophical film. Tadeusz Sobolewski, for example, who regards *Blind Chance* as "Kieślowski's key film" states that it

> broke radically with the system, not just on the level of politics and ideology, but in its very way of conceiving man and his destiny. It expressed a philosophical disenchantment with life as such, not the system. The road to the *Decalogue* lay open. Paradoxically, Kieślowski needed the experience of the martial law along the way to free himself of the last vestiges of the political engagement. (Tadeusz Sobolewski, "Ultimate Concerns," 27)

14. Krzysztof Kieślowski, *Blind Chance*.
15. Ibid.
16. Ibid.
17. *Krzysztof Kieślowski: I am so-so . . .*, Dir. Krzysztof Wierzbicki; Written by Krzysztof Wierzbicki; Videocassette; Prod. 1995 Kulturmode Film (Denmark); Dist. 1998 First Run Features (USA).
18. Joseph Kickasola, *The Films of Krzysztof Kieślowski. The Liminal Image* (New York: Continuum, 2004), 146.
19. Paul Coates, "'The inner life is the only thing that interests me': a conversation with Krzysztof Kieślowski," in *Lucid Dreams,* ed. Paul Coates, 168.
20. Danusia Stok, *Kieślowski on Kieślowski,* 150.
21. "Is . . . the entire film not the flashback of a person who, aware that he is close to death, quickly runs not only through his life . . ., but through *three* possible lives? The scream that opens the film—the desperate 'Nooo!' of Witek falling to certain death—is thus the zero-level exempted from the three virtual universes" (Slavoj Žižek, *The Fright of Real Tears,* 80).
22. Tadeusz Sobolewski, "Ultimate Concerns," 26.
23. Václav Havel, *Letters to Olga. June 1979–September 1982.* Translated by Paul Wilson (New York: Henry Holt, 1989), 240.
24. In *I am so-so*, a Catholic priest has the following to say about Kieślowski: "I think he succumbed to the temptation which has existed since Creation: Who is God? The Lord or myself?" (*Krzysztof Kieślowski: I am so-so . . .*)
25. Agnieszka Holland, quoted by Joseph Kickasola, *The Films of Krzysztof Kieślowski,* 34.
26. Joseph Kickasola, *The Films of Krzysztof Kieślowski,* x.
27. Ibid.
28. Ibid., 32.
29. In "Ultimate Concerns," Tadeusz Sobolewski offers a remarkably perceptive philosophical reading of *Blind Chance*. For him the film transcends politics, ideologies and social concerns, and touches on a set of fundamental philosophical

issues. Sobolewski depicts insightfully the transition from political to philosophical that takes place in *Blind Chance*.

30. Some critics have seen in Witek an *alter ego* of Kieślowski himself. Tadeusz Lubelski, for example, draws a convincing parallel between the two: Witek

> has the same birthday as the film's author—27 June—albeit fifteen years later, in 1956. Kieślowski, too, as a chronicler of the authorities, had had a flirtation with them. . . . He, too, had sympathized with the opposition: a number of his films, headed by *The Calm*, had been shelved for years. But the variant basically closest to him was the third—that of the man who stands on the sidelines. He said as much outright on more than one occasion. (Tadeusz Lubelski, "From *Personnel* to *No End:* Kieślowski's political feature films," in *Lucid Dreams*, ed. Paul Coates, 67–68.)

31. Danusia Stok, *Kieślowski on Kieślowski*, 122.
32. Ibid., 141.
33. Ibid.
34. Ibid., 138.
35. Ibid.
36. Václav Havel, *Disturbing the Peace. A Conversation with Karel HvíŽďala*. Translated by Paul Wilson (New York: Alfred A. Knopf, 1990), 181.
37. Danusia Stok, *Kieślowski on Kieślowski*, 138.
38. Ibid., 113. See also, Kickasola: "Kieślowski, quite literally, marked this film as his shift from the outside world of documentaries to the inner world" (Joseph Kickasola, *The Films of Krzysztof Kieślowski*, 130).
39. Krzysztof Kieślowski, *Blind Chance*.
40. Mircea Eliade, *The Myth of the Eternal Return or, Cosmos and History*. Translated by Willard R. Trask (Princeton, NJ: Princeton University Press, 1971), 152.
41. Ibid.
42. Danusia Stok, *Kieślowski on Kieślowski*, 69.
43. Mircea Eliade, *The Myth of the Eternal Return*, 152.

6 The Evidence of Things Not Seen
Sound and the Neighbor in Kieślowski, Haneke, Martel

Paul Coates

INTRODUCTION

This chapter has two alternative starting points, a different one for each of the comparisons that form its double backbone: that between Krzysztof Kieślowski's *Trois couleurs: bleu* (*Three Colours: Blue* [1993] [hereafter *Blue*]) and Michael Haneke's *Code Inconnu* (2000); and that between Kieślowski's *Trois couleurs: rouge* (*Three Colours: Red* [1994] [hereafter *Red*]) and the films of Lucrecia Martel. Each comparison was sparked by noting moments of strong echo between the Haneke film and *Blue*, on the one hand, and *Red* and Martel's *The Headless Woman* (*La mujer sin cabeza*) (2008).[1] The main common denominator between these films is the relationship between sound and the categorical imperative of love for neighbor, sound being the primary means whereby the known and visible extends into an off-screen invisibility redolent of mystery, other people, or an Other ranging from the human degraded by a process of othering to the Divine. In the Christian context, of course, the Divinity itself takes upon itself the most extreme effects of othering—human degradation and abjection—in Christ's Crucifixion, prompting the writer of the Letter to the Hebrews to enjoin fellow Christians to "go forth to him without the camp, bearing his reproach" (Heb. 13:13; AV).

Another relevant denominator, of key importance to this volume, is the question of the definition of "the European," which widens to include "the beggar at the gate" connecting Eastern and Western Europe (in each case, Eastern Europe and Paris) in the films of Kieślowski and Haneke, and whose suffering through class-positioning recurs in Martel's films where the bourgeois view of neighboring indigenous populations in Argentina may be called colonially Eurocentric. Also analyzed in this essay is Rachid Bouchareb's *London River* (2009). Although less resonant than the above-named works, it merits juxtaposition with them as a test case of explicitly relating neighborhood to ethical demand in a manner reminiscent of the philosophy of Emmanuel Levinas, whose thoughts on the neighbor will be contrasted with those of Slavoj Žižek.

"EUROCENTRISM" UNBOUNDED

Because the "matter of Europe" is central to this volume, I will begin with the question of the Eurocentric and the sense in which it forms part of my justification for including Martel's films (my others being the degree of her concern with the sociology and even epistemology of religion and their relation to sound, a dimension of particular interest to Kieślowski and Haneke, whose stature as filmmakers I would see her as beginning to approach).

Just where "Europe" begins and ends is moot, with geographic definitions more disputable than ideological ones. Critiques aimed at an ideology identified as "Eurocentrism" discern it in North America as well as Europe.[2] These critiques are not, as one might expect, nativist North American denunciations of such a prodigal son as Henry James, with his fascination with Europe's possession of institutions more venerable than those of the United States. Instead, they denounce a world-wide colonialist enterprise that first emanated from Europe and used the Enlightenment reason of certain West European Caucasians as the yardstick whereby other cultures were declared locked in an irrationality, backwardness, and "savagery" a few Europeans nevertheless valued (as in Rousseau's counter-myth of "the noble savage"). Insofar as "Eurocentrism" appears outside Europe, as its theorizations usually assume it does, it is in classes descended from colonists and still defining themselves as superior to indigenous groups whose undeveloped world could never be a developing one. The reason/unreason distinction is mapped onto, reinforces, and is reinforced by a class one. Thus the Northern Argentinian bourgeoisie depicted by Martel denigrate credulous indigenous groups and, in *The Swamp* (*La Ciénaga*) (2001), stare continually at the television screen reporting a vision of the Virgin supposedly experienced by a member of just such a group. Their fascination is with an Other that is a half-separated projection, as the Other of social strata of European descent is fused with a belief-system they both know and disavow, the Catholicism that is part of their own past. Europeans may have left Europe, but the religious belief system they brought with them, and which they now consider irremediably past, comes back to haunt them. The persistent shadow of Catholicism troubles their confirmation in their own identity by the visible Otherness of those natives. As if as a consequence of this, the regime of the visible in general, that realm in which the look is used to assert and maintain control, begins to crumble, conceding an increasing importance to sound. Krzysztof Kieślowski's Poles—especially the hairdresser in Paris in *Trois couleurs: blanc* (*Three Colours: White* [1994] [hereafter *White*])—could be seen as victims of a similar half-separated projection. As that hairdresser himself asks in the Parisian courtroom where his wife is seeking a divorce: "where is equality?" (that lynchpin of an Enlightenment that has declined into bourgeois ideology).

If I begin with Martel, it is because my reflections originated in part in the similarity between a moment in Martel's *Headless Woman* and an early scene in *Red*, that film strongly concerned with European identity (and its tendency to spread, as in it the colors of the French flag and the maxims of the French Revolution shape a story set primarily in Switzerland). The central narrative thread of each film begins with a female driver, distracted by an audio device within her car (for Kieślowski, a radio; for Martel, a cell-phone), hitting something on the road. In one case (*Red*'s) it is clearly a dog; in the other, less clearly so. Although we have a distant rear-view image in Martel's film, its very remoteness seems to correspond to a doubt that then blossoms as Martel's protagonist, Vero, becomes convinced she has killed a person. This doubt is fed in spectators' minds by her relatives' hollow assurance that it was a dog—as they were not with her at the time and clearly wish to hush-up the matter—and the degree to which that doubt becomes plausible localizes spectators and focalizes the narrative uncomfortably close to Vero. In each film, the female driver reacts very differently: Valentine, Kieślowski's protagonist, gets out of the car, loads the injured Alsatian onto her back seat, takes it to a vet, and then restores the dog to the owner. Vero, however, drives on, replaces her sunglasses, and only stops much further on. Once she has stepped outside the car, as she paces beside it and a storm begins, the frame cutting across her body emphasizes the importance of this moment by rendering her headless indeed, echoing the film's title. This coincidence of beginning is not the only overlap between the films' diegetic worlds as the emphasis on "Accidents and Miracles" noted in a chapter largely devoted to Martel in Jens Andersen's study of the new Argentinian cinema[3] recalls Kieślowski's concern with occurrences of this kind. Each deals with the afterlife of religion amidst a sedulously preserved surface secularism. Each also maps a concern with sound onto one with the neighbor: after all, an inveterate concept of the neighbor, and not just alliteration, links the words "noise" and "neighbor." This concern is also related to one with the religious, as divine interventions disturb the lives they penetrate, and, in such a religious text as that of the Old Covenant, very often emerge via the sound that indicates the defining ability of the divine to surround one, checkmate one's efforts at scrutiny, and meet one on terms it alone defines, as phenomena delivered up exclusively to sight, and limited by visible locations, would not do. Locating the supernatural, therefore, is echo-location.[4] The sound's disturbance of the auditor's life rests, among other things, on the possibility that hosting to the neighbor may involve "entertaining angels" (Heb. 13:2; AV), those entities Rilke was not alone in deeming "terrible."

In terms of the human dimension, the other "entertained" thus, through sound's capacity to cross or penetrate walls, may belong to another ethnic group or class. Here the work of Martel contrasts strongly with that of Kieślowski. In *Blue*, crossing the class divide plays the same role as border crossing in the subsequent film in Kieślowski's Trilogy, *White*, and in many films of the 1990s. Here Kieślowski's work is paradigmatic. Class division reveals itself as substitutable for the divisions between countries, often involving the frontiers of wealth and indigence. *Blue* is unusual, however, in focusing less on aspiration and ambition than on someone (Julie) leaving a higher class and coming closer to the street: to a homeless flautist, for instance. Is this because there is a sense in which music "belongs" nowhere, its point of origin so difficult to perceive as to render it both utopian and alienated?[5] Julie, for her part, crosses a class divide again when extending sympathy to the stripper Lucille, resisting another tenant's request to sign a petition to secure Lucille's eviction from the apartment building. Such class barriers, of course, are never breached in the world of *La Ciénaga*, a film ultimately far darker than Kieślowski's as its protagonists remain locked in their Eurocentric contempt for the indigenous other, and only a child within it (Momi) is able to conceive of a different view. In *The Headless Woman*, which revisits that film's world, cynicism is no longer directed towards the mystical but towards a bourgeoisie disdainful of the indigenous communities already shown to be receptive to the mystical.

MYSTERIES

In *The Headless Woman*, Vero stumbles into a mystery, which then closes around her like a trap as her fatal initial refusal of the risk of knowing plunges her forever after into a half-light of ambiguity and unknowing. In locating itself close to her consciousness, the film plunges the spectator into a mystery, while at the same time maintaining sufficient distance from her to allow an irony also. Thus, the object Vero leaves behind her on the road is sufficiently distant for its nature plausibly to be categorized as unclear: it seems to be a dog—but Vero herself thinks she hit a person, and the very visible hand-prints on the car window (made not by the child inside the car earlier, but in fact by Martel herself) might seem to corroborate her suspicion. Our subsequent discovery that an Indian child has ceased going to work fits in with this scenario. We are meant to recall the children playing with a dog at the roadside at the film's beginning. When her aunt Lala talks of ignoring the dead so that they will go away, this too could be read as significant. Spectators are given the same possibly deceptive clues that lead Vero herself into deducing her own guilt. If she stumbles into a mystery, it appears to be a false one—unlike the true one experienced by Kieślowski's Valentine, which involves different lives repeating themselves and the extent of human knowledge and control of the future.

The question of how much one sees, and the degree to which the visible is mysterious, recurs in Martel's work, emblematically summed-up in Momi's statement at the end of *La Ciénaga*, *a propos* of the visions of the Virgin Mary seen by Catholic members of the indigenous population, that "I didn't see anything." One implication of Momi's remark may be that, for all her rebellion against her parents and attachment to the Indian maid Isabel, in the end she is constrained by her origins, adopting a "Western"/"European" approach to the sacred. (Will her quest continue?) In terms of the presuppositions of Martel's work as a whole, the bourgeois environment shows an older generation not only set in its ways but tending towards the immobility of life in and around the bed. Momi, who thanks God for Isabel at the start of *La Ciénaga,* might be aligned with Kieślowski's Valentine, for whom "accidents" do indeed hover on the border of "miracles." Religion may be present less explicitly in *Red* than in Martel's films, but the frequency of critical comparisons between Judge Joseph Kern and a God-like figure arranging encounters indicates a strong implicit presence. At the same time, Kieślowski's omission from the completed film of the published script's reference to Valentine crossing herself on entering a church intertwines the dimension of mystery with a secular European public sphere from which invocations of the supernatural have been banished. In Martel's Argentina, by way of contrast, the Otherness of religion preserves visibility in the public sphere through the Otherness of an indigenous population which has taken up what Nietzsche termed, and the bourgeoisie Martel depicts would also probably view as, "a slave religion": Christianity.

That view is one Martel herself appears to flirt with in her second film, *The Holy Girl (La niña santa)* (2004), where the previous film's identification of religion with the open-mindedness of youth gives way to its alignment with childish delusion. *The Holy Girl* indicates the depth of Martel's capacity to battle herself. Perhaps because her mode of working is highly intuitive, she fails to see her attack on Catholicism as implicitly one on the Indians distinguished elsewhere in her work from the "shipwrecked Europeans" by their capacity for spirituality. It is as if there were no difference between the alcohol abused by Mechio in *La Ciénaga* and a spirituality conceived as "the opium of the masses." The film seems to conclude "it's just as well Momi didn't see anything, as otherwise she'd have become as deluded as this girl." One may suspect a compensatory move to deny the pain of disillusion by embracing cynicism, a move whose excessive simplicity is underlined by the knotty involution of the subsequent *The Headless Woman.*

VARIETIES OF THE UNSEEN: THE NOISE OF THE NEIGHBOR

Relationships with the neighbor notoriously become problematic in the context of encounter with the auditory signs of his or her presence, causing that presence to occupy the edge of absence, as one is unsure how to react, uncertain both of the sound's source and of what exactly it attests to. Thus, in one of the two conjunctions of comparable moments in which this chapter originated, Juliette Binoche plays a person listening to sounds on the other side of her wall or door in Kieślowski's *Blue* and in Haneke's *Code inconnu.* In the former, she hears a street brawl spill over into her apartment building's stairwell, into which a man undergoing a beating flees. The auditory experience ends with a pounding on her door one assumes is his, to which she fails to respond for reasons as defensible as indefensible: after all, her loss of both husband and daughter in a car-crash has numbed her in detachment from the world, and she is a lone woman whose apartment may be engulfed by dangerous male violence. The upshot, however, is the sound of something being slid away. It is hard to avoid thinking it can only be the (possibly dead) body of the victim. In Haneke's film, meanwhile, while ironing and listening to the television, Binoche's character (Anne) puts aside the iron and turns down the television, to attend more closely to noises somewhere beyond her apartment wall suggestive of a child's abuse. The noise then stops, and she turns the TV's sound back up again. Later, she attends a funeral for a girl called Françoise, whose death appears to have been the consequence of the abuse.

As noted above, more than alliteration connects the words "noise" and "neighbor." When neighbors speak a foreign language, or even a cognate one rendered "foreign" by Freud's "narcissism of small differences," their words become "noise," like the "barbar" sound whereby ancient Greeks represented the tongues of their neighbors, who became "barbarians" (*barbaroi*). Speech perceived as noise becomes the discourse of the Other. Jacques Attali therefore criticizes the argument that "there is no music before language";[6] indeed, language could be said always to be music, even if perceived as "rough music" before its classification as language as it is apprehended pre-semantically by infant and fetus. Music epitomizes that which lacks paraphrasable meaning but has effects that retrospectively prompt one to construe and construct from them a system of implicit meanings, a coherently rising and falling scale of moods. When music and noise become mutually translatable, it is often because the scale has become locked into a tonality of pain: either the emptiness of monotony (the repetition of "bar" and "bar" that blocks the advent of any new meaning) or the stab of a sound so sudden and unexpected as to solicit classification as an accident. In the case of Julie in *Blue*, is it the noise of the car-crash she alone survives that allows her to cast the half-completed score of the Concerto for the Unification of Europe into a garbage truck, where its groans during its crushing link noise and death? In terms of the Girardian theory of sacrifice, the fact that Julie sees this music as sacrificeable reflects her experience of it as noise even before she discards it as it disturbs the empty space she erects around herself both to mourn and to protect herself against further shocks. During the actual sacrifice described by Girard, the removal of the element—or person—designated unnecessary to the social system is that of a disturbance that indeed, in a self-fulfilling prophecy, becomes noise when sacrifice itself causes the victim to scream. The birth of tragedy is that of noise out of the spirit of music: the birth of the Žižekian Thing or monster (of which more later) out of the human reality of the neighbor.[7]

The mutual translatability of music and noise is ambiguous, however, as it can be linked also to the opaque experience of prophecy, oracular speech being constitutionally unreadable within the present. Thus Attali is excessively laconic in stating that "Music is prophecy" without appending any definition of prophecy. If its "styles and economic organization are ahead of the rest of society because it explores, much faster than material reality can, the entire range of possibilities within a given code" and if it "makes audible the new world that will gradually become visible,"[8] the very abstraction that grants it this role can be seen as opposing present material reality. Consequently, after the accident, Julie refuses to develop the music that represents her future; indeed, it is as if it has been overlaid by, braided with, or translated into the auditory afterimage of the crash, which contaminates all acoustic reality. The pervasiveness in memory of the noise of the accident defies the possibility of ordering sounds harmonically. Her violent tugging at one of the strands of colored beads on the glass ornament in her dead daughter Anna's room registers its tinkling's transformation into noise. Her suicide attempt therefore involves a "creation of noise" as she shatters a window to distract the nurse in the pharmacy so she can raid it for pills she then crams down her throat. Later, she experiences the music welling up within her as an assault by alien sounds whose meaninglessness she underlines instantaneously, for instance by consigning its scored form to a garbage truck or by slamming down a piano-lid. However, increasingly those sounds become associated with other people whose demands are harder to resist, in part because they can no longer simply be cast as the accidental event that is noise. Julie may refuse to open the door upon which an assault victim pounds, but in the end she responds to Olivier's probes, which she also views at first as violations of solitude and which she may take account of in the first instance simply to put an end to the music and so restore a deathly peace. The unknown neighbor may be defined as noise, but the one from within the building knocking at one's door (Lucile) is more resistant to such categorization. When Lucile then enters Julie's apartment and reaches up to the glass ornament, Julie's sole tangible memento of her old life and of Anna, the image of Julie's reaction is blocked by her shooting from behind (the darkness of her head recalling the black screens that silently rehearse her trauma and render the narrative as discontinuous as any one line of those crystal beads) (see Figure 6.1): Julie could not bear their tinkling, their mockingly apparent evidence of the unseen presence of Anna. What she cannot bear, of course, is the love that leads to pain. That principle of love arguably becomes bearable only when sublimated into the spiritual love identified as *agape* in the setting of I Corinthians 13, which accompanies the final roll-call of the film's characters. Given the New Testament identification of God as love and *agape* as love's highest form, Julie's resistance may also be a Job-like contestation of the divine, the point of origin of all prophecy, the eternity that may penetrate time wherever it finds it undefended, receptive. Until the very end, Julie's defense mechanisms are too strong; only then does she break down and weep.

98 Paul Coates

Figure 6.1 Julie's expression can only be imagined as she stares at Lucille and the crystal ornament whose tinklings recall Anna, Julie's dead daughter, in whose room it once hung.

When Julie finally agrees to work on the score of the Concerto for the Unification of Europe, it may also be because she recognizes, in the spirit of Attali, that music's channeling of the violence of noise renders it a simulacrum of sacrifice,[9] as if using the means of sacrifice to bring sacrifice to an end. This is all the more so inasmuch as the degree of her authorship of the music we hear remains unclear, and any "statement" it might be said to make lacks the relatively clear semantic import of a language. Rather, its repetition places it in the realm of the "barbar" and of ritual, to which sacrifice is central. In the recurrent musical motifs of *Blue*, the self-assertion associated with expressivity becomes indistinguishable from that of a collectivity within which the individual disappears (or becomes one with neighbors), almost as if Julie is less a composer than a film director, even a stand-in for Kieślowski, who once defined the director—in other words, himself—as the only person on set without a proper job. Thus the melody developed in the Concerto is shaped not only by Patrice (Julie's dead husband), Julie herself, and Olivier but even turns up in the work of flautist who is a street person. Whereas Mariola Jankun-Dopartowa reads this echo, possibly crassly, as a sign of Patrice's theft of the flautist's melody,[10] the phenomenon resembles a case described by Pierre Simon Laplace in 1829 in which a man

> to his own surprise, sang an old forgotten song under his breath while he walked on the street of Saint Germain in serious thought. After two hundred steps he saw a blind man standing playing this song on his violin.

For Theodore Reik,

> the sounds of the violin must have reached his ears without his having been aware of it in a semi-perception du son. Laplace concludes that our sensory apparatus can perceive impressions which are too faint to be felt, but sufficient to determine actions whose causes we don't know. [11]

Less rationalistic explanations may be possible, however. It may also be that the relative abstraction of music, its dependence on the mathematical development of patterns, lends it an objectivity that allows it to become less a product of individual expression than one issuing possibly from various people, or a *Zeitgeist*. And that coincidence of different voices itself can generate a sound that is perceived as noise, the uncertainty of origin obscuring what is sound, what is counterpoint, and what is echo. However, there is also an infernal version of such non-expressive music: muzak, hearing which prompts Sabrina in Phil Kaufman's *The Unbearable Lightness of Being* (1988) (one of Kieślowski's inter-texts as Juliette Binoche leaps into a swimming pool in both films) to comment that "everywhere music is turning into noise." At the same time, an alternative multiplication of musicians opens onto the mystical, as in the phenomenon within the four-part a capella Sicilian music referred to as the Quintina: when the four singers achieve optimal harmony, a fifth voice is believed to emerge and to belong to the Virgin Mary approvingly joining in their song.[12]

THE NEIGHBOR AND ETHICAL DEMAND

The privileging of the figure of the neighbor, and the ethical demand he or she embodies, involves an imperative to extend families beyond the nuclear and nations beyond the bounds of one ethnic group, dispelling the malign specter of nationalist tribalism. This specter is particularly strongly present in *Code inconnu,* whose director's origins in Austria, a country located at the hinge between the most widespread European notions of "West" and "East" and with a history of recent integration with Slavic culture through the Austro-Hungarian Empire whose phantom limbs may be said to haunt it, furnish a basis and rationale for destabilizing the distinction between neighbors and strangers. Both Kieślowski and Haneke further attack that distinction by temporary moves to another country, France, where they will do some of their most significant work. Among other things, each considers the effect of the ending of the Cold War and its transformation of former strangers into possible neighbors and the intensification of movement out of economically less privileged areas in response to globalized capitalism. Each considers also the issue of where the human begins and ends, though Kieslowski stages the transition from human to non-human as possibly transcendent in certain cases, whereas the dehumanization as which it figures for Haneke never becomes demonization.

The neighbor/stranger distinction is overthrown also in the passage from Paul's "Letter to the Galatians" which is a touchstone for recent philosophical reflection on the idea of the neighbor, such as that of Alain Badiou: "There is neither Jew nor Greek, slave nor free, male nor female, for you are all one in Christ Jesus" (Gal. 3:28; NIV). Similarly, Jesus states that anyone doing the will of the Father is kin to him. The family is one of spirit, not blood, and the theology one of adoption.[13] Theodor Adorno's critique of Kierkegaard's concept of the neighbor, however, another *locus classicus* for recent work on this topic, critiques Pauline Christianity's dissolution of neighbor/stranger distinctions. For Adorno, "the concept of the 'neighbor,' the foundation of Kierkegaard's ethics, is a fiction. The concept is valid only in a society of direct human relations, from which Kierkegaard well knows that he is separated."[14] Adorno's critique invites categorization as a Judaic one of Christianity. Ironically, to the extent that Adorno himself is Kierkegaardian, and hence anti-Hegelian (albeit *dialectically* anti-Hegelian much as Bogart is an anti-hero . . .), his objection is to the Christian sublation of the neighbor/stranger opposition into a new, synthetic conception of Everyone and Everyman. In modernity, he would point out (that condition central to the work of Haneke and Kieślowski with their interest in screens and surveillance), instead of stranger becoming neighbor, neighbor becomes stranger. The laws of accident, migration, mobility, and the experience of the city-street crowd—that key experience of the modern for Adorno's cousin Walter Benjamin—render people strangers even when neighbors. However, for the dialectician, there should also be the possibility of strangers becoming neighbors: thus, in *Red*, the paths of Auguste and Valentine, near-neighbors in Geneva, repeatedly approach an intersection the god-like Judge Joseph Kern seems to foreknow before a ferry accident throws them together. *Red*'s movement is a microcosm of that of the multi-strand narrative, whose recent prominence suggests recognition of the difficulty of achieving significant interconnection in a society whose members are increasingly mobile, be it in search of performative self-shaping or under the lash of a capitalism compelling abandonment of homes and homelands in search of employment. Inasmuch as those narratives, like the more traditional ones crowned by marriage and the assertion that "they lived happily ever after," provoke skepticism regarding the stability of the newly achieved relationship, Kieślowski both sidesteps and accommodates it by the cunning of a scenario in which the new relationship both reworks and reincarnates a failed one, past failure becoming the price of a success whose delay also underlines its hard-won, even possibly accidental status, or simply varies a minor-key theme musically into the major.

Where Kieślowski traces a movement of succession, from stranger to neighbor, within the stranger-neighbor combination, Haneke, more pessimistically, places the neighbor always under the aegis of the stranger. His protagonists, be they fellow metro riders or Anne interrupting her ironing to listen to the apparent sounds of abuse coming through a wall, freeze in paralysis, unable to know what to do or how to counter the violence installed with apparent impunity at the heart of society; thus relationships always disintegrate. At the end of *Code inconnu*, Georges, unable to enter the apartment because the code has changed, phones Anne, gets no response or a rejection, and hails a taxi to leave, while the final image is of a deaf child using a sign language, which codifies meaning in a manner unknown to spectators. Insofar as Haneke is vulnerable to criticism, it is in the tendentiousness of this pessimism, which arguably allows no countervailing values, whereas Kieślowski, although recording the pain, tears, and rejection of the Judge, finds a growing point of de-traumatization, at least for some, as if through a musical inversion of the reality manifest up to this point, its re-scoring in another key. (An Adornian commitment to the dialectical quality of music, therefore, can yield a hope not usually associated with that philosopher.)

The relationship between the categories of stranger and neighbor lies at the heart also of the different theorizations of the nature of the ethical demand embodied in the face offered by Levinas and Žižek, who criticizes the Levinasian version. Žižek's critique of Levinas's work, which he describes (and arguably simplifies polemically) as identifying the ethical with face-to-face encounter with another, is of considerable relevance here:

> the limitation of Levinas is not simply that of a Eurocentrist who relies on a too narrow definition of what is human, a definition that excludes non-Europeans as 'not fully human.' What Levinas fails to include into the human is, rather, the inhuman itself, a dimension which eludes the face-to-face relationship of humans.[15]

Žižek's rejoinder, problematic itself when it speaks of an inherent monstrosity of the neighbor rather than of projective thought-patterns that glue a mask of monstrosity to his or her face[16] becomes salutary when it mentions both the "Musselman" of the concentration camps—the figure whose loss of the will to live led fellow-inmates to describe him or her as almost zombie-like—and the degree to which Levinas's focus on the single individual practices a selection that omits a crowd of others[17] (here one could go further and speak of the essentially unjust and irrational quality of a selection usually dependent either upon the unconscious of one individual or the idiosyncratic beauty norms of a single culture). As Žižek puts it, "the elementary gesture of justice is not to show respect for the face in front of me, to be open from its depth, but to abstract from it and refocus onto the faceless Thirds in the background"[18] (note the cinematic metaphor of "focus" employed here). Nevertheless, this abstraction itself replicates the pernicious gesture of selection with something of the automatism of a Marxist privileging of the collectivity over a one-on-one encounter, deemed either individualistic or quasi-existentialist, vitiated by proximity to what Adorno excoriated as Heidegger's "jargon of authenticity." The complementary blind-spots of the two positions render both necessary: Levinas focuses on the face that commands one's attention, and hence presents itself as the heart of a visual or social and psychic field; Žižek, however, privileges the overlooked, the crowd-member who, as such, may be deemed "faceless." Cinema, for its part, suggests the ideal venue for a dialogue of these opposites. Irrespective of whether compositions are centered, or how wide the screen may be, the photographic image is usually all in focus: in other words, the distinction between center and periphery, the faced and the faceless, undergoes potential destabilization. Mechanisms of melodrama and casting (which insist on the survival of certain figures considered lynchpins of "identification") may counteract this equalizing potential of the image. Certain forms of cinema may do so also: thus the silent cinema's iris isolates, privileges, and even transfigures certain faces—reflecting the prevalence of melodrama within it despite its radicalization of composition. Nevertheless the "equalizing potential" is hard to expunge entirely and is central to such theories of the cinematic as that of Siegfried Kracauer, valorizing contingency, indeterminacy, and the crowd, or Walter Benjamin, who viewed the crowd and its promotion in documentary in particular as the seed-bed of an art of the future (what is at stake in cinema for Benjamin becoming not the "redemption of physical reality" of the subtitle of Kracauer's *Theory of Film* but redemption of human relations per se.) This potential is activated in Kieślowski's *Dekalog* (1988), which abstracts certain faces from the faceless crowd of windows of the housing block but allows one to dream of ones at other windows, like that student of mine who lamented that the existence of only Ten Commandments prevented Kieślowski adding more films. His transformation of two parts into longer films—each haunted by the idea of shortness—and his unfulfilled plan to extend yet another (*Dekalog 9*) suggests a similar regret in Kieślowski himself. The degree to which each work inscribes endlessness, and builds it in before its own end, becomes the next best thing.

EXCURSUS: CROSSING BORDER/CROSS-CUTTING: A "LEVINASIAN" FILM?

One example of a film that might be called "Levinasian" is Rachid Bouchareb's *London River* (2009), which foregrounds obligations to neighbor from the very outset, as Elisabeth Sommers (Brenda Blethyn)—one of the work's two protagonists—arrives at a church whose minister is expounding Jesus's teaching on this subject in the Sermon on the Mount. Thus the theme of the interrelationship of two of the "religions of the Book"—the degree of their similarity and difference—informs the film's sub-structure. Breaking into Jesus's quotation of the Old Covenant, the minister gives Jesus's amplification and correction of its dictum that "You shall love your neighbor and hate your enemy": "But I say to you, love your enemy, and pray for those who persecute you" (Matt. 5:43). In the film to come, a person likely to be categorized in the immediate aftermath of the London bombings of 2005 as a potential enemy—the Muslim Ousmane (Sotigui Kouyaté)—becomes in various ways Elisabeth's "neighbor."

Bouchareb's film traces the parallel quests for their children, by Elisabeth and Ousmane, just after that bombing. Elisabeth, alarmed by her daughter Jane's failure to respond to anxious phone messages, travels to London and is admitted to Jane's flat by the Muslim butcher who owns it. Ousmane's journey to London from France is motivated by a desire to bring back Ali, the son he last saw when he was six years old. The film's form, therefore, moves from cross-cutting to two-shot. Elisabeth comes from Guernsey, Ousmane from France. The choice of Guernsey as the starting point is intriguing as it lies close to France yet has primary ties with the United Kingdom. The suggestion is of the naturalness of the connection that comes into being between the African Muslim working in France and the English-speaking Christian, who also knows French and converses with Ousmane in that language. As so often in European cinema since the fall of the Berlin wall, a crossing of borders does not just ground a story of contemporary relevance: the scenario is widely used because the differences between the protagonists' societies favors dramatic encounters of potential extremes and feeds the multiple investments required for co-production, that new norm.

One day, Ousmane sees one of Elisabeth's posters declaring Jane missing. He recognizes the girl he had seen sitting beside his son in an Arabic class photograph and calls Elisabeth. She is happy to receive the photograph but worried by Jane's involvement with Ali. She is also suspicious of Ousmane, informing the police about him. In subsequent scenes, the two frequent many of the same places, casting surreptitious glances at one another, until Elisabeth meets him at a mosque where the Arabic class had been held and where he is enquiring about his son. The film's movement from cross-cutting to two-shot is sealed as Elisabeth and Ousmane converse on a park bench after learning that Jane and Ali were leaving London for a French holiday on the morning of the seventh and would probably have departed after the nine o'clock bombings. The camera is directed alternately across the face of one and towards that of the other as each confesses his or her fears: Elisabeth's, that Ali had manipulated Jane; Ousmane's, that his own son—a stranger to him, whose motives he could not know—might have been among the bombers. Jane then invites Ousmane, whose hotel is expensive, to sleep on the couch of the flat Jane and Ali had shared.

Shortly thereafter, however, their hopeful relief is disrupted by the return of the police who had investigated Jane's flat earlier. The DNA samples found there show that both died on the bus that was bombed. Hearing this, Elisabeth reels away into a private pain Ousmane does his best to assuage. She may clasp him briefly as they part, but her pain will persist. The final shots show each of them back in the nature where they had worked,

Elisabeth despairingly hacking at soil and hurling stones aside, Ousmane having to hear that one of the elms he had struggled to save will need to be felled and asking his assistant to do so. Solidarity, life's rearguard action against its darkest moments, can only do so much: Elisabeth and Ousmane must return to their separate worlds, and deal with their loss as best they can. Suspicion—Elisabeth's of Ousmane, Ousmane's of his son—may have been dispelled, but the logic of the story of momentary encounter requires a return to separation. Religion, for its part, appears to console Ousmane more than it does Elisabeth. His account of Ali's death over the phone to his wife Aja says "he is no longer with us," adding "it is God's will." Elisabeth does not enter a church, as does the bereaved father Krzysztof at the end of Kieślowski's *Dekalog* 1, and if she did it would surely be in a spirit of anger, possibly even unbelief, like that of Krzysztof. In the orbit of death, Christianity becomes the images of cross and Virgin placed centrally in the waiting room of the morgue. They are images the waiting relatives can only look past, their own pain compelling them to focus instead on the door behind which they fear, or know, the bodies of their own loved ones to lie—each one of them like the Virgin herself confronted with the cross.

EUROPE, THE NEIGHBOR, AND THE MIRACLE

The different Europes presented by Kieślowski and Haneke share the habit of conceiving the neighbor primarily in terms of the ethical, as the object of obligations one might prefer not to have to meet. However, the relentless exclusion of mystery in Haneke's work prevents any linkage of the atrophy of love of neighbor to the withering of the love of God that is the other pillar of the Law, alongside that of love of neighbor (Matt. 22:35–40). If, for Haneke, contact with the stranger is no longer conceived as a possible "entertaining of angels" (Heb. 13:2), Kieślowski's *Red* begins to reconceive the neighbor as possibly a mask of an otherness that partakes of, or is controlled by, an unseen dimension that could be supernatural, even divine: the Other might bear good news from beyond time's wall, from the other space figured by the positive dream of her future recounted to the Judge by Valentine.[19] In Haneke's work, as in the case of the visit by angels to Sodom on the eve of its destruction and the rescue of Lot and his wife and daughters, the inhabitants of the city might conceivably be able to perceive the beauty of the visitors (Haneke's Parisians do not), but they would not grasp its link to holiness—unless that very holiness unconsciously motivated their attempt to violate it. Thus the Romanian woman begging beside the street is mocked by the Parisian, and the black who defends her is frog-marched away by police. This may be the definition of Sodom: a city ripe for destruction because of its blindness to the neighbor as a possible angel, to the imprinting of the transcendent in an apparently merely human face. The only beauty it might recognize is its own narcissistic ethnic reflection. Accompanying this reduction of humanity is one of the family to the merely nuclear: Lot's sons-in-law resist the temptation to leave the city and so resemble the other inhabitants of Sodom, who deem Lot not really "one of us." Amidst the bourgeoisie studied by Martel, meanwhile, the extended family is another version of one's class, replicating it in microcosm, with strictly policed borders against the admission of less-favored others. Among these denied others are the dead, regarding whom Aunt Lala in *The Headless Woman* states, "don't look at them and they'll disappear." Willed ignorance of the past is directed also towards the previous inhabitants of the land, who are also invisible: hence Lala's stated preference for modernity in architecture, unlike the older buildings in which "you move and everything creaks." Others may declare Lala an "absolutely loony lady," but, ironically, she expresses the ruling principle of her class's world, which hopes that ignoring things will make them vanish. Similarly, Vero's relatives tell her "nothing happened" on the road. Her own unwillingness to know, apparent at the moment of the accident, recurs when she visits the hospital to enquire about her X-rays, only to walk away before an answer can come. It is thus that, to revert to Adorno's critique of Kierkegaard, the neighbor becomes a fiction. The fiction then becomes the story of unsolvable crime in which Vero entraps herself. As in Haneke's work, suspending obligations to the stranger in the name of personal freedom deprives one of the neighbors who could really help one, as the lack of evidence prevents her believing relatives' reassurances that it was only a dog.

Given the significance in *Blue* of the words written by St. Paul in I Corinthians 13, whose Greek text is orchestrated at the film's end, it is worth noting the extent to which the structure of *Red* matches that of Giorgio Agamben's explication of "the messianic *kairos*" in his book on St. Paul. For Eric Santner, Agamben's analysis accords with "the semiotic structure of miracle" in which a moment of the past is recognized as "a *typos* of the messianic present" and, indeed, "constitutes the present *as* messianic." In other words: "the element of the past that is at issue has the structural status of trauma, a past that in some sense never fully took place and so continues to insist in the present."[20] It haunts the present through the failure of self-fulfillment that makes it an uneasy past, not content to die, for it has never lived out its potential fullness. To quote Agamben himself: "two times enter into a constellation which the apostle calls *ho nun kairos*, where the past (the complete) again finds its actuality and becomes incomplete, while the present (the incomplete) acquires a sort of completeness or fulfilment."[21] Agamben's words are uncannily suggestive of an abstract summary of the plot of *Red,* in which the appearance of Valentine at Judge Joseph Kern's house offers an opportunity for a typological replay of events associated with his love and betrayal during youth, except that on this occasion Kern's past role of newly graduated barrister passes to Auguste, and the auguries intimate success, not betrayal, in the relationship between his younger incarnation and Valentine, which is incipient at the film's end. For Santner, such a haunting of one time by another is discernible in Walter Benjamin's enigmatic "Theses on the Philosophy of History": one whereby "the past makes a claim on the present and future precisely insofar as that past is marked by a certain void or lack of being which persists into the present."[22] When Benjamin speaks of past voices finding their echo in the ones we now hear, or women courted having sisters they no longer recognize, the experience he invokes—a spectralization of both past and present—sees mutual strangers, separated in time, redeemed by understanding themselves as neighbors. In the films of Haneke, Kieślowski, and Martel, the interrelated questions of Europe's relationship with other cultures and the nature of the boundaries of "Europe" put flesh on the more abstract formulations of Agamben and Benjamin.

For Santner, too, such ideas evoke the image of the neighbor, as the miracle would occur when an opportunity arises to rectify a past failure with regards to the neighbor, and this opportunity is taken. The failure would typically involve either a refusal of compassion or aid or active demonization of the neighbor as Other.[23] Where the films of Haneke and Martel document such failures, with the small exception of the aid given Anne in *Code inconnu*, when an older Arab berates the young one who has spat at her in the metro, those of Kieślowski allow for the possibility of a reparation suggestive of the mystical, where resurrection or reincarnation generate openings for recompense. Whereas Santner designates the possibility of miracle in terms that simultaneously all but withdraw the word, preferring to describe it not as "a form of religious thinking" but as "*postsecular*,"[24] the inherent vagueness of the content of a notion of "the postsecular" is problematic as both the reference to miracle and the assertion of secularity's obsolescence suggest religiosity. Santner might be accused of frustrating, through dogmatic attachment to the vocabulary of materialism, the logic both of his argument and his terminology as the opposition to the "secular" within the reference to "the postsecular" implies a somewhat substantial divergence from its predecessor. The "postsecular" seems to be either secularity sublated in an incomplete dialectic, or even "the secular" itself by another, obscurely denied name—with the invisible supports superadded amenable to nonmention just because unseen.

Whether Kieślowski might have described his own endeavor as postsecular cannot be determined, of course, though various statements suggest a preference for a different one: "mystery." Asked about the significance of the word "mystery" in the many interviews extorted from him by his fame near the end of his life, he replied that its connotations were less "religious" than "existential":

> It is purely and simply the mystery we actually face every day. The mystery of life, of death, of what follows death, of what preceded life: the general mystery of our presence in the world at this particular time, in this particular social, political, personal and familial context, and any

other context you might think of. Strictly speaking, every question contains a mystery. And it doesn't seem to me to be an issue whether or not we succeed in deciphering it, since obviously we won't. [. . .] Of course, within the framework of the film, the story one tells, what appears on screen, these mysteries often involve very small things or things that are inexplicable, things the heroes do not want to explain, or things about the heroes I do not want to explain myself. They are often very tiny, insignificant things. But I think that there is a point at which all these trifling matters, all these little mysteries, come together like droplets of mercury to form a larger question about the meaning of life, about our presence here, what in fact went before and what will come after, whether there is someone who controls all this, or whether it all depends on our own reason or on someone or something else. That mystery is there all the time. Of course it has certain religious connotations, but those connotations fundamentally arise out of the existential questions, rather than the other way around.[25]

One such element of mystery may be linked to the moment in Martel's *Headless Woman* that first suggested the productiveness of a comparison with *Red*: the key role of a dog in both works. For Martel, the dog running alongside the Indian children at her film's start, and which Vero probably kills, represents almost the bourgeois image of the children it accompanied: the death of either would count for little, and there is no social requirement for any accounting. Vero is alone with her conscience. Kieślowski, however, has the dog Valentine rescues (Rita) lead her into a church, though no event of any great significance transpires there. (In the published script, meanwhile, Valentine's crossing of herself at this moment suggests faith.) If Rita's role here is mysterious, it may be because it raises the specter of alternative realities pursued in some of Kieślowski's other works, notably *Blind Chance (Przypadek)* (1981), discussed elsewhere in this volume, and *The Double Life of Véronique (La double vie de Véronique)* (1991). Thus, in the light of such texts as William James's *The Varieties of Religious Experience* and such films by Andrei Tarkovsky as *Stalker* (1979) and *Nostalghia* (1983), Rita casts a shadow of possibly religious dimensions. Her appearance may intersect with James' description of the sudden conversion "of M. Alphonse Ratisbonne, a free-thinking French Jew, to Catholicism at Rome in 1842." Ratisbonne had entered a church with as little religious intention as Valentine. In a later retelling of his conversion, Ratisbonne remarked that "I passed my eyes mechanically over its interior without being arrested by any particular thought. I can only remember an entirely black dog which went trotting and turning before me as I mused. In an instant the dog had disappeared, the whole church had vanished":[26] a moment later he experienced a vision of the Virgin Mary. Reading Ratisbonne's words, one may imagine a camera movement less mechanical than that of his eyes, crossing the church and finding him weeping on the floor ("I was there prostrate on the ground, bathed in my tears"[27]), convulsed with a sense of transcendence, seeing the Virgin visible only to indigenous peoples in the shipwrecked European world Martel depicts, and to no one in Haneke's Europe. In Tarkovsky's universe, of course, dogs trail behind them the aura of tutelary presences, like the animals accompanying or representing gods in Classical Greek or Egyptian mythology, and signaling the characters' movement through a liminal space of possible fundamental transformation. Meanwhile, both real and symbolic, secular and religious, Kieślowski's dog guards a gate of ambiguities, like that earthly entrance to another world that employs a dog able simultaneously to look more than one way.

NOTES

1. My sense of the potential productiveness of such a comparison stems in part from the juxtaposition of *Code inconnu* and *Red* executed already by Georgina Evans. See Georgina Evans, "Social Sense: Krzysztof Kieślowski and Michael Haneke," in *After Kieślowski: The Legacy of Krzysztof Kieślowski*, ed. Steven Woodward (Detroit: Wayne State University Press, 2009), 99–112.
2. Robert Stam and Ella Shohat, *Unthinking Eurocentrism: Multiculturalism in the Media* (London and New York, Routledge, 1994), 114–21, "The western as paradigm," on this genre's role in the justification of imperialism.
3. Jens Andersen, *New Argentine Cinema* (London and New York: I.B. Tauris, 2012), 155–74.
4. Critiques of religion in European films may also focus on sound: in Andrzej Wajda's *A Generation (Pokolenie)* (1955), the Catholic hymns intoned by Polish women as Avram, a Jew, enters a building after curfew during World War II suggest that his imminent rejection by a former neighbor is linked to a hostility to Jewishness in a space sound demarcates as Catholic.
5. The playability of CDs and DVDs in different regions may reveal something about the particular status of sound itself. If a CD from one region can be played anywhere else in the world, whereas a DVD cannot, does this reflect a lack in the former case of a *necessary* inscription and preservation of local tradition? Does it reflect the degree to which sound is able to give the lie to the walls it penetrates, among other things, through its possible counterpoint with the visual?
6. Jacques Attali, *Noise: The Political Economy of Music* (Minneapolis: University of Minnesota Press, 1985), 25.
7. Slavoj Žižek, "Neighbors and Other Monsters: A Plea for Ethical Violence," in *The Neighbor: Three Enquiries in Political Theology*, ed. Kenneth Reinhard (Chicago and London: University of Chicago Press, 2005), 134–90.
8. Attali, *Noise: The Political Economy of Music*, 11.
9. Ibid., 26.
10. Mariola Jankun-Dopartowa, "Trójkolorowy transparent: Vive le chaos!," *Kino* 29:6 (June 1995), 5.
11. Theodor Reik, *The Haunting Melody: Psychoanalytic Experiences in Life and in Music* (New York: Grove Press, 1953), 242.
12. Daniel Levitin, *This Is Your Brain on Music: The Science of a Human Obsession* (New York: Dutton, 2006), 106.
13. This is an issue of some interest to Kieślowski: Filip Mosz, in *Camera Buff* (1979), is an orphan, and Tomek's story, in *A Short Film About Love* (1988) literally evokes a thematic of adoption.

14. Theodor Adorno, *Kierkegaard: Construction of the Aesthetic,* trans. and ed. Robert Hullot-Kentor (Minneapolis and London: University of Minnesota Press, 1999), 50.
15. Žižek, "Neighbors and Other Monsters," 158.
16. Ibid., 162.
17. Ibid., 183–5.
18. Ibid., 183.
19. For more on the aura of the religious surrounding the Judge, see my *Cinema, Religion and the Romantic Legacy* (Aldershot: Ashgate, 2003), 160–1.
20. Eric Santner, "Miracles Happen: Benjamin, Rosenzweig, Freud, and the Matter of the Neighbour," in *The Neighbor, Three Enquiries in Political Theology,* ed. Kenneth Reinhard (Chicago and London: University of Chicago Press, 2005), 126.
21. Ibid., 127.
22. Ibid., 87.
23. Ibid., 88–90.
24. Ibid., 133.
25. Paul Coates, "'The inner life is what interests me . . .: Interview with Krzysztof Kieślowski," in *Lucid dreams: The films of Krzysztof Kieślowski,* ed. Paul Coates (Trowbridge: Flicks Books, 1999), 167–8.
26. William James, *The Varieties of Religious Experience: A Study in Human Nature,* ed. Martin E. Marty (Penguin: Harmondsworth, 1984), 225.
27. Ibid.

7 Bruno Dumont's Cinema
Nihilism and the Disintegration of the Christian Imaginary

John Caruana

INTRODUCTION

When thinking about an earlier generation of auteur filmmakers like Ingmar Bergman, Robert Bresson, Carl Dreyer, Roberto Rossellini, and Andrei Tarkovsky, one is struck by the intensity of their fascination with religious themes and questions. Perhaps it was their proximity to the death knell—sounded only decades earlier by Nietzsche's madman—announcing the demise of God that placed these questions at the forefront of their imagination. But time does not seem to have diminished the compulsion to respond to the significance of the proclamation of a certain conception of the death of God.[1] A newer generation of cineastes seems just as engrossed by similar concerns. Despite the increasingly secularized cultural landscape of the last three decades, as one finds in regions like Western Europe, we have nevertheless witnessed the release of religiously inflected films by important filmmakers like Krzysztof Kieślowski, Terrence Malick, Lars von Trier, and the Dardenne brothers. Much has already been written about the religious aspects of these particular filmmakers. One noteworthy contemporary auteur, however, whose work is thoroughly preoccupied with religious questions, and yet has not always received the same critical attention, is the French director Bruno Dumont. The reason for that may have something to do with Dumont's uncompromising philosophy of art. His films deeply divide audiences between those who admire his minimalist aesthetic craft and those who are frustrated by his unwillingness to provide his audiences with any interpretive key. Dumont's cinema, I argue, deserves the attention of anyone interested in the interstices of religion, secularism, and art. His paradoxical stance—an atheist who is haunted by religion—represents a refreshing alternative to the one-dimensional views of many religious fundamentalists and their equally stifling counterparts, the New Atheists—two groups that receive disproportionate attention in our shallow media-saturated culture. Eschewing the dogmatism that beguiles so many on either side of the divide, Dumont prefers to linger on liminal and even, I dare say, spiritual experiences that resist simple classification. He forcefully attests to Julia Kristeva's claim that a secular humanist culture intent on purging itself of the sacred runs the risk of undermining the psychic coherence of its subjects by drawing them closer to the edges of an existential void. Indeed, the power of Dumont's cinema may well come from its intent of showing us that we have already crossed that threshold.

In our age of secularist complacency, Dumont stands out as a creative figure who manages at once to fascinate, provoke, and even irk his audiences. Most conventional theists will probably not get past the grim and violent world he represents; they will thus fail to recognize the serious engagement with religious concerns that are at the heart of his films. Overt religious practices and symbols are for the most part absent in his work. When he does represent the Church, as in *Hadewijch* (2009), for example, Dumont chooses to represent it via the more marginalized tradition of Christian mysticism, which has generally eschewed positive religion for a conception of the absent divine that at times appears to border on the irreligious.[2] Likewise, those atheists who might hope to find validation for their own unquestioned disbelief will be confronted, if not irritated, by his repeated, unapologetic attempts to signify the sacred. If his films are deeply unsettling, they are so because Dumont refuses to indulge the conceits and well-worn assumptions of our age. While repeatedly reminding interviewers that he belongs squarely to the ranks of unbelievers, he nevertheless goes out of his way to rebuke what he takes to be the mindless rejection of religion *tout court*. In fact he goes further still, for the films of this ultramodern French artist, brought up on the unquestioned tenets of *laïcité*, powerfully convey that the nihilism that afflicts many quarters of Western culture is directly linked to the disintegration of the religious imaginary.

AN UNORTHODOX ATHEIST

Dumont's cinema, like the person himself, is thoroughly paradoxical. Nowhere is that paradox more evident than in the title of his impressive debut film, *La Vie de Jésus*. Released in 1997, the film strikingly represents the moral and psychological nihilism of a group of young people in the northern French community of Bailleul. Amongst its many discordant features, viewers are confronted with the fact that the film's title seems to bear virtually no relation to the narrative itself. Aside from one very brief pictorial reference to the resurrection of Lazarus, a shot of a faded print of Giotto's painting of the story, there is little to suggest that this film has anything to do with Jesus, let alone his life.

La Vie de Jésus represents Dumont's first major attempt to represent the crisis of belief in postindustrial Western Europe. The film, as is the case with the rest of his oeuvre, draws on several major and varied sources. These include the Bible; the history of painting, especially the vast tradition of pictorial representations of Christ; the radical and controversial ideas of Ernest Renan (the nineteenth century Bible scholar whose most famous book *La Vie de Jésus* serves as the title for Dumont's film); and the unsettling, unconventional Christian aesthetics of Fyodor Dostoevsky and Robert Bresson.

Like many French intellectuals and artists, following in the wake of the tradition of the great *philosophes,* Dumont is decidedly anti-clerical. He makes it a point to declare himself no friend of institutional religion. At the same time, however, Dumont unabashedly and openly proclaims his endless fascination with religion in general and the Bible in particular. He understands the Bible's singular achievement to be its commanding communication of fundamental universal truths about what it means to be a human being. For Dumont, scriptures represent a powerful poetic expression of the tribulations of the human subject. In his view, the Bible offers faithful testimony to the travails of human suffering, patience, and longing. It captures the sacred dimension of the intersection between our finite, embodied selves, and our desire for transcendent experiences that might transfigure and dignify our existential forlornness.

As one might well imagine, Dumont's appreciation for the Bible and spirituality in general provokes a good deal of confusion on the part of both his admirers and critics. During one of his many interviews, Dumont is asked point blank "so you're not a believer then?" To which he responds "no not at all. God interests me only in a poetic manner. *But,*" he quickly adds, "at the same time, there is something inconsolable about atheism that doesn't suit me."[3] Dumont is not persuaded that a wholly secularized language can do justice to the challenges and travails of being human. By contrast, the spiritual language of grace and transcendence manages to express, for him, something important about the human condition that is all too frequently lacking in most secular depictions or accounts. In the wake of the announcement of the "death of God," Dumont is worried that we are in danger of completely abandoning the religious vernacular that for centuries has guided our thinking and lives on matters relating to the intractable anxieties of human existence. So while he is clearly no friend of mainstream religion, he does not at all share the desire or wish held by atheists like Christopher Hitchens or Michel Onfray for the complete erasure of the religious imaginary from our modern horizon. To abandon wholesale the religious symbolic system of signs, parables, and metaphors is in Dumont's mind tantamount to the rejection of a critical truth. His unromantic depiction of the effects of nihilism is a response to what he takes to be the refusal of secular culture to confront its existential limits.

In the same interview, the perceptive interviewer prods Dumont on what he perceives to be the filmmaker's equivocation surrounding the word "spiritual." The interviewer feels that Dumont wants to have his cake and eat it too. He suspects that the filmmaker wants to affirm the supposed truth associated with spirituality, all the while dissociating himself from a belief in the divine. Dumont's response demonstrates that he is fully aware that he is walking on a thin line:

> I recognize the ambiguity. But one must recover words like 'grace,' holiness,' for the profane world; we should not simply grant organized religion a monopoly over this language. I desire a sacred humanism, indeed a spiritual life, transcendence, but without God or the Church.[4]

Dumont, therefore, has no interest in restoring the former powerful status of institutional religion in the West. Rather, his stated ambition is to visually express, in secular form, the life-affirming insights that he feels are embedded in religious intuitions. For Dumont, spiritual categories like "grace" and "redemption" adequately convey fundamental truths without which we risk sinking into the quicksand of meaningless nihilism. While he does not personally believe in God, or at least any conventional notion of the divine,[5] Dumont nevertheless feels that a minimum engagement with religious symbols and images is a necessary pre-condition for the moral and psychological well-being of both the individual and society.

REPRESENTING THE LIMITS OF THE SYMBOLIC UNIVERSE

The close observer of Dumont's cinema will be impressed by the numerous direct and indirect references to the history of painting. He is particularly drawn to the history of pictorial representations of Christ as well as landscape paintings, especially in the Flemish tradition. These interests are linked in his mind. Painting, like cinema, holds the potential to register the invisible through the visible. The creative image, for Dumont, can speak to us in ways that are far more powerful than the conceptual and measured language of philosophy.[6] Dumont makes explicit this conviction in relation to the representation of Christ when he states:

> I believe that the story of Christ is one of the most beautiful poetic expressions of the human tragedy. I believe in it like I believe in a poem. I believe in the frescoes of Giotto, the Passion of Bach. Christ is merely a means of expression. Painting interests me a great deal. In Flemish painting Christ is a peasant, he is a man of the people. This is not the royal Christ, etc. Christ is an ordinary man. So in my film I tell the story of a man. A small man who lives, who takes the same road. What counts in life is to ascend from where one is. Without the title, the film loses something. It is a very mystical film. Film has the power to touch something mysterious in the body, its secrets.[7]

Dumont's interest in certain representations of Christ is fused with another genre: namely, the spiritual portrayals of landscapes from the Renaissance to the late modern European period. In these paintings, he recognizes the artist's capacity to pierce through the ordinary perception of the world in order to reveal in the visualization of habitat, faces, and bodies the invisible spiritual matrix that permeates life. The Flemish landscape that Dumont's camera records appears to us to be infused with a shimmering effervescence suggestive of an invisible excess within the confines of the immanent natural world. Here he is emulating his great Flemish compatriots, like Pieter Brueghel, who have the power to make us aware that a landscape might be saturated with more than one can intuit or synthesize. Similarly, the filmic representation of bodies, flesh, and faces simultaneously captures the finitude of material, organic life—its vulnerabilities, incessant needs, and drives—at the same time that it reveals or intimates at disavowed spiritual needs.

Dumont maintains that the immediate catalyst for *La Vie de Jésus* was an exhibition that he attended in the 1990s featuring some of Georges Braque's post-cubist paintings. So moved was Dumont by these representations that he confesses in his working notes for *La Vie de Jésus* to having been overcome by tears.[8] The paintings induced in him a visceral self-immersion into the very pictorial content of Braque's frame. The experience prompted within him a vision of a cinematic narrative shortly thereafter actualized in *La Vie de Jésus*. One can see how the two genres of paintings—portrayals of Christ and landscapes—are melded into a singular creative vision:

> The expression on my face had all but disappeared; my body was inflected. I was lying in the soil. In the silt of the earth, its labours. When I sat up, there were other people around me. We were kneeling, arms held rigidly above our heads, backs bent; my hand had acquired dirt beneath its nails. . . . I had no choice but to take pity, there on the tiling. It was so beautiful. Here was our Freddy in his trench, torso bare, kneeling. His consumption. A chrysalis. The expression on his face all but vanished. His image, eminently sensitive, sorrowful, Christian, magnificently simple. Sanctified. . . . The corpse [of Christ] in painting, its contortion, suffering, that is what moves me. In my mind, Freddy's torso is just that. It's the representation of man, of his misery, but also of his hope.[9]

The film itself contains one direct reference to an actual historical painting; it serves as a kind of silent link to the title. Early in the narrative, as Freddy and his comrades visit their dying friend, Cloclo, we see a discolored reproduction of Giotto's painting hanging in the hospital room. The painting (see Figure 7.1) adopts a compositional logic common to many medieval and renaissance depictions of biblical events. In this particular case, the painting conveys temporally distinct moments of the Lazarus narrative within the confines of a single frame. Particularly noteworthy is the man in the green robe who occupies the frame's center. His gesturing hands capture two distinct moments of the story's unfolding. The first moment expresses doubt and skepticism as signaled by the way his hand is positioned in relation to his face. The other hand gesture registers a later, second moment, after Jesus resurrects Lazarus from the dead. Now his hand rises in unison with those behind him as they collectively acknowledge the miracle that they have just witnessed.

Dumont, I argue, uses this painting to telegraph at least two points. The first is to register the religious illiteracy of the film's subjects. One of Freddy's companions turns to him and whispers: "Look at the poster, isn't that the guy who was raised from the dead." A story or image that formerly spoke to countless millions of people across Europe now goes barely recognized.

Figure 7.1 Giotto, *The Raising of Lazarus*

Here Dumont reminds us of the once powerful religious imaginary which is now quickly receding into oblivion. The second point is more significant. Unlike Giotto's own faith in the veracity of this miracle, the characters of the film have no reason to believe that the harsh finality awaiting their friend—whose face bears the ravages of sarcoma—can be overcome. But we must be careful here. Dumont is not simply using this as an occasion to underscore the brutal truth of our finite being. His deeper point is to get us to reflect on the consequences of an impoverished symbolic order that fails to adequately help contemporary subjects navigate the limits of their being. In doing so, Dumont manages to also shake our comfortable secular confidence that all that is needed is a little stoic fortitude in the face of death.

While Dumont remains a nonbeliever, he nevertheless finds something wanting in atheism's refusal to recognize the challenges posed by our existential predicament. A similar point is developed brilliantly in Julia Kristeva's analysis of another painting, Hans Holbein's *Body of the Dead Christ in the Tomb* (1521)[10] (see Figure 7.2). Kristeva maintains that Holbein's painting

116　*John Caruana*

Figure 7.2 Hans Holbein the Younger, *The Body of the Dead Christ in the Tomb*

signals both the audacity and fragility of the emergent modern epoch. The painting represents an important moment in the development of the Western individual. Earlier representations of the dead Christ gave viewers no reason *not* to believe in his immanent resurrection and the subsequent removal of the sting of death for mortal beings. Holbein's painting, however, offers no such reassurance. For how is it possible to believe that *this* corpse could ever come back to life? Rather than depicting Christ triumphantly overcoming the chains of death, Holbein abandons his compatriots to one of the most unnerving depictions of death in the history of painting. Unlike, for instance, the painting by Giotto discussed above, the artist in this case provides no psychic support for the confrontation with death.

For Kristeva, Holbein's representation paradigmatically captures the limits of human subjectivity; it brings us to the very verge of who we are—these ever decaying mortal coils. It also confronts us with our often-unacknowledged need to believe that suffering, evil, and death are not without redemption; that these limits do not represent the finality of human existence. Recently, Kristeva has called this deep desire that underwrites human subjectivity the "incredible need to believe."[11] The great challenge of the modern age—already signaled by Holbein's painting—is to dare us to confront these limits by way of our own internal resources. But Kristeva claims that our epoch consistently fails to appreciate the tremendous demands this places on modern subjects. Coming into direct contact with our limits without the idealizations formerly provided by the religious symbolic order exposes the subject to the brutal indifference of the death drives, the potential meaninglessness of it all that Holbein's painting more than hints at.

Dumont frames Cloclo (see Figure 7.3) in a manner that is eerily similar to Holbein's representation of the dead Christ. In both cases, we witness an emaciated figure whose flesh is ravaged by the contingent violent circumstances that befall him. One might even say that the terror in these depictions does not simply concern our fear of death, but something more horrifying. Interestingly, both figures are represented with their eyes wide open, in death, in the case of Christ, and, on the verge of lifelessness for Cloclo. More than Heideggerian anxiety in the face of death, their countenances evince a primal horror. To put it in an idiom we would associate with Maurice Blanchot or Emmanuel Levinas, existence makes mockery of the conceit that a resolute stance towards our mortality remains within our range of possibilities. Death does not present itself as the self's utmost

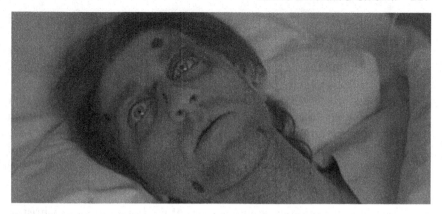

Figure 7.3 The dying Cloclo in Bruno Dumont, *La Vie de Jésus*

possibility, but rather as Levinas puts it in *Time and the Other,* it "marks the end of the subject's virility and heroism."[12] The utter and complete disregard of indeterminate being—of existence without existents—seizes us with the terrifying awareness of the "no exit," namely, that there is no ready escape or resolution to existence and its vice-grip hold on us. The wide-open eyes of Holbein's Christ and Dumont's Cloclo—the living dead—drives home the ineluctability of being's callous indifference. Far from liberating us, the affirmation of a radical immanence merely serves to accentuate the sense of hopelessness that the self undergoes in relation to indeterminate being.

No rigidly secular solution to our predicament presents itself to us. The opposite of faith is not enlightenment. For Dumont, as for Kristeva, the fragile incredible need to believe has to be taken seriously. What is at stake is nothing less than the establishment of the psychic lining that envelops and sustains our subjectivity. This is why Dumont adamantly dissociates himself from the sort of upbeat atheism—bordering on Pollyannaish—that intends to disabuse us of our idealizations. By contrast, Dumont, in line with Kristeva, grasps that necessity for a minimum level of idealization—without which the subject collapses in on itself. Neither view such idealizations as a mere sort of heuristic device meant to assuage our mortal fears. If these idealizations are to have their intended effect, they must be experienced as heartfelt, real convictions by the subject.

La Vie de Jésus testifies to a society that lacks the proper ritualistic spaces and discourses for helping its members to navigate the tumultuousness of the semiotic—Kristeva's special term for the prelinguistic maternal body, the fluid realm of biological drives and rhythms. The dramatic disintegration of the religious imaginary in the West has created a void in the symbolic landscape. Formerly, the Christian narrative, with its vast repertoire of images and stories, made it possible for subjects to confront their awareness of the fragility of enfleshed existence without succumbing to psychic paralysis. The centerpiece of the Christian vision revolves around the kenosis: God's self-emptying, the Son made flesh. Through an intense identification, the believer passes through the stations of suffering, humiliation, and finally death. None of this is muted or sentimentalized: Jesus experiences abandonment and finally dies on the cross. But the idea of the love of the Father telegraphs to the subject the idea that death will not have the last word. Christ's resurrection suggests more than the miracle of returning from the dead. For Kristeva, it also supplies the believer with a sense of the meaningfulness of human existence beyond (and even, despite) the vicissitudes of the biological cycles of generation and degeneration.

> For the interruption, even momentary, of the bond that links Christ to his Father and to life, this caesura, this "hiatus," offers not merely an image but also a story for certain psychic cataclysms that lie in wait for the presumed balance of each individual and, because of this, make a dressing for them [*les pansent*]. Each and every one of us is the result of a long "work on the negative": birth, weaning, separation, frustration. For having staged this rupture at the very heart of the absolute subject, Christ, for having presented it in the figure of a Passion, as the other, supportive side of the resurrection, Christianity brings to consciousness the essential internal dramas of each person's becoming.[13]

In the absence of such assurances, these perennial cycles give rise to the sort of fatalism encountered in the mythological worldview of the ancients—what the Greeks called the *Moirae* and Romans the *Parcae*. Even so, the Greeks and Romans undoubtedly were shielded from thoroughgoing despair as a result of the psychological succor afforded by other features of their religious practices and narratives. But in our contemporary context, the exposure to these cycles is virtually unmediated. Consequently, it plays a significant role in the spiritual malaise of Dumont's *jeunesse perdue*. Increasingly, young people must rely on their own internal resources to navigate the perilous upsurge of drives and affects. In some cases, these threaten to overtake the individual. In more extreme cases, the failure is signaled by the fact that the self itself becomes a site of abjection. Ideally, this should not happen. For Kristeva, the incipient self undergoes a perilous transition from biological organism to speaking agent. If successful, this passage results in the formation of a fairly intact psychic envelope, what she calls "narcissism," not to be confused with the autistic universe occupied by Ovid's famous character. Narcissism, in Kristeva's sense, is the interior space that allows the subject to negotiate the ever-threatening vicissitudes of the drives. In order to secure its proper psychic lining, the infant must abject what is undeniably also a part of itself: mucous, feces, etc. Narcissism is the clean haven that results, the necessary psychic pre-condition for becoming a symbolic mediator. But the process is extremely fragile.

For the child must be *assured* that it can safely traverse the gap separating the semiotic (maternal, biological realm) from the symbolic without being abandoned in the process. For Kristeva, this raises the important question of the role of idealization, the very basis of belief in general. The child must sincerely believe that everything will be fine as it crosses over into the social symbolic space of speaking subjects.

In order to flesh out this idea, Kristeva turns to an underdeveloped notion first introduced by Freud: the "father of individual prehistory."[14] What this agent relays to the child is the sense that it will not be abandoned in its hour of need. If one discerns a parallel here with religion—Christianity, in particular—then this is so for a reason. According to Kristeva, religion has in the past served as the primary agent or proxy of the father of individual prehistory. In the case of Christianity, the notion of a loving Father has served as that stabilizing agent, ensuring the proper embedding of the narcissistic substructure of subjectivity. But in our world, very little is in place at the social level to replicate this function. If the work of the social symbolic is to bring meaning where none exists (semiotic), then our age, which prides itself on demolishing any title to truth, gives rise to a crisis in meaning. Combined with the crassness and cynicism of late capitalism, where everything is commodified—including meaning itself—one can perhaps better appreciate why our era has become an incubator for psychic instability.

In the case of Dumont, nihilism results in a culture that has given up on spiritual idealizations because it can no longer believe in the possibility of a goodness or truth that does not so much exceed our finite limitations as treats them in relation to an irreducible sense of dignity and hope. By contrast, this nihilistic age, for Dumont, *reduces* us to the status of mere organisms, consisting of nothing more than the conglomeration of clusters of particles, genes, and bio-chemical states—anonymous organic systems inhabiting a completely indifferent universe. When human beings are deprived of idealization, they revert to the repetition of base drives devoid of any meaning. This might explain why in almost all of his films, Dumont's representation of lovemaking is reduced to its mechanics. As he portrays it, physical intimacy is expressed as raw copulation without the least hint of tenderness. The reversion to the drives in turn exposes us to the constant threat of catastrophic and senseless violence—a thread that unites every single one of Dumont's feature films: ruptures of violence as in the brutal murder of Kader in *La Vie de Jésus*, the savage rape of an 11-year-old girl in *L'Humanité*, the explosion of unimaginable hatred and sadism at the end of *Twentynine Palms*, the savagery of war in *Flandres*, and, more recently, the perverse terrorism of religious fanaticism in *Hadewijch*.

Under such circumstances, Dumont's cinema shares Kristeva's intuition that an "atheism without nihilism"[15] must "take up this [religious] heritage once again, to give it meaning, and to develop it in the face of the current explosions of the death drive."[16]

AN ATHEISM WITHOUT NIHILISM

An appreciation of Dumont's religiously informed atheism-without-nihilism requires us to also take stock of the combined influence of Dostoevsky and Bresson. They offer him, I maintain, the means to communicate his desired "sacred humanism," an atheism that readily acknowledges the need for a religious imaginary. Ironically, Dumont relies on two Christian artists in order to make this possible.

Like other contemporary art-house filmmakers, the Dardenne brothers and Michael Haneke in particular, Dumont explicitly acknowledges his cinematic indebtedness to Bresson.[17] The director of *Pickpocket* (1959) and *Mouchette* (1967) employs an aesthetic style that is clearly inspired by Dostoevsky.[18] In order to circumvent the egoistic dispositions of his readers, their desire to be confirmed rather than challenged, Dostoevsky constructs his stories using the technique of deformation. Characters and settings are deliberately deformed through a process of overstating or exaggerating certain characteristics; as a result, they do not quite match, to use phenomenological language, our anticipatory expectations. Everything else about the story follows conventional narrative and plot structures. Everything appears by and large as it should be, except that, for example, the central character's behavior might come across as overdone, hyperbolic—just not quite altogether there. Bresson adopts a similar method but with some notable differences. Where Dostoevsky deforms his characters by means of exaggeration, the French filmmaker moves in the direction of austerity or understating. Characters are stripped of inessentials, emotions, even segments of their speech or utterances. They appear to us as automata. In Bresson's case, both storylines and characters are made deliberately incomplete. A typical narrative is peppered with inexplicable gaps or ellipses. Bresson's ultimate objective for deploying this style was spiritually motivated. Regardless of these differences in the deployment of the technique of deformation, Bresson's films, brief aphorisms, and interviews strongly suggest that he shares Dostoevsky's unconventional Christian outlook.[19] For both of them, the divine is not some supreme entity out there in a timeless region of perfect being; rather, it is deeply intertwined with profane life, so imbricated as to be otherwise unnoticeable. The point of using the deformation rests, then, on the hope that something of the invisible world of grace might break through the visible which is otherwise attended to by a habitual and routinized seeing. Just as Dostoevsky desires to prepare the reader for the capacity to be surprised, to apprehend the role of grace in the transformation of certain of his characters, similarly, Bresson sets out to unsettle the viewer's ossified perceptions in the hope that she will descry something other than the workings of the human will.

Dumont's cinematic style equally exploits the technique of deformation. His films, *La Vie de Jésus* included, seem on the surface, at least, to have an air of realism to them. They deal with real people confronting concrete problems. Yet, they are not simply just that. Dumont is persistently vexed by those critics who insist that his art be understood as a form of political analysis, a commentary on reality. He returns the favor by reminding—albeit hyperbolically—them that he is not in the least bit interested in reality. If he were interested in reproducing reality, he tells them, he would not have chosen to become an artist.[20] For Dumont, the artist glimpses things that are not visible in reality. One notices that things are not quite all there in his representational universe. The streets of Bailleul, for example, which are normally bustling with life, seem conspicuously empty in his films. Streets are devoid of cars and people. In such instances, Dumont is emulating his cinematic mentor, Bresson. Dumont's style is to understate, or better yet, to subtract from reality; "subtraction" is a term he himself uses to describe his particular use of this technique. He divests his characters of superfluous features. He slows down the rhythm of their movements and speech. The resulting minimalist aesthetic is Dumont's unmistakable signature. This minimalism has the effect of producing characters who seem incomplete. It thus invites audience members to fill in the void and the gaps, which is another way of saying that Dumont confronts his viewers with their own existential void.[21]

Dostoevsky and Bresson present us with characters who, through a process of psychological attrition, arrive at an abyssal region of being. What happens next to them is critical. Rather than abandonment, they—or, at the very least, we, the readers and viewers—see that their forlornness is not dissimilar to that faced by Jesus at the low-point of the narrative arc of the Gospels: the torment that culminates in the crucifixion. Within the Christian framework, that low-point also represents its invisible redemptive apex: it is only in the going under that one learns the absolute necessity of a love that is stronger than death. In the depths of his disavowals and anguish following the murder of a pawnbroker and her sister, Raskolnikov meets the self-sacrificing Sonya, a redeeming Mary of Magdalene figure.[22] In a pivotal moment of the story, Raskolnikov pleads with Sonya to read the story of Lazarus to him. The resurrection of Lazarus foreshadows Raskolnikov's own return from spiritual death. Likewise, Bresson's *Pickpocket*, loosely inspired by *Crime and Punishment*, follows Michel's spiritual imprisonment, which is made literal in the film with his actual incarceration after a period of successfully eluding the police. Jeanne, Michel's dying mother's neighbor, seeks to save him from his self-imposed confinement. He initially rebuffs her words and actions. His moral rebirth is powerfully communicated at the end of the film when he, utterly unexpectedly, kisses Jeanne though the prison bars and exclaims "oh Jeanne, to reach you, what a strange path I had to take!" In both instances, the male protagonists who are left for "dead"—morally and spiritually—find themselves resurrected, not through their own efforts but through the patient and undeserved love of someone who unexpectedly enters their lives.

Following in the steps of Dostoevsky and Bresson, Dumont chooses as his protagonist a young man who is equally ensnared by his circumstances and actions. Freddy's life—like those of his immediate peers—strikes us as utterly aimless. One of the few things that punctuates his existence is the fleeting exhilaration that he and his friends experience speeding down the country roads outside of Bailleul on their motorcycles. Otherwise, his existence is marked by an overwhelming tedium. Towards the close of the story, his life takes a dreadful turn after he viciously attacks a North African young man, Kader, who has been making advances on his girlfriend. Like Dostoevsky's Raskolnikov and Bresson's Michel, Freddy's criminal actions underscore his psychic despair. But while Marie, Freddy's girlfriend, bears the namesake of Mary Magdalene, she, unlike Sonya and Jeanne, does not serve as a catalyst for his redemption. There is no obvious transfigurative moment for Freddy. His symbolic universe is deeply impoverished—his is a wasteland of televisual vacuity and virtual illiteracy. By contrast, both Raskolnikov and Michel still inhabit a world of books, discourse, and religious symbols that arguably, at least, retain the real potential to transform troubled souls. For Freddy, however, the story of Lazarus cannot achieve the effect it has for Raskolnikov: the Giotto print he sees on the hospital wall is just an empty artifact, devoid of significance. Yet something enigmatic happens at the end of *La Vie de Jésus*. In the final moment of the film, we see Freddy lying in a field after undergoing what appears to be an epileptic seizure.[23] He stares directly at the sky. What does he see? What do we see? Is it simply the sky? Or is the sky a metaphor, an idealization for something transcendent? It is not clear. Even if we lean towards a non-spiritual reading, the film's conclusion is not simply atheist in a conventional sense. This final shot resonates for the viewer with an earlier scene when Kader and Marie, the illicit lovers, are standing, embracing each other, in what appears to be the shell of an abandoned, roofless church. The camera shows us a close-up of Marie who says, "forgive me," perhaps for feeling guilty for betraying Freddy. Then, the camera turns to Kader, who suddenly looks up, and fixes his (and our) gaze at the sky. That scene is symbolically linked with the final one (see Figure 7.4). With that in mind, I think that Dumont desires to register, in the final moment of the film, the notion of the "incredible need to believe." He represents it with a rudimentary gesture, looking up at the heavens—a classical symbol of transcendence. For Dumont, like Kristeva, there is an intractable need to believe that we are more than just what our biological, material reality suggests—without that sense of the *more*, our subjectivity risks being either stillborn or aborted altogether.

Figure 7.4 (Left) Kader and Marie embracing; (Right) Freddy staring at the sky in Bruno Dumont, *La Vie de Jésus*

It is interesting to note that Dumont himself has recently acknowledged a spiritual aspect to his artistry. After the release of his penultimate feature film, *Hadewijch*—named after the thirteenth-century female mystic—Dumont has on more than one occasion described his own cinematic technique as a form of "spiritual exercise," going so far as to liken it to a kind of mystical experience. Dumont notes:

> I'm very interested in forms of mysticism. I think mysticism is essentially cinematographic. It's present in my form of expression, it's a vision that is very rich and something that I think has a lot in common with cinema. In fact, I think that mystical experience helps me understand cinema better. When you're approaching mysticism, then you're dealing with something that has nothing to do with the rational, logical mind. It reaches zones or areas touching on ecstasy, ecstatic experiences that I find absolutely astonishing. And I feel that when I'm making a film very quickly, I reach over into this other side, I attain this nonlogical, nonverbal area. It's an experience I don't entirely understand, but which interests me deeply.[24]

When he speaks this way, Dumont's unorthodox atheism makes contact with the discommoding religiosity that one finds in Dostoevsky and Bresson. Dumont gives expression to an indistinct zone that eludes the simple categories of belief and unbelief. In a very Bressonian mode, Dumont notes "cinema is not reality. Reality does not interest me. What interests me is its unveiling."[25] What his films unveil is admittedly not always entirely clear.[26] Dumont's generosity as a filmmaker leaves it to the viewer to decide for him or herself what they might encounter in the emptiness and gaps of his films. Regardless, his is a rare form of artistic expression today, an exploration of the very preconditions for the believing subject—which is to say the subject in general.

NOTES

1. Here I am in agreement with John Caputo who maintains that what is at stake in this context is "a *certain* death of God." John D. Caputo and Gianni Vattimo, *After the Death of God*, ed. Jeffrey Robbins (New York: Columbia University Press, 2007), 66 [my emphasis]. Caputo's understanding of the significance of the death of God—as is also the case with Gianni Vattimo, Jean-Luc Marion, and others—clears the way for more innovative ways of conceiving the divine. The "death of God," in other words, need not necessarily be heard in an atheistic register.
2. The classic example here is Meister Eckhart's famous prayer requesting of God that he "rid me of God," *The Essential Sermons, Commentaries, Treatises and Defence*. Translated by Edmund Colledge and Bernard McGinn (New York: Paulist Press, 1981), 83.
3. Jean-Marc Lalanne, "*Bruno Dumont: Mystique or Profane?*" [My trans.; my emphasis]. Available at www.lesinrocks.com/actualite/actu-article/t/41633/date/2009-11-25/article/bruno-dumont-mystique-ou-profane/. Last accessed November 21, 2013.

4. Ibid.
5. Dumont's atheism is indeed unorthodox. What are we to make of the fact that the protagonist of *L'Humanité* appears to be levitating in one scene? How are we to understand the resurrection scene in *Hors Satan* (2011)? Despite his denials of the existence of God, such representations and his oft-repeated enthusiasm for Christian mysticism might even suggest an inversion of Eckhart's prayer: *help me to rid myself of my absence of faith.*
6. Prior to becoming a filmmaker, Dumont was a philosophy professor at a *lycée* in French Flanders.
7. David Walsh, "Interview with Bruno Dumont, Director of *The Life of Jesus*," World Socialist Web Site. Available at www.wsws.org/arts/1997/sep1997/freddy.shtml. Last accessed October 20, 1997.
8. Some of these paintings include *Le champ de Colza* and *La Charrue* (1956–57).
9. Bruno Dumont, "Director's Notes," in *La Vie de Jésus*, directed by Bruno Dumont (1997; DVD release London: Masters of Cinema, 2008).
10. Julia Kristeva, *Black Sun: Depression and Melancholia*. Translated by Leon S. Roudiez (New York: Columbia University Press, 1989), 105–38.
11. Julia Kristeva, *This Incredible Need to Believe*. Translated by Beverley Bie Brahic (New York: Columbia University Press, 2009).
12. Emmanuel Levinas, *Time and the Other*. Translated by Richard A. Cohen (Pittsburgh, PA: Duquesne University Press, 1987), 72.
13. Kristeva, *This Incredible Need to Believe*, 94–95.
14. For Kristeva's novel reading of the "father of individual prehistory," see "Freud and Love: Treatment and Its Discontents," in *Tales of Love*, trans. Leon S. Roudiez (New York: Columbia University Press, 1987), 21–45.
15. Julia Kristeva, *Hatred and Forgiveness*. Translated by Janine Herman (New York: Columbia University Press, 2011), 210.
16. Kristeva, *This Incredible Need to Believe*, 97.
17. Michael Brooke, "Robert Bresson: Alias Grace," *Sight & Sound* 17:11 (2007), 26–28.
18. Two of Bresson's films are adaptations of novellas written by Dostoevsky: *A Gentle Woman* (*Une femme douce*, 1969) and *Four Nights of a Dreamer* (*Quatre nuits d'un rêveur*, 1971). Other films, like *Pickpocket* and *Au hasard*, also bear the imprint of the Russian novelist's influence.
19. The normally reticent Bresson made the connection between his work and Dostoevsky explicit in an interview with *Sight and Sound*. Reprinted in Bert Cardullo, *The Films of Robert Bresson: A Casebook* (London and New York: Anthem Press, 2009), 127–30.
20. "I would even say that reality does not interest me, it tells me nothing. Art is precisely invention, the representation of our truth. Some people have said to me 'But that is not reality. People aren't like that in Bailleul.' I don't give a damn about reality, it doesn't interest me. I am not a documentarist." [My trans.]. André Lavoie, "Entretien avec Bruno Dumont," *Ciné-Bulles*, 16:3 (1997), 20.
21. Dumont notes in an interview:

> Emptiness may be the condition necessary for the audience to change. Violence, cruelty, roughness are also regressions, a return to something primary to alter the sophistication in which we live today. That is why I choose rustic people. And my characters are so expressive because they are all unfinished. . . . [T]he audience completes them. I must be drawn to this roughness. It is the shapeless matter placed in front of the spectator's face.

Valérie Jouve, Sébastien Ors, and Philippe Tancelin, Bruno Dumont (Paris: Dis voir, 2001), 75.

22. Fyodor Dostoevsky, *Crime and Punishment*. Translated by Richard Pevear and Larissa Volokhonsky (New York: Vintage Books, 1993).
23. It is not clear in that scene if he has experienced a seizure or if he is deliberately thrashing himself into the ground. Though, earlier in the film we are made to witness one of his epileptic fits. Freddy's epilepsy might not be entirely insignificant, especially in light of the twin influence of Renan and Dostoevsky on Dumont. Renan interpreted—interestingly, in the context of an analysis of the story of Lazarus—Jesus's visible grief for his dead friend as a sign of his alleged epilepsy. It is also worthwhile to note that Dostoevsky's principal protagonist of *The Idiot,* Prince Myshkin, a holy-fool figure, was an epileptic. The two ideas have been historically linked: epilepsy as a sign of a mystical visionary. See Harriet Murav, *Holy Foolishness: Dostoevsky's Novels and the Poetics of Cultural Critique* (Stanford University Press, 1993), 80–81.
24. Damon Smith, "Bruno Dumont, 'Hadewijch'," *Filmmaker.* Available at www.filmmakermagazine.com/news/2010/12/bruno-dumont-hadewijch/. Last accessed Nov. 21, 2013.
25. Walsh, "Interview with Bruno Dumont, Director of *The Life of Jesus.*"
26. His most recent film—*Hors Satan*—is a case in point. The enigmatic protagonist is at once angelic and demonic. The film reveals an eerie, numinous world, one beyond good and evil.

8   Religion Against Religion in Lars von Trier

Camil Ungureanu

SECTION I   INTRODUCTION

Lars von Trier's cinema deals with religious themes such as sacrifice, faith, transfiguration, conversion and evil, most notably in *Breaking the Waves* (1996) and *Antichrist* (2009). However, Trier's relation to religion is puzzling. His public persona is a moving target echoing different religious figures. Pendulating between deep depression and clownery, extreme vulnerability and haughtiness, Trier has constructed his persona as a trickster[1] and a holy fool[2]—as a jester-like figure often dealing, tragically and farcically, with unsettling images and ideas. Born in a Protestant country, Trier was, in his youth, proud of what he believed to be his Jewish heritage.[3] In a dramatic switch, Trier's mother revealed, on her deathbed, that his real father was a different man and not Jewish at all. As a result, *l'enfant terrible* of the Danish cinema went through a religious crisis and raised eyebrows by converting, at 33, to Catholicism.[4] To further complicate matters, while the three main forms of Christianity share with Judaism the belief in the goodness of creation—"God saw all that He had made, and behold, it was very good" (Gen. 1:31)—in a variety of his most representative movies (*Dogville, Dancer in the Dark, Antichrist* and *Melancholia*), Trier intimates quite the opposite. This has led commentators to uphold that Trier celebrates a perverse satanic theology.[5] In *Dogville*, the inhabitants of the little American village are so evil that they are deemed "lower than dogs" and then exterminated; as if this weren't drastic enough, in *Antichrist*, creation itself becomes—in the words of the female protagonist—nothing less than "Satan's Church." Disconcertingly though, *Antichrist* is dedicated to Tarkovsky, a director who, as Trier claims, deeply influenced him and whose cinema was decisively shaped by faith in God and Christian Orthodoxy.[6]

How then to interpret Trier's puzzling relation to religion?

First, Trier's cinema shares with a long tradition of religious and non-religious filmmakers—from Bergman, Bresson, Dreyer, Pasolini and Tarkovsky to Sokurov and Dumont—a deep interest in religious experience and a discontent with secularist rationalism of Enlightenment extraction. For secularist rationalism, religion is irrelevant for understanding current ethical and socio-political issues; these are to be made sense of through what Charles Taylor calls "immanent frame,"[7] a view that discards as irrelevant any reference to transcendence and the correlative experiences of conversion, faith, transfiguration and sacrificial gift. In contrast, some of Trier's most representative movies—*Dogville, Mandeville, Antichrist, Melancholia*—transpire or surface his discontent with the self-sufficiency, if not the conceit, of reason. This critique takes the most extreme form in *Antichrist*, where it is not the sleep but the active role of a conceited reason that creates monsters and leads to disastrous consequences (see Section III).

On the other hand, despite the presence of some recurrent themes,[8] it is artificial and futile to search into Trier's cinema for a unique and coherent view and experience of religion. While not succumbing to the "myth of coherence"[9] in interpreting Trier's changing oeuvre, I argue that, despite Trier's conversion to Catholicism, his cinema can be understood as being nourished by a changing and original mix of reinterpreted religious topoi and experiences; this variable mix either echoes in part radical Protestant themes (e.g., *Breaking the Waves*) or an extreme revolt against religion (as theodicy), Gnostic and other elements (e.g., *Antichrist*). "Religion against religion" is a "religion without God":[10] God or Transcendence—be it as palpable presence—as in Dreyer's *Ordet* and Tarkovsky's *Mirror*—or riveting silence—as in Bergman's *The Seventh Seal*—disappears as such, in particular in Trier's most recent movies, *Antichrist* and *Melancholia*. And even in *Breaking the Waves*, the well-known final aerial scene of a Church whose bells are tolling conveys neither the belief in nor the paradoxical yet "absolute certitude" (Kierkegaard) in the existence of God, but rather the directorial high-order approval to Bess' "selfless" sacrifice (see later, Section II).

In the following, I will focus on two of Trier's films most explicitly evocative of religion—*Breaking the Waves* and *Antichrist*. First, I will analyze *Breaking the Waves* and the interpretative hypotheses concerning Bess' sacrifice either as Abrahamic (in Kierkegaard's reading) or Christ-like.[11] Bess's sacrificial gift does display relevant affinities with Christ's and Abraham's; together with Tarkovsky's last film, *Sacrifice (Offret)* (1986), *Breakings the Waves* dwells on the link between salvation and selflessness or/and unconditional self-sacrifice. Nonetheless, selfless sacrifices come under different guises and are to be valued differently. As Jacques Derrida argues, strictly speaking there are no pure, unconditional sacrifices.[12] Sacrificial gifts occur and are made sense of in relation to a logic of conditionality. It is therefore worth distinguishing the specificity and ambivalence of Bess's immoral yet sublime offering[13] and separating it from Abraham's or Christ's. I will do so by introducing Derrida's discussion of the paradox of sacrificial gift as caught between unconditionality and conditionality[14] and by distinguishing different examples of selfless sacrifice—that of a *moral saint* (Christ), of a "*criminal devotee*" (Abraham) and of an *immoral "saint"* (Bess).

Second, despite the continuity between *Breaking the Waves* and *Antichrist*, I will analyze the latter as a parable of therapeutic reason and radical evil—a parable resonating with elements of Gnostic or Marcion-like anti-cosmism (see Section III).[15] In *Antichrist*, what I call "religion against religion" takes its most radical form: the power of evil become so radical that it can be expressed only obliquely through a "religious" imagery of an evil *demiourgos*. It also eclipses completely the Christian God—be it palpable presence (as in Dreyer's *Ordet* and Tarkovsky's *Mirror*) or a riveting silence (as in Bergman's *The Seventh Seal*).

The thrust of this chapter, however, does not consist in arguing that *Antichrist* is a Gnostic-Marcionic movie any more than *Breaking the Waves* is a radical Protestant one.[16] Trier is a gadfly who shares with his compatriot Kierkegaard a taste for unsettling paradoxes but not his "absolute certitude" in and the relentless affirmation of the existence of God and Transcendence. Likewise, *Antichrist* does not champion, as in a streak of Gnosticism, that an evil God or Creator[17] exists any more than supports a black or satanic theology. Antichrist or Satan—Trier uses these names interchangeably—is a *real fiction* conveying the experience of the excessiveness and non-representability of a radical evil and of our deepest fears of it as well as of the limits to cure it therapeutically by means of reconciling reason and dialogue.

SECTION II *BREAKING THE WAVES:* THE AMBIVALENCE OF BESS'S "SUBLIME OFFERING"

> For . . . I am the whore and the holy one.
> I am the wife and the virgin. . . .
> I am the silence that is incomprehensible . . .
> I am knowledge, and ignorance. . . .
> I am shameless; I am ashamed.
> I am strength, and I am fear. . . .
> I am foolish, and I am wise. . . .
> I am godless, and I am one whose God is great
> ("Thunder, Perfect Mind," in
> *The Gnostic Gospels*)[18]

The unsettling story of *Breaking the Waves*, written and directed by Trier as part of the "Golden Heart" trilogy,[19] unravels in a forlorn village in a corner of Northern Scotland in the 1970s. The movie is centered on a female character, Bess (wonderfully played by Emily Watson), a simple woman who lives in a closed, traditional community. Bess is an ardent believer, belonging to a rigorous and closely-knit group of women who "do not speak in church." She marries Jan (played by Stellan Skarsgård), a worker on the oil rigs in the North Sea. All seems routine until Jan gets badly injured in a work accident, as a result of which he becomes almost completely paralyzed. The doctor is certain that he will never be able to walk again.

The dramatic twist of the story is yet to come: one day the immobilized Jan asks Bess, without any explanation or justification, to find a man and give herself to him—as he says: "for my sake. And then tell me about it." Naturally, Bess is at first reluctant to fulfill her husband's unexpected wish. Yet, eventually she obeys; she does precisely what her beloved asks of her in the conviction that her sacrifice would please God, and it could bring his salvation. Spurned by her ever more desperate desire and a belief in the possibility to save Jan, Bess gradually gets to the point of boarding a ship where even prostitutes would refuse to go. The community and the Church's reaction is, predictably, ruthless. The latter banishes Bess, Church elders condemn her and the village children throw stones at her. Yet, while defiling her body, Bess maintains the faith in Jan's salvation and her purity of heart in spite of going through the hardest of ordeals and the community's moral condemnation. Bess subjects herself to brutalization at the hands of a shipful of sailors, faithful that in so doing, Jan's life will be saved, and he will be made able to walk again. She tragically dies as a result of her injuries, yet Jan is "saved": he is miraculously cured. The final scene of the movie—a slow-motion aerial shot of a Church while bells are tolling—suggests the commendation of her behavior in the eyes of a higher authority.

The clash of Bess's sacrifice and faith, on the one hand, and the conventional moral-religious norms, on the other has invited the interpretation of *Breaking the Waves* as Protestant-Kierkegaardian. The confrontation between Bess's faith and community/Church norms appears to display a striking resemblance to Kierkegaard's Protestantism of non-reconciliation that takes Abraham's sacrifice of Isaac as a "model" of faith. But are Bess's faith and sacrifice Abrahamic-Kierkegaardian? It is worth dwelling on Kierkegaard's view given the controversy it stirred. Kierkegaard's brand of Protestantism is quite specific as it rejects radically both the Protestant and Catholic theologies of reconciliation between faith and reason, individual and community and the immanent world and the transcendence. An example of Protestantism of reconciliation is the Pietist vision of a "union of hearts," which inspired Immanuel Kant's philosophical theodicy—that is, his harmonizing view of faith and reason, morality and religion. Kierkegaard's *Fear and Trembling* represents an opposite strand of Protestantism, one based on an agonistic view of the relation between rational-universal morality and faith, reason and religion and the immanent world and the transcendence.[20]

There have been various attempts to water down Kierkegaard's seemingly outrageous claims regarding the essence of faith as "revealed" in Abraham's promptness to sacrifice his son.[21] Abraham's readiness to take Isaac's life at God's command has often been a source of embarrassment for believers, even theologians. Some see the story as part of an antiquated image of the vengeful and jealous God of the Old Testament; others see it as referring to a merciful God given that Isaac is not sacrificed but replaced at the last moment with a lamb. Yet Kierkegaard does not dilute Abraham's story at all, instead he goes to great lengths to develop its most puzzling and dramatic elements, which he regards as conveying the *mysterium tremendum* of faith. In so doing, his goal is to "retrieve" God as *das ganz Andere* (Absolutely Other), namely as what cannot be reconciled and mediated on account of immanent categories—rational or theological—of essentially limited creatures. As Kierkegaard (or Johannes de Silentio) asserts, the "paradox [of decision and faith] cannot be mediated." Attempting to tame *das ganz Andere*, to translate the transcendence into our immanent and fallible categories—from selling indulgences to demonstrating rationally the existence of God—fails to grasp God's mysterious and terrible alterity.[22]

In Kierkegaard's reading, Abraham's story goes as follows: after making Abraham await the "child of promise" for a very long time, God eventually spoke to him: "Take Isaac, your only son, whom you love, and go to the land of Moriah and offer him as a burnt offering on a mountain that I will show you."[23] It seemed clear to Abraham that his long waiting had been useless, and that God was deriding him.[24] Abraham was convinced that God's initial promise had been in vain, a mockery really, yet his passionate faith in Him and the "child of promise" remained, paradoxically, unshaken. According to Kierkegaard, Abraham "had faith by the virtue of absurd, for human calculation was out of question, and it certainly was absurd that God, who required it of him, should in the next moment rescind the requirement."[25]

Kierkegaard does not make any attempt to moderate the contradiction between the religious obligation to the Absolute Other and the moral obligation towards fellow others. Quite the contrary, and against various interpreters who have attempted to water down Kierkegaard's vision, he is adamant that, at the level of the essence of faith, *no* reconciliation (through community, Church, theological or moral-rational rules, language and conceptual thought) is possible. Abraham's story suggests that his unconditional obligation to God entails killing one's most beloved: the paradox of faith entails the loss of the middle term, or the mediator, between individual and community, i.e., the overcoming of the moral-religious rule.[26] For Kierkegaard, the moment of faith is *superior* to that of morality:[27] to have faith is to believe passionately in the possibility of the impossible: "(f)aith is precisely the paradox that the single individual as the single individual is higher than the universal. . . . This position cannot be mediated, for all mediation takes place only by virtue of the universal; it is and remains for all eternity a paradox, impervious to thought" (*Fear and Trembling*, 55–56).[28] In the essential moment of experiencing God, the faithful acts against what he cherishes the most in the immanent world. Abraham has, thus, a "dreadful responsibility" and his only "assurance" is "pain"[29] as he is absolutely alone in his decision. He cannot explain, justify or even communicate it; this entails that, in the eyes of humanity, he is murderer.

Now, is Bess an Abrahamic figure? Her experience does display striking similarities with Kierkegaard's version of Protestantism. First, there is a core element of "blind" obedience and devotion in both Bess and Abraham.[30] Abraham's faith is based on unconditional obedience: what God demands (sacrificing the "child of promise") is absurd and incomprehensible, yet Abraham neither questions it nor asks for an explanation. He obeys—unconditionally so. On the other hand, when Jan asks Bess to sleep with another man, Bess accepts it without asking for any reason whatsoever. Why does Jan, who seemingly loves and respects his wife, ask Bess to fulfil his "sick fantasies" (as Bess's sister calls them)? This remains an enigma. Neither does he provide a plausible justification nor does Bess ask for one: she appears to act on blind faith and submission. Faith and sacrifice are, further, lived by Abraham and Bess in anguished and utter solitude; they are individual acts and not the result of communion and sharing with other members of community of believers.

As Kierkekegaard underlines, the moment of faith is revealed as a private experience, as an intimate communication with God. Yet Abraham has a "private conversation" with God and is His "confident." Kierkegaard refers to the "intimation of the wondrous glory the knight attains in becoming God's confidant, the Lord's friend . . . in saying <You> to God in heaven."[31] Not unlike Abraham, Bess is completely alone with respect to her community, yet she appears to communicate with Him. It is a private communication, not one mediated by community or any third (e.g., her sister or Jan): she talks alone and aloud in a dialogue between her voice representing God as a severe father and authoritarian figure and her voice as a trusting child.[32]

Despite these common points, Bess's example cannot be simply understood as Kierkegaardian. Given the centrality of the conflict between individual faith and community/Church norms, *Breaking the Waves* is interpretable as an echo of the tradition of a Protestantism of non-reconciliation. Yet, the comparison with the Kierkegaardian version of it is limited. To begin with, what is at stake for Bess is *both* her marriage and God, her love for Jan and her faith in God. In contrast to Abraham, Bess does not break her bond to the immanent world in order to obey the transcendent God. Further, it is not God who asks her to break the moral law. It is Jan. Only after Jan makes his request, she searches desperately to harmonize her love for him with her faith. In other words, Bess attempts to reconcile her relation to Jan with her faith in God and immanence with Transcendence; in contrast, in *Fear and Trembling*, faith manifests itself when the most intimate family bond is "broken," namely Abraham's love for his son Isaac. The *analogon* of Isaac's sacrifice would have been sacrificing Jan at God's request.

Bess's behavior is, I argue, an example of the *ethically sublime*.[33] Her acts are not simply immoral, but morally ambivalent. I call "ethically sublime" those supererogatory acts that are excessive and overwhelming with respect to the limited powers, reason and imagination of the common moral agent. More generally, sublime acts—be they ethical or aesthetic—are awe-inspiring: they simultaneously overpower and elevate the observer beyond herself. The ek-stasis, being-taken-out-of-oneself is an essential part of the experience of both the ethical and the aesthetical sublime.[34] And just as what is aesthetical sublime need not be identified with perfect beauty, so the ethical sublime need not be identified with moral perfection. Seeing a storm from the top of a mountain can provide a sublime aesthetical experience; or such an aesthetic experience, drawing on Edmund Burke's line of argumentation, is deeply ambivalent—it combines attraction and fear, fascination and recoil, harmony and dissonance, symmetry and asymmetry.[35] Likewise, Bess' example suggests that imperfection and even morally questionable behavior can sometimes square with the ethical-sublime. Bess's moving fortitude and commitment is, on the one hand, sublime in its excess, in its immeasurable and tragic love for her crippled love. Her behavior strikes and overwhelms moral reason and imagination and stirs up admiration for what is noble, uncommon and even grandiose. Bess's submission generates, however, an ambivalent reaction in the audience: the result is an audience torn between discomfort (regarding Bess's "blind" obedience) and admiration for her resilience, faith and dedication to her crippled husband.[36]

The experience of sublime is, according to Kant's classic argument in *The Critique of Judgment* (1791) pure and disinterested.[37] But, as critics like Derrida persuasively argue, there is no such thing as a purely disinterested or unconditional act or experience. Kant's conception of sublime is anchored in the old and questionable metaphysical opposition between empirical and noumenal, and it overlooks the social conditions of possibility of experience. In particular, sublime sacrifices such as Bess's are not absolutely pure and disinterested: such acts can aspire to disinterestedness and unconditionality, yet they are also embedded in specific material and symbolic contexts that condition them. Sublime sacrifices are caught between the aspiration to unconditionality, on the one hand, and a specific context that conditions it, on the other. In particular, in spite of Bess's "purity" and childish naïveté of heart, her supererogatory behavior is conditioned by her husband's dubious desire for her to prostitute herself and her acceptance to pursue it, as well as by a patriarchal God, a stern Father "expressing" Himself through her childish voice.

The end of *Breaking the Waves* suggests that the "sublime offering" of Bess's love, even if it leads her to immoral behavior, is superior to it.[38] But this does not make the movie Kierkegaardian. From the perspective of morality and community, as Kierkegaard acknowledges, Abraham *is* a criminal. Bess is, in contrast, neither a criminal nor does she aim to overcome morality; she is an immoral "saint."

In Kierkegaard's *Fear and Trembling,* the emphasis is on God as the Absolute Other and on the certitude of the solitary and individual faith in Him; in contrast, in *Breaking the Waves,* the emphasis is on Bess's sublime sacrifice. Yet, more than the "absolute certitude" of the faithful in the existence of God as Absolute Other (Kierkegaard) and, consequently, more than the view that the religious contradicts and is superior to the moral, the final aerial scene of a Church whose bells toll after Bess's death commends her behavior in the eyes of a higher authority, while the ethical-sublime appears to overcome the norms of the moral-religious community; the taste of ambivalence, of simultaneous admiration and recoil, cannot be erased.

One different interpretation is that Bess's sacrifice is not Abrahamic but Christ-like in nature. There are, indeed, commonalities between Bess's sacrifice and Christ's.[39] For one thing, their self-sacrifice is driven by a desire of, and an aspiration to, someone else's salvation. Their self-sacrifice is therefore other-centered: it is aimed not at their own salvation, but at the salvation of the other—the paralyzed Jan or sinful humanity. What's more, in their quest for redemption, both Christ and Bess challenge and flaunt the moral norms of their community. They are ridiculed as "mad"[40] and despised and condemned by their community. It is, however, overstretched to regard Bess's behavior as an *imitatio Christi*. Christ famously reached out to the "wretched of the earth"—the sick, the poor, the prostitutes, etc.—to teach them that "God is on their side" (Matt., 4–6). Yet there is nothing in The New Testament suggesting that Jesus would have condoned the continuation and even intensification of sinful behavior as a way to salvation. If he reached out to prostitutes, he did so in order to convert them to the real faith and a radically different mode of living. Transformation and conversion mean giving up prostitution, not persevering in it. Christ challenged the moral norms of his time, and still challenges ours; yet he does so in order to expand moral and religious imagination in novel and radical ways. Jesus's behavior is a paramount example of moral sainthood and perfectionism. To imitate Christ, then, is to aspire to a demanding ideal, namely to moral sainthood.[41]

In short, *Breaking the Waves* resonates only in part with a Protestant-individualistic and agonistic interpretation pitting Bess's faith against her community and Church. Bess's selfless sacrifice should be distinguished both from Abraham's and Christ's. I turn now to *Antichrist*, where the Gnostic echoes become so strong that they silence the Protestant ones. While in some of Trier's most representative movies community is oppressive and evil (*Breaking the Waves, Dancer in the Dark, The Idiots, Dogville, Mandeville*), in *Antichrist* the creation itself becomes "Satan's Church," and seems brought about by an evil God. The consequence is that one of the most common motifs in Trier's cinema, namely that of woman's sacrificial gift, tends to vanish.

SECTION III *ANTICHRIST*: FROM SACRIFICE TO VICTIM AND PERPETRATOR

"Nature is Satan's church."

(*Antichrist*)

In *Breaking the Waves*, Trier conveys an agonistic vision of religion and sacrifice that is at odds with conventional religion and common morality. There is significant continuity between *Breaking the Waves* and *Antichrist*, Trier's most explicitly "religious" movies.[42] Both deal with the issue of evil, with a link between violence and sexuality, and portray a limit-situation centered on a woman's suffering. They also propose a vision of transfiguration beyond the seeming oppressiveness of being-together either as a community or as a couple. But *Antichrist* radicalizes so much the treatment of these themes that, compared to *Breaking the Waves*, it becomes a violently anti-religious movie. Interestingly enough, Trier's most sweeping rejection of religion does not resort to the tools of secularist rationalism; instead, it expresses it through religious images and a vocabulary resonating with the Gnostic theme of the evil of creation, in addition to being a critique of self-sufficient rationalism. The very making of *Antichrist* by a profoundly depressed Trier can be read at once as a therapeutical act *and* an inner religious journey, an act of *descensio ad infernum* so as to confront and overcome his demons, phobias and traumas.[43] The movie is structured in a way that is evocative of religious ritual. It is a ritualic voyage made of the three stages distinguished in Arnold van Gennep's *Rites of Passage:* the normal stage; the liminal stage (a *descensio ad infernum*), which is generally accompanied by some form of violence and finally, the transformation and re-emergence.[44] Furthermore, the actors' (Charlotte Gainsbourg and Willem Dafoe) account of their time filming strikes one as being reminiscent of ritualic experiences. Their acting was not based on impersonating a clearly specified character with previously defined emotional reactions and views. The experience of acting orchestrated by Trier was more like the plunging into a liminal stage of a religious ritual, that of radical questioning of one's identity, of vulnerability and of "chaos."

The ritualic journey of the film starts with a prologue in which a married couple—named in the credentials as He and She[45]—makes love passionately in the bathroom of their fourth-floor flat. Like in *Breaking the Waves*, the drama of the *Antichrist* is triggered by an accident.[46] Their young son, Nick, opens the gate of the cot, sees his parents making love as he passes the open bathroom door and climbs on to a table beside a window. Forestalling the evil to come, Nick knocks over three statuettes, which symbolically bear the inscriptions "Grief", "Pain" and "Despair." He then precipitates from the window to his death in the street below, his woolen rabbit falling with him. The ominous tension amplifies as the movie unfolds. During Nick's funeral, She has a mental collapse, blaming herself for her son's death. Given her state of mind, He decides to help her and so takes on the role of a psychotherapist. He entrusts reason and sensible dialogue to allay his wife's guilt over the boy's death and reconcile her with her moral feeling of guilt and responsibility. Armed with good intentions, He makes her give up the medication prescribed by the doctor, and applies in exchange an alternative therapeutic technique. This method is based on introspective communicative exchanges, and is aimed at bringing to light her deepest fears so as to face and bring them under rational control. He soon discovers that chief amongst the roots of her fears is the forest that surrounds their holiday cabin, which they call Eden, and urges her to return there.[47] She questions this therapeutic strategy, yet eventually agrees to it. Upon their arrival, the audience quickly realizes that Garden of Horrors would have been a more appropriate name for the environment in which they find themselves. The forest, which surrounds the cabin, becomes a source of palpable terror, and the anxiety mounts in the confined, decaying cabin until it escalates into terrible violence. He helplessly contemplates how his good intentions and therapeutic technique have come to naught, as she gradually falls towards "the dark side": from a loving wife she converts into a disconcertingly violent enemy—into Satan's or the Antichrist's tool.

Once the couple reaches Eden, the religious and mythical symbols and images become central to the movie. *Antichrist* acquires surrealist undertones, which corresponds to a partial change in the cinematographic technique. Trier begins to deform reality almost immediately upon their arrival. Standard, well-balanced, medium shots are intercut with distant, shaky, hand-held camera shots as if to suggest that they are being watched, presumably by a malevolent and invisible spirit (the Antichrist?). The frame distorts from time to time, conveying a hallucinatory dark state and anticipating the breakdown of the "natural" order of things. We tend to presume that things go from bad to worse, but things go even worse than that. In the biblical Eden, God gives dominance over animals and plants to man and woman. In contrast, in Trier's Eden, those animals and plants retaliate against their lords. The ground burns her feet and she fears the tall grass and a stream. In *Antichrist*, Eden trees produce not fruit but hailing acorns. The male protagonist has surreal interactions with ominous animals; they seem to be both in cahoots and at war with each other. In one shot, an army of militant ants devour a dead bird; yet in another, it is revealed that a talking fox, a deer carrying a half-delivered still born, and a violent raven all seem to be working together against the man, standing by each other staring menacingly at him. The talking fox announces: "Chaos reigns." (This is an element based on Trier's presumably shamanic experience.)[48] The relentless violence between man and woman sets in, and all seems to indicate the presence of the Antichrist. At one point, she leaves him bemused by saying "nature is Satan's church." Their relation degenerates into surprising and shocking scenes of attempted emasculation and maiming her sex.

Antichrist is at once a reflection on therapy and an inner (quasi)religious journey—that is, an act of *descensio ad infernum* so as to violently confront and overcome one's demons, phobias and traumas. This relation between excessive violence and evil, on the one hand, and therapeutic reason, on the other, is not a new theme—it is dealt with, for instance, by S. Kubrick in *A Clockwork Orange* (1971) as inspired by Anthony Burgess. "Ultraviolence" is the way in which Alex DeLarge, the central character of the movie, calls this gratuitous violence, a violence devoid of any moral inhibition or manifest finality (social change, revenge, etc.). Kubrick shows how the transformation of a moral problem—a crime and the responsibility that should accompany it—into a question of therapeutic technique generates the danger of a political dystopia. Kubrick satirizes the pretense to cure moral evil by means of a scientific technique and shows how therapeutic reason can produce a surplus of political unreason and domination. While Trier is not primarily interested in political aspects but dwells on question of the limits of representation of the origin and phenomenon of evil in its disruptive forms, he shares an analogous interest in the paradox that the reduction of a moral problem to a matter of therapeutic reason, control and technique is flawed and can produce an increase in irrationality and evil.

In Trier's *Antichrist*, the therapist is doubly hubristic. First, He aims to reduce a moral problem—that of guilt and responsibility related to Nick's death—to a technical one, to a question of emotional management. Second, He pretends that by rational-therapeutic means, one can have control over and be in command of her deepest fears and passions. But his strategy is a complete failure. Once the Pandora's box of Her deepest fears is opened, the therapist's reason turns out to be powerless. Unwittingly, He makes hell break loose, and is soon forced to abandon the overconfidence in his therapeutic "game" and fight against his wife's increasing aggressiveness. The confrontation with his most-beloved turned worst enemy becomes a matter of life and death. In the end, he has to kill her in order to survive and to deliver her from excruciating suffering and self-inflicted violence. Trier's cinematic experience mirrors his personal experience of depression, and his misgivings as to the limits of the therapeutic method. Trier tells a story based on a rhetoric made of visual and narrative figures of amplification and hyperbole. The accidental death of one's child can leave indelible scars on a mother's soul, and therapy can have perverse consequences, yet few women would probably react like the female character in *Antichrist*. However, Trier's misgivings about the "new priests" cloaked as therapy experts and positive-thinking professionals are spot-on. The point here is not the rejection of therapy as such, but what Trier does is to place a critical magnifying glass on a more general and problematic trend of approaching moral issues and traumas from a managerial-rationalist perspective.[49]

A paradox shapes these scenes of escalating violence. Violence is explicit, direct and often shot in a quasi-documentary style with a hand-held camera. This creates a feeling of uncanny proximity with the audience: we are drawn into the scenes, and pushed back by their appalling violence. But evil is as much explicit as it remains inscrutable, it is as intimate as it is transcendent. Confronted with its exorbitant and "disproportionate" character—that is, with evil as event that cannot be reduced to seemingly relevant causes (her guilt, his misplaced therapeutic strategy)—reason's perception loses its clarity. In order to approximate it, to grasp what seems to be ungraspable and transcends all expectation, Trier cannot but resort to an indirect symbolic language—just as mystics resort to a symbolic, analogic language to gesture towards a Gnostic demiourgos and invisible evil God.

To better understand the relevance of the evil god (Satan, Antichrist, demiourgos) in Trier's film, it is useful to distinguish it from two other ways of going about radical evil. The first one is theological; it takes the Antichrist as referring to a real character and an embodied force playing a specific role in the Christian narrative. The second one is rationalist. To illustrate, for Kant religious and mythical symbols are a superficial crust of a truth unveiled, codified and mastered by reason. Despite the presence of radical evil (conveyed by the symbols of Satan and the Antichrist), Kant regards it as an accidental and subordinated element with respect to his projection of a universal rationalist morality involves the "rational faith" in a "union of all hearts" under the same God. The evil God is, from this perspective, a symbol that has a fictive or unreal referent; it is a symbol (or image) of something that is adequately grasped and properly conveyed by the faculty of reason, in conceptual terms. In spite of their differences, what the two approaches have in common is that they aim to inscribe evil in a world saga of religious and rational order and reconciliation. As such, they negate the possibility of its disruptiveness. Trier's filmic experience is a life-and-death confrontation with "radical evil" beyond the conventional religious and rationalistic ways of dealing with it.[50] "Radical evil" refers not only to the problem of the root of evil (I. Kant), but also to that of an evil that is by "nature" unruly and exorbitant. A good part of the strength of *Antichrist* is that it challenges the self-complacency of the religious and philosophical sagas of goodness and order, including Kant's own, which have attempted to domesticate, reconcile and do away with the disruptive or "transcending" character of radical evil as event. It is worth noting that *Antichrist*'s reinterpretation of the Book of Genesis does not unambiguously "sow" the seed of evil in the nature of women. In *Antichrist,* the conceit of reason (whose carrier is the male protagonist) generates, in good part, the outpour of irrationality, evil and violence. It is not the sleep of reason but its hubris that creates monsters.

These two approaches claim to domesticate the irruptiveness and radicality of evil by inscribing it into religious or rationalist theodicy. In contrast, the referent of the symbol of the evil God is neither real nor unreal, it is a "real fiction" through which Trier expresses the inexpressible and infinite anxiety in the face of a radical evil and the difficulty of identifying an ultimately acceptable rational or theological explanation, justification or therapeutic cure through reasonable dialogue.[51]

While in *Breaking the Waves* Bess' faith overcomes the worldly evil and attains a high-order reconciliation with the "divine" or transcendence, in *Antichrist* evil is so powerful that it appears to undo any link with God and to unsettle the pretense of rational control.[52] Trier's filmic experience has, as I've pointed out, some affinities with Kierkegaard's anti-rationalistic and anti-theological vision of religion. Yet *Antichrist* is so much a radicalized experience that it turns against God and religion: in *Antichrist,* the Protestantism of non-reconciliation converts into a cry of anguished protest against the worldly evil. If for Kierkegaard faith is a paradox, at once an impossibility and an unshakeable certitude, for Trier the presence of radical evil undoes any hope in the rational or religious reconciliation with world and God.[53]

Tarkovsky—to whom the *Antichrist* is disconcertingly dedicated—conceived cinema-making as a prayer and often used images of nature and visual symbols as epiphanies of the divine. In contrast, in Trier's *Antichrist*, God—as opposed to the demiourgos—is utterly absent, and instead the evil is alive and thriving.[54] The "epiphanies" are of a god that exists only in his antithetic form. In *Antichrist*, the oppressiveness of being-together becomes generalized, and it turns into the evilness of the whole creation; such evil becomes so powerful that the female protagonist loses her status of sacrificial victim, as in *Breaking the Waves*, and becomes a tool and victim of Satan. While Bess sacrifices herself by defiling her body for Jan's redemption, the female protagonist in *Antichrist* goes as far as to self-destructively maim her sex and to attempt at her husband's life.

Still, after the life-and-death struggle between the two protagonists, He undergoes an experience of transcendence and transfiguration. To convey this heterodoxic (quasi)religious vision, Trier uses close-ups of the male protagonist taken from below and light effects that suggests that their source comes from inside; these close-ups of the glowing, haloed and ecstatic appearance unmistakably bring to memory other cinematic scenes of Jesus's transfiguration. This transformation of the representative of reason is conveyed as a surreal and cryptic vision of a several women climbing up slowly towards the bedazzled and ecstatic male protagonist. The movie ends not with a clear-cut message, but with a cryptic mystic vision whose connection with the life-and-death struggle between the two remains an enigma. These final images of the movie convey an experience of transcendence beyond any conventional religion and affirmation of the existence of God and which is not reducible to propositional ennunciation.[55]

SECTION IV CONCLUSION

The relationship between Trier's cinema and religion is ambivalent and multi-layered. 1) *The movie per se can be seen as religious experience.* Antichrist has, for instance, the tertiary structure of religious ritual (a. the normal stage; b. the descent into chaos (the liminal stage), which is often marked by violence and sacrifice and c. the emergence of a new order based on an experience of conversion and transfiguration). 2) *Making the movie is a religious experience in itself.* The making of *Antichrist* by a profoundly depressed Trier can be read as an inner religious journey, i.e., an act of *descensio ad infernum* so as to confront and overcome his own demons, phobias and traumas. In addition, as Charlotte Gainsbourg suggested, acting in *Antichrist* did not take the form of interpreting a ready-made role; instead, the filming experience resembled plunging into the second liminal stage of a religious ritual, that of radical questioning of one's identity, vulnerability and "chaos." 3) *The movie as reinterpretation of religious topoi.* The movie echoes and reinterprets traditional religious motives in novel ways that are not simply traditional Christian, Protestant-Kierkegaardian or Gnostic. 4) *Movie as a polemic rejection of conventional religion and theology.* 5) *The spectator's cinematic experience as experience of the sacred.* The reaction of the spectators and commentators to this difficult film has often been one of straightforward rejection; yet the movie can generate in the audience of an experience of the sacred in Rudolf Otto's sense of revulsion, fear and fascination in face of what's not fully representable and comprehensible: this is an experience of the *mysterium tremendum* of the radical evil (Antichrist, Satan) and an experience of *mysterium fascinans* with respect to the final transfiguration and "mystical" vision of the male protagonist. In short, Trier's cinema includes eclectic and original visions of transcendence, sacrifice, faith, guilt, conversion and transfiguration. By simultaneously echoing and breaking with the different religious traditions, Trier's filmic experiences under examination occupy the unstable space between the subjective and heterodox appreciation of the relevance of religion and a radical protest against it.[56] His cinematic experience is thus deeply ambivalent in relation to religion—it is an attitude of rejection, fascination and recreation beyond Church dogmas and the certitude of the existence of God.[57]

NOTES

1. The trickster is a central figure in dualist religions (e.g., Gnosticism). See Ioan Culiano, *The Tree of Gnosis: Gnostic Mythology from Early Christianity to Modern Nihilism* (San Francisco: HarperCollins, 1992).
2. For an analysis of the development of the image of holy fool in Russian cinema, see Alina Birzache's chapter in this volume.
3. For valuable biographical details, see Jack Stevenson, *Lars von Trier,* (London: British Film Institute, 2002); Jan Lumboldt (ed.), *Lars von Trier Interviews,* (Jackson: University Press of Mississippi, 2003); Hilaro J. Rodriguez, *Lars von Trier. El cine sin dogmas* (Madrid: Ediciones JC, Madrid, 2003).
4. Trier's conversion does not appear to have a significant bearing on his cinema which, as I will argue, is evocative of Protestant and Gnostic themes.
5. This misleading interpretation is at the basis of some of the most disparaging reviews against Trier's *Antichrist*. For a more balanced yet still disconcerted reaction, see Joanna Bourke in Xan Brooks, "Antichrist: a Work of Genius or the Sickest Film in the History of Cinema?" *The Guardian,* July 16, 2009. Last accessed March 22, 2013.
6. *Breaking the Waves* is much closer to Tarkovsky's *Sacrifice*. These two films connect the themes of salvation and selfless sacrifice, even if the goal of the sacrifice and the way it is enacted are different. See later, Section II.
7. For a detailed analysis of "immanent frame" at the basis of "exclusive humanism," see Charles Taylor, *A Secular Age,* (Harvard: Harvard University Press, 2007).
8. Such recurrent themes in Trier's movies are: sacrifice (normally of the female protagonist), the oppressiveness of living-together, the experience of transcendence and transfiguration.

9. I borrow the phrase "myth of coherence" from Quentin Skinner's work on the history of ideas. Skinner refers to forcing a complex and shifting body of work into the straitjacket of one set of ideas an intellectualist illusion. See Q. Skinner, *Visions of Politics, Vol. I, Concerning the Method,* (Cambridge: Cambridge University Press, 2000).
10. I borrow the phrase from Ronald Dworkin, "Religion without God," *The New York Review of Books,* April 4, 2013. Available at www.nybooks.com/articles/archives/2013/apr/04/religion-without-god/?pagination=false. Last accessed May 12, 2013.
11. For an interpretation of *Breaking the Waves* as Kiekegaardian, see Donna Yarri, "Lars von Trier," in *Encyclopedia of Religion and Film,* ed. Eric Michael Mazur, (ABC-CLIO, 2011), 433–43; Slavoj Žižek, *The Paralax View (Short Circuits),* (The MIT Press, 2009); Laura Llevadot Pascual, "El individuo singular: El cine de Lars von Trier a la luz de Kierkegaard," *Themata. Revista de Filosofía,* 39 (2007), 435—41. For discussion of Bess as a Christ-like figure, see, for instance, Linda Mercadante, "Bess the Christ Figure?: Theological Interpretations of *Breaking the Waves,*" *Journal of Religion and Film,* 5:1 (2001), 221-39; Michael P. Murphy: "Breaking the Waves," in Michael P. Murphy, *A Theology of Criticism* (Oxford: Oxford University Press, 2008), 91–126; Carleen Mandolfo, "Women, Suffering and Redemption in Three Films of Lars von Trier," *Literature and Theology,* 24:3 (2010), 285–300.
12. Jacques Derrida, *The Gift of Death,* (Chicago: University of Chicago Press, 1995); Jacques Derrida, *Given Time: Counterfeit Money* (Chicago: University of Chicago Press, 1992).
13. I take the phrase "sublime offering" from Jean-Luc Nancy. He uses it in a different context and with a different meaning. See Nancy, "The Sublime Offering," in *Of the Sublime: Presentation in Question* (Albany, NY: State University of New York Press, 1993).
14. See, for instance, Derrida, *The Gift of Death* (Chicago: University of Chicago Press, 1995); Derrida, *Given Time: Counterfeit Money* (Chicago: University of Chicago Press, 1992).
15. I take this phrase from Culiano, *The Tree of Gnosis: Gnostic Mythology from Early Christianity to Modern Nihilism.* For a critique, see Michael Allen Williams, *Rethinking "Gnosticism." An Argument for Dismantling a Dubious Category* (Princeton: Princeton University Press, 1996). It is noteworthy that Williams' critique is aimed against the view that Gnosticism in general is anti-cosmic without denying the relevance of anti-cosmic beliefs.
16. For an analysis of *Dogville* in terms of Gnosticism, see Costica Bradatan, "'I Was a Stranger, and Ye Took Me Not In': Deus Ludens and Theology of Hospitality in Lars von Trier's *Dogville,*" *Journal of European Studies,* 39:1 (2009), 58–78.
17. Generally speaking, in Gnostic texts the Creator or Demiurge is not evil, but rather ignorant. See Elaine Pagels, *The Gnostic Gospels,* (New York: Vintage), 1989.
18. Pagels, *The Gnostic Gospels,* 55–56.
19. Trier's second trilogy, "Gold or Golden Heart," is named after a book Trier read as a child (for details, see Stevenson, *Lars von Trier*). Apart from *Breaking the Waves*—which is the only overtly religious movie of the trilogy—this is made of *The Idiots* and *Dancer in the Dark. The Idiots* is about a group of young adults who form a community in which they act as if they are mentally challenged. *Dancer in the Dark* is about a young Czechoslovakian immigrant woman who struggles to make a life for teenage her son and save him from the genetic eye problem he inherited from her. It is noteworthy that even if *Breaking the Waves* is the only explicitly religious movie in the trilogy, all three

deal with experiences of transformation and self-transcendence. Furthermore, all three of the films in this trilogy feature a self-sacrificing woman. In *Antichrist*, the theme of evil becomes even more radicalized; one of the consequences is that the woman is not a sacrificial offering anymore; she becomes a perpetrator and a victim.

20. In the following, I make use of Søren Kierkegaard, *Fear and Trembling. Repetition* (Princeton: Princeton University Press, 1983). (Original work published 1843.)
21. The exegetic literature on Kierkegaard's short book *Fear and Trembling* is impressive. See, for instance, Mark Dooley, *The Politics of Exodus: Kierkegaard's Ethics of Responsibility* (New York: Fordham University Press, 2001); Harvie Ferguson, *Melancholy and the Critique of Modernity: Søren Kierkegaard's Religious Psychology* (London and New York: Routledge, 1995); Jaime Ferreira, *Transforming Vision: Imagination and Will in Kierkegaardian Faith* (Oxford: Clarendon Press, 1991); Ferreira, "Faith and the Kierkegaardian Leap," in *The Cambridge Companion to Kierkegaard,* eds. Alastair Marino and Gordon Marino (Cambridge University Press, 1998), 207–34; Alastair Hannay, *Kierkegaard* (London: Routledge & Kegan Paul, 1982); Mark C. Taylor, *Journeys to Selfhood: Hegel & Kierkegaard,* (Berkeley, Los Angeles, London: University of California Press, 1980).
22. Kierkegaard, *Fear and Trembling. Repetition*,18.
23. Ibid., 19.
24. Kierkegaard reads:

> (s)o God was only mocking Abraham! . . . All was lost! Seventy years of trusting expectancy, the brief joy over the fulfillment of faith. . . . Now everything would be lost! All the glorious remembrance of his posterity, the promise in Abraham's seed—it was nothing but a whim, a fleeting thought that the Lord had had and that Abraham was now to obliterate. . . . [T]he fruit of Abraham's life, sanctified by prayer, matured in battle . . . this fruit was now to be torn prematurely and rendered meaningless, for what meaning would it have if Isaac should be sacrificed! (Kierkegaard, *Fear and Trembling. Repetition,* 19)

25. Ibid., 35–36.
26. Ibid., 71.
27. For Kierkegaard, the moment of free decision can neither be justified nor communicated since that would imply its inscription in general categories and in a body of knowledge. Thus, Abraham never explains to Isaac or to his wife the real purpose of the journey to the mountain. "Abraham cannot be mediated; in other words, he cannot speak. As soon as I speak, I express the universal" (Kierkegaard, *Fear and Trembling. Repetition,* 60). It is thus not by chance that Kierkegaard signed the book as Johannes de Silentio.
28. Kierkegaard does not demonstrate this superiority; however, he points out that if Abraham's story and "singularity" makes sense at all, then it has to prevail over the universal rule: "faith is this paradox . . . or else Abraham is lost" (Kierkegaard, *Fear and Trembling. Repetition,* 55–56). Further: "[t]his paradox cannot be mediated, for it depends specifically on this: that the single individual is only the single individual" (Kierkegaard, *Fear and Trembling. Repetition,* 70). And: "(f)aith itself cannot be mediated into the universal, for thereby it is cancelled. . . . Faith is this paradox, and the single individual cannot make himself understandable to anyone" (Kierkegaard, *Fear and Trembling. Repetition,* 71). Here I cannot enter a critical discussion of the metaphysical presuppositions of Kierkegarrd's view of the relation between morality (the universal) and faith (the singularity, the exception). Kierkegaard's reading of

142   *Camil Ungureanu*

Abraham's situation is based on a metaphysics of exception which is the mirror image of Kant's universalist rationalism. This metaphysics of exception is constructed on a series of rigid dichotomies between, on the one hand, communicable reason, universal and equalitarian moral rule and, on the other, the absolutely singular and incommunicable experience of faith in the Absolute Other. The latter are deemed to be revealing of a superior "essence."

29. Kierkegaard, *Fear and Trembling. Repetition,* 80.
30. It is known that Trier puts his female protagonists (Grace, Selma, Bess, She) through the ordeal of limit-situations that often break them physically or spiritually. But it is hasty to argue that there is a clear-cut anti-feminist pattern in Trier's cinematography. Trier often identifies with his female protagonists—or with part of their experience. *Antichrist* is a case in point. In her interviews, Charlotte Gainsbourgh underscores that Trier is, by and large, identifying himself with the woman under therapy. Moreover, contorted as their destinies may be, women are often Trier's heroes confronting a hostile world and the objects of his admiration. For instance, Selma in the musical *Dancer in the Dark* displays the extraordinary capacity to confront and transform the unfair and brutal reality by means of art and imagination. Selma is quite different from a typical male hero—she is weak and vulnerable. Yet what makes her a hero worthy of admiration is her sacrificial gift to her son and her strength to face death with a song and a dance—a strength that nourishes her fragility and sensibility. *Dancer in the Dark* is a hymn to imagination and art in the most adverse conditions; it is a hymn to the power of the weak over injustice and of art over death. For more detailed discussions, see Alydia Faber "Redeeming Sexual Violence? A Feminist Reading of *Breaking the Waves,*" *Literature and Theology* 17:1 (2003), 59–75; Stephen Heath, "God, Faith, and Film: *Breaking the Waves,*" *Literature and Theology* 12:1 (1998), 93–107; Caroline Bainbridge, *The Cinema of Lars von Trier: Authenticity and Artifice* (New York: Wallflower Press, 2007).
31. Kierkegaard, *Fear and Trembling. Repetition,* 77.
32. See Robert Ebert's review of *Breaking the Waves.* Available at www.rogerebert.com/reviews. Last accessed May 3, 2013.
33. From Longinus to Kant, the notion of sublime was applied to aesthetic experience. Here I use the term with reference to moral experience, more specifically in relation to supererogatory acts. For an analysis of "sublime" in the aesthetical *and* moral contexts, see Paul Crowther *The Kantian Sublime: From Morality to Art* (Oxford: Clarendon Press, 1989); Paul Crowther, *Critical Aesthetics and Postmodernism* (Oxford: Clarendon Press, 1993); Jean-François Lyotard, *Lessons on the Analytic of the Sublime* (Stanford, CA: Stanford University Press, 1994).
34. For Longinus, the sublime involves transcending the baseness and ignobility intrinsic to merely finite being. This is why Longinus goes on to suggest that those who achieve the sublime in literature are more than mortal; they lift us towards the Deity.
35. Edmund Burke, *A Philosophical Enquiry into the Origin of Our Ideas of the Sublime and Beautiful* (London: Penguin, 1958). (Original work published 1757.)
36. The immorality of Bess's behavior is per se ambivalent: on the one hand, the immorality is just what it is, namely something ethically negative. On the other hand, it is precisely her willingness to go at such lengths in sacrificing herself for her crippled husband that contributes to the ethical-sublime quality of her behavior, and so to a feeling of elevation and self-transcendence. As a consequence, as it often happens with Trier's movies, the audience experiences a ("Brechtian") dialectic between identification and distance, attraction and revulsion, self-transcendence and rejection (for another example, see below the discussion of *Antichrist*).

37. Immanuel Kant, *The Critique of Judgment*. Translated by J.C. Meredith (Oxford: Clarendon Press, 1973). (Original work published 1790.)
38. Nancy, "The Sublime Offering."
39. Becky McLoughlin, "Playing Ball with God: Breaking the Law in *Breaking the Waves*," *Textual Ethos Studies* 26 (2005), 85–100; Suzy Gordon, "*Breaking the Waves* and the Negativity of Melanie Klein: Rethinking 'the Female Spectator'," *Screen* 45:3 (2004), 206–25.
40. This is well-known recurrent motif in the Pauline theology.
41. In turn, Alexander, the protagonist of Tarkovsky's *Offret*, a film centered as well on the bond between sacrificial gift and salvation, is probably closer to a Christ-like figure. Alexander is a deeply anguished intellectual (i.e., journalist, theater and literary critic) with the acute, apocalyptical sense that humanity is on the verge of self-destruction due to the triumph of materialism and technology. Indeed, the movie places the story of Alexander against the background of a global technological war and the imminence of the end of the world. Can the world be saved? Can humanity be saved? In what is clearly a filmic allegory, it emerges that the world can be saved by a sacrificial gift. Not unlike Christ, Alexander comes to the realization that sacrificing himself could save the world and humanity. Even Alexander does not necessarily aspire to moral "sainthood"; he "imitates" Christ by sacrificing his ties to this world whose self-destructive sin is materialism and forgetting the spiritual-religious dimension of existence by symbolically burning down his house. The movie ends by showing him, apparently turned into a madman, being carried away by an ambulance. This extreme gesture echoes Christ's to the extent that salvation is ensured by means of dying for this materialistic world of self-destruction that humanity itself has generated. Alexander, an alienated and apprehensive intellectual, is a Christ-like figure of the modern technological-materialist age; by his sacrifice, Alexander aims to retrieve the spiritual-religious dimension of the world. In so doing, he aims to put an end to humanity's self-destructive alienation, and save it. By the end of Tarkovsky's movie Alexander's sacrifice saves humanity; he then turns into a Holy Fool who is taken to the madhouse.
42. This thematic continuity is visible in other movies by Trier (*Dogville, Dancer in the Dark,* etc.)
43. As Trier says: "I would like to invite you for a tiny glimpse behind the curtain, a glimpse into the dark world of my imagination: into the nature of my fears, into the nature of Antichrist." Trier pronounced these words at the premiere of *Antichrist* at the Cannes Film Festival in 2009. Available at www.antichristthemovie.com. Last accessed May 20, 2013. It is futile to claim to be able to *completely* disentangle between the psychological and the religious dimension of films such as *Breaking the Waves* and *Antichrist*. I am not, therefore, supporting any of the two opposite hypotheses, i.e., that these movies are either essentially religious or accidentally so.
44. Arnold van Gennep, *The Rites of Passage,* (Chicago: University of Chicago Press, 1961). In *Antichrist,* the final stage takes the form of a surreal and mysterious vision of transfiguration, a vision that is rather cryptic and obscure if compared with the final aerial scene in *Breaking the Wave*.
45. This is how I am going to call them. They are played by Willem Dafoe and Charlotte Gainsbourg.
46. For the original texts, see Bentley Layton, *The Gnostic Scriptures* (n.p.: SCM Press, 1987).
47. Together with the fact that the two protagonists do not have proper names, this indicates that von Trier aims to construct an exemplary story echoing the beginning of the Book of Genesis.
48. In an interview published in *Rotten Tomatoes,* Trier acknowledges the influence of Shamanism. "[Interviewer] Is the fox a joke? [Lars von Trier] No, it

comes from these Shamanic journeys that I did.... You have a drum beat and you go into a trance that takes you into this parallel world. And there, I talked to this fox and it demanded to have a line. [Interviewer] Did he say anything else? [Lars von Trier] Well, the first fox I met was a red fox. And it started to split itself to pieces. And afterwards, I met a couple of other foxes. Silver foxes with little cubs. And they said to me, 'Never trust the first fox you meet.' So it was interesting." Lars von Trier in Jonathan Crocker, "RT Interview: Lars von Trier on *Antichrist*," *Rotten Tomatoes*, July 29, 2009. Website. Last accessed May 9, 2013.

49. Elaine Pagels, *Adam, Eve and the Serpent: Sex and Politics in Early Christianity*, (New York: Vintage Books, 1988).
50. I have made use of Immanuel Kant, *Religion Within the Boundaries of Mere Reason* in "*The Cambridge Edition of the Works of Immanuel Kant*" *(Religion and Rational Theology)*, eds. Allen W. Word and George di Giovanni (Cambridge: Cambridge University Press, 2005). Kant does not identify radical evil with extreme evil. "Radical" refers, for Kant, to the root or origin of the evil. The extreme or "diabolic" evil is, therefore, one of the facets of the radical evil.
51. The talking fox's words "chaos reigns" is resonant of Nietzsche's dictum *chaos sive natura*. Yet for Nietzsche, "chaos" is not the expression of evil.
52. In the *Antichrist*, the Kierkegaardian-Protestant ethos of Trier's *Breaking the Waves* is reduced to a radical protest against the complacencies of religion as theodicy.
53. Trier's story of a boy's accident and critique of the conceit of rationalism is resonant of the first part of Kieslowski´s *Decalogue One* ("You shall have no other gods before me"). Despite the similarity between the two stories around a child's accident and the related critique of reason's conceit, Kieslowski´s movie affirms, albeit obliquely, the existence of a superior instance (God), while Trier appears to deny it.
54. The radicality of evil lies in its excessive, gratuitous and unpredictable character. As a result, the shocking and the monstrous are not an ersatz of the lack of substance of the cinematographic experience, but are "inherent" to the phenomenon as such.
55. I call this "positive transcendence" because, while cryptic, it does not appear to be an "epiphany" of evil.
56. For an interpretation of this double-bind logic as postsecular, see my "Final Remarks" in this volume.
57. For useful observations on this chapter, I thank Alina Birzache, Costica Bradatan and John Caruana.

9 The Banalities of Evil
Polanski, Kubrick, and the Reinvention of Horror

Nathan Abrams

INTRODUCTION

> "Some day, he thought, I would like to meet a monster who *looks* like a monster."[1]

Conventional wisdom has it that Jewish director Stanley Kubrick intended to make a film about the Holocaust but never did because Steven Spielberg beat him to it with *Schindler's List* (1993). Those closest to Kubrick say the results of his vast research depressed him too much to complete the film. Geoffrey Cocks, however, has argued that Kubrick indeed completed his film about the Holocaust; that film was *The Shining* (1980).[2] Cocks' analysis can be extended to argue that *The Shining* bookended a period, beginning in 1968 with Roman Polanski's *Rosemary's Baby*, in which secular and agnostic Jews, taking advantage of the changes in Hollywood, in particular the loosening of the Production Code, used the horror genre to grapple with the nature of evil in a post-Holocaust world. But these Jewish directors, who had rejected their *conscious* ties to any religious commitment and tradition, did not draw upon Judaism for their influences and conceptualization of evil. Rather, they detached evil from any religious moorings, preferring not to rely on God or the Devil for their secular eschatology. As a result, their updating of evil uncannily echoed the key insights of Holocaust scholarship of the 1960s, in particular Raul Hilberg's *The Destruction of the European Jews* (1961) and Hannah Arendt's *Eichmann in Jerusalem* (1962).[3]

Consequently, while their films explicitly and implicitly reference the immediate domestic and international violence of the late 1960s and 1970s, they also contain subliminal Holocaust allusions. Henry Bial, *inter alia*, has argued that minority ethnic and religious cultural texts are frequently marked by specialist knowledge unavailable to majority audiences.[4] Such an approach relies on the director (and often the actors) placing, both consciously and unconsciously, characteristics, behaviors, beliefs, and other tics, all of which require a prerequisite and prior knowledge. In this way, directors (and actors/actresses) encode clues that can be read in terms of Jewish specificity, producing what Jon Stratton has called "Jewish moments,"[5] but which a general audience decodes as universal. This requires a strategy employing a "complex of codes that cross-check each other,"[6] of which the Jewish identities of actors/actresses is a key, but by no means the only, part.[7] Other important clues include historical and cultural references; looks; intellect; behavior; profession; names; physiognomy; foods; verbal and body language; phenotype; aural, visual or emotional/genre signs, speech patterns and accents; hairstyles; anxieties; neuroses; conflicts; and tradition. This strategy of "directing" or "acting Jewish" relies on the viewer to locate, identify and decode those clues. Consequently, the individual viewer is given the possibility of *"reading Jewish"* but not with certainty.[8] This approach will be applied to argue that, if the Holocaust genre borrowed from horror as Caroline J. S. Picart and David A. Frank have posited, then the horror genre surely borrowed from the Holocaust.[9] This chapter, therefore, suggests that what was witnessed in the New Horror of the 1960s and 1970s was the incorporation, albeit oblique, of what has been labeled a "Holocaust consciousness," which is a much greater awareness in the United States and elsewhere, of the Nazi genocide into mainstream Hollywood horror film.[10]

In so doing, these directors and their films helped to reinvent the horror genre. Indeed, it has been argued that *Rosemary* heralded the birth of horror in the modern cinema. Ron Rosenbaum described the films as the "New Horror" to distinguish them from "Old Horror."[11] Crucially, in Old Horror evil was incarnate, inhering in such embodied figures as Dracula, Frankenstein, and the Mummy. The Old Horror's evil was present in figures that could only be evil. In contrast, Polanski and Kubrick, as two modern European Jews, disembodied evil in their New Horror films to produce an evil that is almost never seen, but always present. Evil becomes metaphysical and able to attach itself to ordinary men and women in the right circumstances, even the most liberal and understanding people, who could thus become evil themselves. Furthermore, evil, whether supernatural or psychological, is assisted by human collaborators, and without which it would not be nearly as effective. Evil needs help in order to triumph. In this way, both movies updated evil from Old Horror's something seen and embodied to a largely off-screen source. In so doing, Kubrick and Polanski removed God from the equation. God is conspicuously absent in both of their films to be replaced by a post-Holocaust theology of sorts in which the Holocaust took on a quasi-religious symbolism in the minds of Jews for whom Judaism no longer held any religious attachment. As novelist Stephen King said of *Psycho* (dir. Alfred Hitchcock, 1960), from which both directors drew inspiration, "It is not outside evil, predestination; the fault lies not in our stars but in ourselves."[12] And where Polanski in his *Rosemary's Baby* introduced Satan and a lapsed Catholic protagonist, in *The Shining* religion is nowhere mentioned at all. Nonetheless, both proceeded by misdirection, producing a paradox in which both break with religion but use religious or para-religious stories as vehicles for expressing their respective thematics nonetheless.

OLD EUROPEAN MASTERS

While Polanski was a European director working inside the Hollywood system, Kubrick was an American who had escaped Hollywood to make his films in Europe. Yet, like Polanski, Kubrick exuded a very European sensibility. He was acutely aware of his Central-European origins and, in terms of cinematic style, setting, and content, rarely strayed far from that continent. *Fear and Desire* (1953), *Paths of Glory* (1957), *Spartacus* (1960), *Clockwork Orange* (1971), and *Barry Lyndon* (1975) were all set in Europe, while *Lolita* (1962), *Dr. Strangelove* (1964), *2001* (1968), *Clockwork Orange, Barry Lyndon,* and *Eyes Wide Shut* (1999) were all adapted from novels by European authors. Indeed, Kubrick manifested a lifelong fascination with Central-European literature, in particular that of Kafka, Freud, Jung, Zweig, Mann, Hesse, and Schnitzler. He also displayed great familiarity with European classical music: Mozart, Beethoven, Strauss (Johan and Richard), Orff, Bartok, Penderecki, Ligeti, Mendelsohn, and Mahler. His work was punctuated by visual references to Gainsborough, Klimt, and others. He was fascinated with European history, in particular that of Ancient Rome, Germany, and Napoleon; the latter two subjects he wished, but never succeeded, to make films about. He admired the work of such European émigrés as Pabst, von Stroheim, Lang, and, above all, Ophuls, whose gliding camerawork influenced Kubrick throughout his career. Roger Lewis went even further to suggest, "Whether by accident or design . . . Kubrick (b. New York) is an English director—and his work shows an interest in the English sensibility, in peculiarly English themes: class, chivalry, hypocrisy, repression, patriotism, xenophobia."[13] Although not always immediately noticeable or obvious in their films, Polanski and Kubrick's Jewishness was indelibly inscribed, forming the bedrock of their filmmaking. As historian Paula Hyman has observed, "Even secularized Jews were likely to retain a strong ethnic Jewish identification, generally internally and reinforced from without."[14] Polanski and Kubrick shared a religious tradition rooted in millennia of European history, what George Steiner referred to as "the pride and the burden of the Jewish tradition."[15] Born in the interwar period (Kubrick b. 1928, Polanski b. 1933) and growing up during the Holocaust, the awareness of their inescapable Jewishness had a significant effect on both of them. Although Polanski and his father escaped extermination, Polanski's mother died in Auschwitz, and though Kubrick said very little about the subject, its impact is apparent in both of their films. The way they were rendered puts them into a single category: the Holocaust is approached obliquely, via analogies and metaphors which explore the very same issues raised by the Shoah. "Kubrick, who never realised his Holocaust film project, nonetheless had a post-Holocaust vision of the contemporary world."[16] A Jewish New Yorker with a Central-European heritage, Kubrick shared with his coreligionist émigré filmmakers—Wilder, Lang, Preminger, and von Sternberg—a reluctance ever to explain his intentions.[17] As Frederic

Raphael, who collaborated with Kubrick on the screenplay for *Eyes Wide Shut,* put it, "S.K. proceeds by indirection . . . [his] work could be viewed, as responding, in various ways, to the unspeakable (what lies beyond spoken explanation)."[18]

NORMALIZING AND POPULARIZING THE HOLOCAUST

In 1961, Hilberg published his magisterial and ground-breaking Holocaust study, *The Destruction of European Jewry.* In great detail, Hilberg laid bare the administrative process that cumulated in the Final Solution and how the Jews of Europe complied and even collaborated in their own destruction.[19] Through the administrative unit of the *Judenräte,* Jewish leaders in occupied Europe obediently selected Jews to be killed by the Nazis; without their cooperation, the extermination would not have been so efficient. Furthermore, Jewish denial and a willingness to be deceived were key components in their genocide. Jews even devised and used their own euphemistic language ("bakery" for crematoria; "Moslem" for someone destined for the gas chambers, and "Canada" for the stockpile of confiscated belongings), mirroring that of the Nazis themselves ("final solution," "solution possibilities," "special treatment," "cleansing operation," "deportation," "displacement," "resettlement," and "evacuation" for murder).[20] Unable to find a commercial publisher and at 800 pages in length, the book did not make a widespread impact. In fact, it was his writing about the role of Jewish Councils in carrying out Nazi directives, in which he was deemed to have gone too far, that led to difficulties in finding a publisher for his work.[21] Following in the wake of Hilberg, German-Jewish émigré philosopher Hannah Arendt published a series of articles that received much more publicity. Observing the trial for war crimes of Adolf Eichmann—one the chief architects of the Nazi genocide—in Jerusalem in 1961, she produced a twin thesis that genocide did not require monsters or pathological anti-Semites, but rather that Nazi bureaucrats like Eichmann were normal, banal even, and that the Jews acquiesced, even cooperated, in the genocide. "One cannot extract any diabolical or demonic profundity from Eichmann," she wrote and "if the Jewish people had really been unorganized and leaderless, there would have been chaos and plenty of misery but the total number of victims would hardly have been between four and a half and six million people."[22]

Arendt had relied heavily on Hilberg's path-breaking work, particularly in her account of the *Judenräte,* much to his displeasure.[23] Nevertheless, both were united in their desire to defy the notion that the Holocaust is beyond belief, that it transcends or resists historical and/or social scientific understanding, that it exists, ontologically, outside of ordinary time and logic. They dismissed any attempt to rationalize the Holocaust as a singular act of insanity. Instead, they sought to reduce the horror down to ordinariness, to find some explanation for it in ordinary, everyday behavior and tasks, rather than the incomprehensible, mystical, irrational, and theological. Their explanations attempted to shatter the notion of the Holocaust as an ineffable mystery of the human capacity for evil. Arendt, in particular, sought to demonstrate that evil was like a fungus, without depth or demonic dimension, and that "Eichmann is in each one of us."[24] As she wrote, "The deeds were monstrous, but the doer . . . was quite ordinary, commonplace, and neither demonic nor monstrous."[25] Consequently, she rejected dualistic and Manichean accounts of good and evil that relied, in effect, on fundamentally and irreducibly theological frameworks.[26] This required Arendt to dispense with metaphysical dualisms and "approach the problem of evil in an entirely secular setting."[27] She acknowledged that "it would have been very comforting indeed to believe that Eichmann was a monster."[28] This would certainly, as a contemporary journalist at the trial, Harry Mulisch, observed, have "allow[ed] us to believe in the Devil even if it was no longer possible to believe in God."[29] But, Arendt warned, what "stared one in the face at the trial" was Eichmann's "sheer thoughtlessness" and "lack of diabolical or demonic profundity."[30]

As a result, in part because of Hilberg and Arendt's efforts, secular Jewish intellectuals, particularly in the United States, became much more conscious of the devastation of the Holocaust. Furthermore, they were vocal about it, using the Shoah to mold US public opinion. Explicit comparisons between the Nazi genocide and nuclear mass death were increasingly frequent in the 1950s and early 1960s, for example.[31] Even Kubrick suggested it in his *Dr. Strangelove* (1964). But perhaps it was Betty Friedan who demonstrated this most strikingly by comparing Nazi concentration camps to American suburban homes in 1963. In one of the most potentially shocking passages of her *The Feminine Mystique,* Friedan claimed that "the women who 'adjust' as housewives, who grow up wanting to be 'just a housewife,' are in as much danger as the millions who walked to their own death in the concentration camps."[32] Friedan went on to explore this analogy for several pages, and then continued to use the phrase "comfortable concentration camps" to refer to suburban homes throughout the rest of the book. In the following years, the Civil Rights and Black Pride movements empowered Jews to focus on their own history. The anti-war movement; the revelation of American atrocities in Vietnam; and the rhetoric of "Nazis" and the "Nuremberg defense" of following unjust orders brought the Holocaust into sharper focus, as did Jewish anxiety before and relief following the Six Day War in May 1967.

Jews appeared to be under threat of annihilation for a second time in the space of quarter of a century, while the world seemingly stood by and gentiles appeared indifferent. Confronted with the horrifying prospect that Israel might be destroyed, comparisons began to be made with the Holocaust. Israel, it was believed, faced the specter of a second genocide within the space of a single generation. After twenty years of Jewish self-confidence in America, suddenly there was a perception that anti-Semitism was a real and present danger, not something of the past. There was a collective resolve against what was seen as the passivity of Jewish victims of the Nazis, a revulsion that spawned slogans like "Never Again." Prior to 1967, Israel, and the Holocaust—which served merely as an illustration of the manifestation of evil and was used to strike at optimistic theologies—possessed no special significance. The Six Day War changed all that, setting a new tone. It was also in 1967 that Hilberg's tome, originally published in hardback in 1961, was released in paperback and widely publicized, gaining a much greater audience than it had originally done. In that same year, Ira Levin published *Rosemary's Baby*.[33]

Meanwhile, between 1959 and 1967, the Holocaust became a much more familiar topic in Anglo-American popular culture. *The Diary of Anne Frank* (dir. George Stevens, 1959), which had been published and serialized in *Commentary* magazine, was adapted for the stage and then made into a major motion picture for which Shelley Winters (who would later go on to star in *Lolita*) won an Oscar for Best Supporting Actress. *Judgment at Nuremberg* (dir. Stanley Kramer, 1961), with camp footage, was released two years later, followed by *The Deputy* (Royal Shakespeare Company 1963, Broadway 1964), *The Pawnbroker* (dir. Sidney Lumet, 1964) (also with camp footage), and *The Man in the Glass Booth* (West End 1967, Broadway 1968), the latter based on the Eichmann trial, and Mel Brooks's *The Producers* (1967) which transmogrified Broadway chorus girls into goose-stepping SS troopers and a drug-fuelled hippie into Hitler. Finally, in 1978, two years before the release of *The Shining*, the landmark NBC miniseries *The Holocaust* hit American television screens.

DOWNPLAYING THE SUPERNATURAL

Rosemary's Baby and *The Shining* were both adapted from previously published novels. In Polanski's adaptation of Levin's novel, Rosemary Woodhouse (Mia Farrow) and her actor husband Guy (John Cassavetes) arrive in New York City where they rent an apartment in the Bramford, an old-fashioned building with a reputation for Satanism and cannibalism. Their new neighbors, an elderly couple, Minnie and Roman Castevets (Ruth Gordon and Sidney Blackmer), take a great interest in them, particularly Guy. Rosemary becomes pregnant. On the night of conception Rosemary imagines Satan raping her in a strange ceremony that includes the Castevets and their circle of friends. The Castevets, overjoyed by the news of Rosemary's pregnancy, take great interest in her condition. They recommend the society obstetrician Dr. Abraham Sapirstein (Ralph Bellamy). However, Rosemary suffers continuous pains, looks pale and withered, and has unusual cravings. She begins to suffer from paranoia, and for most of the film it is never clear whether this is the result of delusions or actual occurrences, until it is revealed that Guy and the Castevets have colluded in a sinister conspiracy to impregnate Rosemary with Satan's semen so she can sire and raise his child.

Kubrick, with the assistance of novelist Diane Johnson (whose *The Shadow Knows* [1974] had impressed him), adapted Stephen King's novel *The Shining* (1977).[34] Jack Torrance (Jack Nicholson), an ex-teacher and aspiring writer, accepts a job as the winter caretaker at The Overlook Hotel, set high in the Rocky Mountains in Colorado, despite the hotel's history of violence and "cabin fever." Jack moves his wife Wendy (Shelley Duval) and son Danny (Danny Lloyd) to the isolated hotel. Because of his ability to "shine"—his capacity to see events in the past and future—Danny fears the hotel. After several weeks, Jack's mental state declines and he experiences delusions, one of which is the hotel's dead caretaker, Delbert Grady (Philip Stone), who murdered his own family with an ax, ordering him to "correct," that is kill, his family.

Both Polanski and Kubrick made significant changes to their source material. Primarily, they downplayed the supernatural. Although Polanski generally stuck very close to the novel, where Levin made it unambiguously clear that witches used Rosemary to sire Satan's child, because Polanski did not believe in the immanent or supernatural, the unmistakably paranormal was unpalatable. He stated: "One aspect of *Rosemary's Baby* bothered me [. . .] Being an agnostic, I no more believed in Satan as evil incarnate than I believed in a personal god; the whole idea conflicted with my rational view of the world."[35] Consequently, as mentioned at the outset, God is absent from Polanski's film. Indeed, a *Time* magazine cover that Rosemary picks up in *Rosemary's Baby* even asked "Is God Dead?" The notion that God was dead was one that gained increasing popularity in the post-Holocaust world. Certainly Holocaust survivor and author Elie Wiesel grappled in his work with the theological significance of the Holocaust as "the site and occasion of [God's] abdication."[36] In 1958, Francois Mauriac wrote of Wiesel, "Dieu est mort . . . le Dieu d' Abraham, d'Isaac et de Jacob s'est à jamais dissipé, sous le regard de cet enfant, dans la fumée de l' holocauste humaine exigé par la Race, la plus goulue de toutes les idoles."[37] Translated in 1960, Mauriac's words became: "For him [Wiesel] . . . God is dead . . . the God of Abraham, of Isaac, of Jacob . . . has vanished forevermore . . . in the smoke of a human holocaust exacted by Race, the most voracious of all idols."[38] Instead, an element of ambiguity was introduced into the screenplay; for example, Polanski never showed the baby, leaving it up to the audience's imagination. In that way, it could all be explained away as paranoid delusions—underscored by the banal cup of tea that Minnie offers Rosemary at the end. This allowed a reading of Rosemary as unsound and hysterical or as a woman driven thus by Satanic forces. Polanski explained "*Rosemary's Baby* was an adaptation of a book which is serious about the Devil, but I had a hard time to be serious about it. That's why in *Rosemary's Baby* I never gave any supernatural hints—it could be all interpreted, in the final analysis, as some kind of neurosis on Rosemary's part: a figment of the imagination of a pregnant woman."[39]

Similarly, Kubrick and Johnson also reduced the supernatural elements of King's novel, which is clearly a ghost story that pits an innocent child against the external evil of the hotel. Although clearly psychologically damaged, Jack in the novel is presented as a decent man overcome by those supernatural forces rather than his own rage and alcoholism. Kubrick and Johnson eliminated much of Jack's back-story, including his anger at his treatment at the hands of his own father. They also removed fire hoses and topiary animals that come alive. As a result, Jack's motivation for murder is never entirely clear. The external conflict becomes an inner one waged within Jack. Where Jack is killed by the hotel's exploding boiler in the novel, in the film he freezes to death in a maze (which Kubrick added) after Danny deliberately bamboozles him. Kubrick certainly felt that "there's something inherently wrong with the human personality. There's an evil side to it. One of the things that horror stories can do is to show us the archetypes of the unconscious: we can see the dark side without having to confront it directly."[40] Where Polanski retained Rosemary's lapsed Catholicism, *The Shining* is explicitly devoid of religion *of any kind*. As Kubrick told King, "I don't believe in hell."[41] The closest Kubrick came to any religious sentiment is Jack's declaration, "God, I'd give anything for a drink. I'd give my god-damned soul for just a glass of beer!" Although a potential Faustian pact, it is hard to derive any sense of belief from it.

Compared to Old Horror, distinctions between sanity and madness, delusion, and reality are deliberately blurred, making us question whether what we are watching is real or the projection of evil possession. Taking off from the earlier *Psycho* and *Peeping Tom* (dir. Michael Powell, 1960)—both thematically post-Holocaust films—both *Rosemary* and *The Shining* can be described as "exercise[s] in the unreliability of subjective cognizance."[42] *Rosemary* is shot strictly from Rosemary's perspective, sustaining the notion that the supernatural is merely a series of coincidences, creating an anxiety about reality itself.[43] Increasingly isolated and alone, not knowing whom to trust, Rosemary is uncertain of even her own mind. Polanski established a strict ambiguity about just about everything. "He only showed parts of the action, often keeping the camera away from the people talking; motivations are hinted at, but rarely explained."[44] For example, the Castevets and their circle might be a coven, or simply a group of old friends to whom Rosemary ascribes in her mind supernatural powers.[45]

Indeed, rather than inhering in evil incarnate, the horror, whether real or imaginary, stems from the invasion of both public and private domestic space. Unlike in Old Horror, evil is no longer confined to the gothic mansion or castle or its inhabitants. Rather, because it attaches itself to ordinary people, which will be discussed in further detail below, it is present among us, in ordinary, mundane circumstances in our cities and neighborhoods, on the very streets where we live, inhabiting the world we know: a universe of apartment blocks, department stores, cafés, doctors' waiting rooms, neighbors' apartments, bedrooms, kitchens, and hotels in contemporary Manhattan and rural Colorado. Even the everyday life of the Third Reich, in which evil became normalized and banal, was characterized by habitual routines:

The Third Reich consisted first and foremost of a multitude of mundane everyday factors that structure people's lives in every imaginable society. Children attended school, and adults went to work or to the unemployment office. They paid their rent, did their shopping, ate breakfast and lunch, met up with friends and talked of sports or politics. While all these dimensions of everyday life may have become increasingly tinged with ideology and racism over the twelve years of the Third Reich, they remained habits and routines.[46]

Likewise, the films are located in domestic places, the setting of the middle- and upper-middle class home and hotel, the bourgeois (the characters are not poor), the *Heimlich* (Kubrick and Johnson both read Freud's essay "The Uncanny" when writing *The Shining* screenplay). The settings were familiar, homey, and right next door even.[47]

Drawing on the genre of the paranoid gothic, both films are set almost exclusively indoors: the Bramford building[48] and the Overlook Hotel. Both *Rosemary* and *The Shining* investigate how buildings and spaces become sites of terror. In this way they drew on the earlier *Psycho*, in particular, how "a clean, bright motel bathroom in the semirural American West becomes a place of sudden, savage murder."[49] Largely rejecting the lonely haunted house on the hill scenario (although this is certainly invoked), the settings are largely dull and domesticated, such as apartments, bedrooms, laundry rooms, doctors' surgeries, and waiting rooms. Both directors insisted on authenticity and realism, as well as the mundane. Kubrick, for example, went to great lengths to base his hotel on a composite of existing templates. Polanski made sure that the Woodhouses' apartment was "a conspicuously bright, clean space, the blandly cheerful vision of a glossy magazine distressingly unmarked by the obscene happenings it is witness to."[50] Like the Bates Motel, the evil hides behind "the constrictive façade of normalcy."[51] Key scenes in *The Shining* occur in "banal spaces."[52] As Cocks notes, "The horrors in *The Shining*, as in *Psycho*, are Kafkaesque since they take place not in the gloomy shadows of an old private home but in the bright public rooms of modern life and activity."[53] Even when Rosemary and Wendy escape outdoors, the settings are oppressive, offering no refuge. Rosemary has the feeling of being stalked and followed—she certainly fears she is as the film progresses. The way in which Kubrick shot the maze sequence similarly conveys that Wendy and Danny are being looked over by Jack, and the use of Steadicam introduces the specter of an unseen presence following Danny through the hotel and ultimately the maze.

Both films are replete with banalities, miscellany, and ephemera. "The characters, their conversations, their situations, and their actions are naturalistic, often to the point of banality."[54] Household brand names, popular culture such as magazines, television, and films are either seen or mentioned. In both films, we see "countless rituals of homemaking,"[55] such as Rosemary doing the laundry ("Pardon me, but I have to add the softener"), arranging throw pillows, measuring out the wallpaper, making meals, hosting a party, assembling shelves, building a home, and starting a family; Wendy preparing and serving meals, watching TV, or involved in childcare. Where "Shelley Duvall creates a figure of wifely banality that is itself frightening to behold,"[56] Rosemary presents the "image of fashionable normality, a character completely in accordance with her blandly pleasant taste in interior design. Her desires are for a child and a stable family life."[57]

The banality of language is also conspicuous, particularly in *The Shining*. The use of euphemism is especially striking. Jack talks of the "White Man's burden"[58] when complaining about his wife to Lloyd the barman who replies with "Women, can't live with 'em, can't live without 'em." Jack's repeated typed refrain is "All work and no play makes Jack a dull boy." When Jack recounts injuring Danny, "he cloaks his guilt in one of those self-exculpating euphemisms Kubrick makes a point of storing away for use in certain kinds of situations."[59] It was not fatherly rage that made him hit Danny: only "a momentary loss of muscular coordination." A similar "loss" will shortly lead him to swing an ax at his family. Furthermore, when he chops through the bathroom door, all he can do is parrot such pop cultural clichés as "Here's Johnny" and "Wendy, I'm home." In addition, Kubrick was insistent Grady "should talk in aphorisms": "Find some clichés about discipline, family."[60] Later he noted, "Euphemism is more frightening" and "Euphemisms not 'kill, kill, kill'."[61] Consequently, in an echo of the Nazis' use of euphemistic language, Grady, with the outward civility and reserve of a proper English butler, orders Jack to "correct" his family. Cloaked in the language of manners, Grady is, in reality, discussing murder.[62] This closely reflected Eichmann, who, Arendt observed, was unable to "utter a single sentence that was not a cliché."[63]

ORDINARY MEN[64]

One of Hilberg and Arendt's key findings was the ordinariness of those who might betray and/or kill that stood out. The Holocaust was carried out by ostensibly ordinary individuals—sane, God-fearing family men, many of whom simply claimed to be following orders. Hilberg, for example, wrote: "The bureaucrats who were drawn into the destruction process were not different in their moral makeup from the rest of the population. The German perpetrator was not a special kind of German."[65] This view surely influenced post-Holocaust horror; *Psycho*, for example, warned that "the true monster resides within us—not in some supernatural external agent (such as a vampire or mummy) foreign to human nature."[66] Polanski and Kubrick took this one step further. In both films, evil people are represented as very ordinary in their tastes and habits, even more down-to-earth than the people whom they try to corrupt. Some of them even possess deeply-held religious beliefs, albeit not God-fearing ones. Margaret Tarratt observes how Minnie "retains a concern for the wellbeing of her new carpet."[67] Even during the denouement, when Rosemary discovers what has been done to her child, Minnie offers her nothing more sinister than a cup of tea. Similarly, in *The Shining*, David A. Cook noticed that "we're being told that true horror is not extraordinary but surrounds us every day and, as Auden wrote of evil, 'sits with us at the dinner table'."[68] Jack begins as a superficially affectionate father and husband, engaging in "Blondie-and-Dagwood banter" with his wife, but which soon falls away to expose his underlying anger and frustration. "The friendly, smiling guy from Vermont becomes a raging fiend who goes after his family with an ax."[69]

Both films feature protagonists who are seemingly liberal, intellectual, artistic professionals. Hilberg observed that "the great majority of the officers of the *Einsatzgruppen*[70] were professional men." This included, for example, a physician, a professional opera singer, a Christian clergyman, and a large number of lawyers. He continued: "These men were in no sense hoodlums, delinquents, common criminals, or sex maniacs. Most were intellectuals. By and large, they were in their thirties, and undoubtedly they wanted a certain measure of power, fame, and success."[71] Guy is an aspiring actor and Jack is a former schoolteacher aiming to become a writer. The significant fact is that, as Arendt showed, like Eichmann *inter alia* both are ordinary, even mediocre, men given opportunities to rise far beyond their stations through Faustian pacts. Even noted Nazi-hunter Simon Wiesenthal was moved to describe him as a

> weak colorless, shabby fellow in a glass cell between two Israeli police officers; they looked more interesting and remarkable than he did.... There was nothing demonic about him; he looked like an accountant who was afraid to ask for a raise.... He wore a cheap dark suit and presented the picture of an empty, two-dimensional cardboard figure.[72]

Lacking the black uniform with the death's-head insignia, Wiesenthal even suggested to the prosecutor, senior District Attorney Gideon Hausner, that Eichmann be dressed in an authentic uniform.[73] Like Eichmann *inter alia*, both Jack and Guy are obsessed with their standing, status, and careers, making them very susceptible to the influence of others, who demand malign sacrifices. Roman seduces Guy with promises of a successful career in entertainment. Grady entices Jack into killing his family with ingratiating, aggrandizing, and toadying comments that Jack is in charge. As Rosemary recognizes that the Satan worshippers' success in their nefarious acts requires the willing participation of her husband, when she spits in his face at the end of the film, "she expresses in this way much greater contempt than she has for any of Guy's Satanic friends."[74] If anything, they at least were motivated by religious fervor, whereas he is driven by pure mendacity. Throughout *Rosemary*, Polanski draws upon recent US culture to suggest the parallel: several times we view William Whyte's study of post-war conformism, *The*

Organization Man (1956), "a study of a certain type of modern-day Faustian man who sells his soul for the collective good of his corporation."[75] In *The Shining,* Jack willingly obeys orders; in the words of that companion book to Whyte's, *The Lonely Crowd,* he is an "other-directed" type.[76] They demonstrated that even the "most civilized minds contain barbarism."[77]

Furthermore, Arendt wrote of the "unspeakable horror of the deeds and the undeniable ludicrousness of the man who perpetrated them," leading her to conclude that "[d]espite all the efforts of the prosecution, everybody could see that this man was a 'monster,' but it was difficult indeed not to suspect that he was a clown."[78] The evildoers of both films are not simply ordinary but comical even. The performances of Gordon and Blackmer produce a laughable effect. Gordon played Minnie with "such humor and eccentricity that she became a small, nosy clown with enough energy to fill a room."[79] Roman appears henpecked and clumsy (as when he spills the drinks onto the new carpet). Minnie berates him, "Sometimes I wonder how come you're the leader of anything" and we wonder, too. As Barbara Leaming argues, "With them, [Polanski] thwarted any assumption on the part of the audience that evil characters would appear grim and sinister. Instead, his witch and warlock are jovial, even zany types, difficult to take seriously as emissaries of Satan."[80] Similarly, in *The Shining,* Nicholson's performance was so over-the-top that, for some, it bordered on the absurd, eliciting inappropriate audience laughter. Kroll, for example, felt that Jack's "metamorphosis into evil has its comic sides as well—which makes us remember that the devil is the ultimate clown."[81] Yet, as Marsha Kinder and Berverle Houston commented, "the silliness of the demonic killers in no way lessens their capacity for evil."[82]

JEWISH COLLABORATION

In both films, Jews play significant roles in collaborating with and assisting evil. I have argued elsewhere that Jack can be read as conceptually Jewish through a series of perhaps oblique signifiers.[83] It is also possible to read the Castevets in a similar fashion. Roman is a wanderer, who has been "everywhere." He has "piercing eyes," and we learn that he has changed his name from Steven Marcato to *Roman*[84] Castavets to hide his dubious origins—all traits with historical Jewish associations. Minnie is a *baalebusteh* who cooks and *kibitzes,* nagging her henpecked husband ("just watch the carpet," she warns him), and browbeating Guy and Rosemary until they cannot refuse. As mentioned above, at one point, she is heard through the walls of the apartment shouting at her husband, questioning his leadership abilities. Minnie manifests other stereotypical Jewish tics. She is nosy; as Rosemary observes, "she's the nosiest person I've ever seen. You know she actually asked the prices of things." She wears glasses, as well as a great deal of jewelry and bangles, which clack together when she gesticulates with her hands. Her taste in interior decoration is vulgar. She displays a lack of civility and decorum. In addition to constantly poking her nose into Rosemary's business, even ordinary conversations are conducted in a loud voice, and her body language lacks reserve. She has poor table manners, consuming her dessert in an uncivilized fashion, an elbow on the table while stuffing large chunks of cake into her mouth, and aggressively chewing. She pronounces "mousse" as "mouse."[85] As Norman Podhoretz wrote, the "association of Jewishness with vulgarity and lack of cultivation" is fairly widespread "not least among Jews."[86]

Dr. Abraham Sapirstein, Rosemary's obstetrician, is more obviously Jewish. Virginia Wright Wexman describes him as "a sinister, bearded Jewish physician."[87] Both his names suggest his ethnicity/religion, even if it is nowhere mentioned in the film. His surname combines two words of Hebrew and German origin respectively to mean "sapphire stone," an item of biblical significance. Crucially, his first name is Abraham, connecting him not only with the biblical patriarch, the father of the Jewish people, but also to the binding of Isaac, which I have argued elsewhere lies at the heart of *The Shining*.[88] In the novel, unlike the other characters, his ethnicity is explicitly foregrounded: Minnie describes him as "Abe Sapirstein. A Jewish man. He delivers all the Society babies," while Roman says, "He's a brilliant man with all the sensitivities of his much-tormented race."[89] It is not clear why Levin specifically draws attention to Sapirstein's origins, but in so doing he suggests that even Jews are complicit in collaborating with evil. Sapirstein certainly aids and abets the forces of darkness.

Finally, Minnie introduces Rosemary to a "famous dentist" named Dr. Shand at a New Year's party. Shand gives Sapirstein, who is also present, a knowing, conspiratorial glance, and we learn that he made the chain for the charm that Minnie gave Rosemary earlier in the film. Shand was played by Phil Leeds, a well-known Jewish comedian and character actor. Together, this group, in seeking to procure a child for Satan, echoes age-old Judeophobic canards.[90] It is also are a sign that the presence of evil can be anywhere and is not confined to a single group. In this way, both films explore the individual or group's complicity and willingness to commit violence in the service of a higher power.

Denial was a key part of allowing the Holocaust to happen. Yet, at the same time, not to the extent that no one knew. Consequently, a key element of both films is the denial of reality. Note how Morrison's comment about the pendant charm Minnie gives Rosemary has uncanny echoes in this respect: "exuding an abhorrent reek that would surely be masked if its benefactors were really concerned to hide anything. Instead they chirp, 'You get used to it!'—a telling phrase since the film is ultimately about how it is possible to adjust to the most unspeakable horrors."[91] Morrison continues:

> The "secrets" of *Rosemary's Baby* are almost entirely rhetorical; from the start, the audience is cued to see through them and invited to participate in the excruciating irony of the fact that Rosemary is the only one who can't. The movie's horror lies not in Rosemary's paranoid

imagining of the ills that are not there but in her inability to image the evils everywhere around her, however instantly visible they are.[92]

Rosemary remarks "there *are* no witches, really." It is significant in this respect, then, that the actor who Guy replaces inexplicably goes blind—a metonym for the denial and blindness with which the couple surround themselves. Jack also denies that much of what he sees is the result of internal delusions and his own ability to shine. At one point, he even denies his violent nature to Wendy: "I'm not gonna hurt ya," he reassures her. "I'm just going to bash your brains in."

QUESTIONING AUTHORITY

The representatives of institutions that sanctify and sanction order—doctors, dentists, psychiatrists, caretakers, etc.—are developed with considerable ambiguity. Authority rooted in professional expertise, scientific knowledge, doctors, and medicine are a source of distrust and called into question in both films, reflecting a dim view of modernity, particularly medicine and psychiatry. Both obstetricians fail Rosemary. Sapirstein is positively sinister, injecting her, and prescribing her unorthodox herbal remedies, while dismissing her concerns and ignoring her deteriorating mental and physical condition. This leads one of her friends to describe him as a "sadistic nut." Sapirstein is part of the Castevets' circle, collaborating to procure Rosemary's child to be used in their devilish plans. Although it is unclear as to whether Dr. Hill is part of the conspiracy or not, and his intervention is relatively minor given that he is only introduced to Rosemary very late in her pregnancy, he deceives her trust and willingly betrays her to Guy and Sapirstein, his superior colleague whom he blindly obeys explicitly against Rosemary's wishes. While medical authorities are less present in *The Shining* and less malign, they are still viewed as incompetent. Danny visits a child psychologist, but she proves no assistance in establishing why Danny is able to "shine." In these ways, both films' "attack on science is part of a larger condemnation of sophisticated, decadent, bourgeoise [sic] culture."[93]

Furthermore, both directors include references which may be read as implicitly invoking Nazi eugenics research, in particular evoking Josef Mengele's notorious pseudo-scientific "medical" experimentation at Auschwitz. When Rosemary first sees her baby, described in Levin's novel as golden yellow with vertical black slits, she believes that his eyes have been subject to medical experimentation:

ROSEMARY: *What have you done to it? What have you done to its eyes?* [They stir and look to Mr. Castavet.]
MR. CASTAVET: He has His Father's eyes. [Rosemary looks at him, looks at Guy—whose eyes are hidden behind a hand—looks at Mr. Castavet again.]

ROSEMARY: What are you *talking* about? Guy's eyes are *normal*. What have you *done* to him, you maniacs?

In *The Shining,* in contrast, Kubrick used subliminal editing to insert images of murdered sisters in blue dresses who, although not actually twins, appear to be such, during visions in which Danny sees torrents of blood, gushing out of elevator doors and daubed over the walls and corridors of the Overlook. Both instances suggest Mengele's "work."[94] He was also fascinated by eye color, specifically heterochromia, a condition that causes one iris to be a different color than the other. By trial and error, he attempted to fabricate blue eyes from brown. Twins allowed Mengele to conduct experiments on one subject, while using the other as a "control."[95] In his *The Boys from Brazil* (1976), Levin explained: "he did thousands of experiments on children, twins, trying to make good Aryans, trying to change brown eyes into blue eyes with chemicals, through the genes."[96]

In his denials that *Rosemary* "should be seen as some kind of allegory about the Holocaust" together with his statement that Polanski "wished to avoid an overly facile analogy between the story content of his film and the Holocaust," Joe McElhaney only seems to confirm the suspicion.[97] While Polanski removed a line of dialogue from Levin's book in which one of Rosemary's friends, distraught over her appalling physical appearance at the hands of Sapirstein, compares her to a concentration camp victim ("You look like Miss Concentration Camp of 1966. Are you sure this doctor knows what he's doing?"[98]), this may have been done to render the parallel less explicit and more oblique, sharing with Kubrick a refusal to tell the audience what to think.[99] As McElhaney put it, but which is just as apt for Kubrick's treatment of *The Shining,* "Polanski's strategy is to mute some of the more overt ethnic, racial, and political elements of the novel."[100] Nonetheless, an audience familiar with Friedan's comparing the perils of domesticity to a "comfortable concentration camp" would have surely made the connection already.

At the same time, McElhaney concedes:

> the treatment of New York in the film is one that is often informed by an experience of urban space shaped by that traumatic historical moment. Rosemary is part of a long line of Polanski characters who are fugitives or exiles from their own cultures, hiding out in broom closets until the inevitable knock of the door arrives [. . .] Rosemary herself functions as the victim of collective terror and betrayal, one who within twentieth-century history has assumed a most vivid enactment through fascism and the Holocaust.[101]

Added to this is Le Caen's observation that to suggest that *Rosemary's Baby*

> drew deeply upon the horror of Polanski's traumatic childhood as a Jew in occupied Poland would, until recently, have been no more than a prime example of the sort of psychologically presumptuous approach

to his cinema that he is so notoriously scathing towards. Yet, this "biographical speculation" is worth mentioning, however inconclusively, simply because is almost impossible that anyone [. . .] could have watched the scenes in Polanski's Holocaust saga *The Pianist* [2002], detailing Wladysaw Szpilman's period on the run hiding in various flats, without a shock of recognition. These approximately three reels provide nothing more than a sort of Ur-text for the earlier horror films. All the claustrophobia of the "apartment" trilogy returns in these images of a persecuted man locked in an apartment, obliged to keep silent out of mortal terror of the neighbours, living or dying on the basis of whom he chooses to trust.[102]

Creatures of their times, Polanski and Kubrick reinvented an old genre both to reflect on contemporary events (Vietnam, the Six-Day War, and other manifestations of contemporaneous violence) as well as to reflect upon what took place several decades earlier. For that reason their works can be seen as Holocaust films, even though the Shoah is never mentioned in them. McElhaney concludes, "Polanski's intervention as a European auteur with a strong visual and dramatic style, indeed a style arguably informed by his specific experience of historical upheaval and trauma, causes *Rosemary's Baby* to assume an even more powerful resonance."[103] Such a judgment is just as apt for Kubrick and *The Shining*.

CONCLUSION

Lacking an eschatological framework, in which secular atheism and agnosticism prevail, both films are gloomy, dark, and pessimistic in outlook. Ambiguity and confusion are privileged over certainty and morality. Thus neither ends happily, in which evil is definitively defeated, or in which cheerful emotions ultimately dominate over dark feelings. While Jack dies at the end of *The Shining*, "[w]hat made *Rosemary's Baby* such a radical break from the past was that unlike almost every other film about the battle with the Devil, there was no fight to the finish at the end."[104] Both also pose more questions than they answer, ending, as Zinoman put it, "with more of a question mark than an exclamation point."[105] We do not know what happens to Rosemary and the baby after the film ends. Although there is a fight at the finish at the end of *The Shining*, unlike King's novel, there is no epilogue to Kubrick's film showing us what happened to Danny, Wendy, or the hotel. Meanwhile, the reincarnation of Jack in a photograph leaves us with a host of queries regarding what we have just seen. Polanski, in ending with a reversal of the opening shot, pulling away from the Bramford to revisit the New York skyline, similarly suggests a repetition of history.[106] Therefore, what Polanski and Kubrick are attacking is the impulse to derive comfort from the familiar while treating the past as static history. Their central message is "that there is no message. The world does not make sense. Evil exists, and there is nothing you can do about it."[107] If there is a God—and it is not clear that either is suggesting there is—then He is dead and there is nothing in His place.

NOTES

1. Ira Levin, *The Boys from Brazil* (London: Corsair, 2011), 145. (Original work published 1976.)
2. Geoffrey Cocks, *The Wolf at the Door: Stanley Kubrick, History, and the Holocaust* (New York: Peter Lang, 2004).
3. Raul Hilberg, *The Destruction of the European Jews* (New York: Quadrangle, 1961), revised and republished in 1967 (all quotations are taken from this version); Hannah Arendt, *Eichmann in Jerusalem: A Report on the Banality of Evil* (London: Penguin Books, 1963).
4. Henry Bial, *Acting Jewish: Negotiating Ethnicity on the American Stage and Screen* (Ann Arbor, MI: The University of Michigan Press, 2005); Nathan Abrams, *The New Jew in Film: Exploring Jewishness and Judaism in Contemporary Cinema* (New Brunswick, NJ: Rutgers University Press, 2012).
5. Jon Stratton, *Coming Out Jewish* (London: Routledge, 2000), 300.
6. Ibid., 70.
7. Joel Rosenberg, "Jewish Experience on Film—An American Overview," in *American Jewish Year Book, 1996* (New York: The American Jewish Committee, 1996), 26.
8. Bial, *Acting Jewish*, 70.
9. Caroline J.S. Picart and David A. Frank Picart, "Horror and the Holocaust: Genre Elements in *Schindler's List* and *Psycho*," in *The Horror Film*, ed. Stephen Prince (New Brunswick, NJ: Rutgers University Press, 2004), 206–23.
10. Peter Novick, *The Holocaust in American Life* (Boston: Houghton Mifflin, 1999).
11. Ron Rosenbaum, "Gooseflesh: The Strange Turn Toward Horror," *Harper's*, September, 1979.
12. Quoted in Stephen Rebello, *Alfred Hitchcock & the Making of Psycho* (London: Marion Boyars, 2013), 192. Significantly, quoting Shakespeare, Hitchcock opened his earlier *Spellbound* (1945) with those very words, "the fault . . . lies not in our stars but in ourselves."
13. Roger Lewis, *The Life and Death of Peter Sellers* (London: Arrow, 1994), 777.
14. Paula Hyman, *Gender and Assimilation in Modern Jewish History: The Roles and Representation of Women* (Seattle: University of Washington Press, 1995), 91.
15. George Steiner, *The Death of Tragedy* (New Haven, CT: Yale University Press, 1961), 4.
16. John Orr and Elżbieta Ostrowska, *The Cinema of Roman Polanski: Dark Spaces of the World* (London: Wallflower, 2006), 142.
17. Michel Ciment, *Kubrick: The Definitive Edition* (New York: Faber and Faber, 2003), 59.
18. Frederic Raphael, *Eyes Wide Open: A Memoir of Stanley Kubrick* (London: Orion, 1999), 150.
19. In 1975, Kubrick asked his brother-in-law, Jan Harlan, to read Hilberg's book; in 1980, he sent a copy to Michael Herr, describing it as "*monumental.*" Herr recalled how Kubrick was "absorbed" by it. Shortly thereafter, Kubrick wrote to Hilberg asking him to recommend a novel on which he could base a film

about the Holocaust. Michael Herr, *Kubrick* (London: Pan, 2000), 10; Geoffrey Cocks, "Death by Typewriter: Stanley Kubrick, the Holocaust, and *The Shining*," in *Depth of Field: Stanley Kubrick, Film, and the Uses of History*, eds. Geoffrey Cocks, James Diedrick, and Glenn Perusek (Madison, WI: The University of Wisconsin Press, 2006), 196.
20. Hilberg, *Destruction*, 652, 658, 668.
21. See Valerie Hartouni, *Visualizing Atrocity: Arendt, Evil, and the Optics of Thoughtlessness* (New York: New York University Press, 2012), 133 n. 25.
22. Arendt, *Eichmann*, 125, 287.
23. Hartouni, *Visualizing*, 30.
24. Hannah Arendt, *The Jew as Pariah*, ed. Ron Feldman (New York: Grove Press, 1978), 251.
25. Hannah Arendt, *The Life of the Mind, Vol. I: Thinking* (New York: Harcourt, Brace Jovanovich, 1977), 4.
26. Hartouni, *Visualizing*, 70.
27. Arendt, cited in Hartouni, *Visualizing*, 71.
28. Arendt, *Eichmann*, 276.
29. Harry Mulisch, *Criminal Case 40/61: The Trial of Adolf Eichmann* (Philadelphia: University of Pennsylvania Press, 2005), 50.
30. Arendt, *Eichmann*, 276.
31. See Jon Petrie, "The Secular Word HOLOCAUST: Scholarly Myths, History, and 20th Century Meanings," *Journal of Genocide Research* 2:1 (2000), 31–63.
32. Betty Friedan, *The Feminine Mystique* (New York; W. W. Norton, 1963), 294.
33. Ira Levin, *Rosemary's Baby* (New York: Pegasus, 2010) (Original work published 1967.)
34. Diane Johnson, *The Shadow Knows* (New York: Penguin, 1974); Stephen King, *The Shining* (New York: Doubleday, 1977).
35. Quoted in Denis Meikle, *Roman Polanski: Odd Man Out* (London: Reynolds & Hearn, 2006), 131.
36. See Naomi Seidman, "Elie Wiesel and the Scandal of Jewish Rage," *Jewish Social Studies*, 3:1 (Fall 1996), 2.
37. Francois Mauriac, *Le Figaro Littéraire* (June 7, 1958), 4. "Cet enfant" refers to Wiesel.
38. Petrie, "HOLOCAUST," 42.
39. Quoted in Meikle, *Roman*, 131.
40. Quoted in Norman Kagan, *The Cinema of Stanley Kubrick* (London: Continuum, 1989), 203.
41. Quoted in Joe Dunthorne, "Was Stephen King Right to Hate Stanley Kubrick's Shining?" *The Guardian*, April 6, 2013. Available at http://m.guardian.co.uk/film/2013/apr/06/king-kubrick-shining-adaptation. Last accessed April 2013.
42. James Morrison, *Roman Polanski* (Urbana, IL: University of Illinois Press, 2007), 61.
43. Jason Zinoman, *Shock Value: How a Few Eccentric Outsiders Gave Us Nightmares, Conquered Hollywood, and Invented Modern Horror* (New York: Penguin Press 2011), 21.
44. Ibid.
45. In the novel, the way that the coven is described, resembles that of the SS: "initiation ceremonies" and "a secret mark of membership somewhere on [the] body." Levin, *Rosemary's*, 194.
46. Sönke Neitzel and Harald Welzer, *Soldaten: On Fighting, Killing, and Dying: The Secret World War II Tapes of German POWs*, trans. Jefferson Chase (London: Simon & Schuster, 2012), 27.
47. Zinoman, *Shock*, 209.

48. In the script, the Bramford has "a main gate."
49. Cocks, *Wolf*, 169.
50. Maximilian le Caen, "Into the Mouth of Madness: *The Tenant*," in *The Cinema of Roman Polanski: Dark Spaces of the World*, eds. John Orr and Elzbieta Ostrowska (London: Wallflower Press, 2003), 122.
51. Ibid., 122.
52. Philip Kuberski, "Plumbing the Abyss: Stanley Kubrick's Bathrooms," *Arizona Quarterly*, 60:4 (Winter 2004), 139.
53. Cocks, "Death," 199.
54. Geoffrey Cocks "Bringing the Holocaust Home: The Freudian Dynamics of Kubrick's *The Shining*," *Psychoanalytic Review*, 78:1 (1991), 110.
55. Morrison, *Roman*, 65.
56. Kroll, "Stanley."
57. Le Caen, "Into," 123.
58. This is taken verbatim from the novel.
59. Walker, *Stanley*, 300–01.
60. Stanley Kubrick, "Annotated Chapters from the Novel," 407, SK/15/1/2, Stanley Kubrick Archives, London (hereafter "SKA").
61. Ibid., 443; Kubrick, "Copy of Annotated Novel Text, 'The Shine'," SK/15/1/3, SKA.
62. Walker et al., *Stanley*, 307.
63. Arendt, *Eichmann*, 48–49.
64. This was later the title of a famous study: Christopher Browning's *Ordinary Men: Reserve Police Battalion 101 and the Final Solution in Poland* (revised edn., New York: Harper Perennial, 1992).
65. Hilberg, *Destruction*, 649.
66. James F. Iaccino, *Psychological Reflections on Cinematic Terror: Jungian Archetypes in Horror Films* (Westport, CT: Praeger, 1994), 39. *Psycho* itself can be read as another sub-textual Holocaust film. In 1945, Alfred Hitchcock served as "treatment advisor" (in effect, a film editor) for a Holocaust documentary produced by the British Army. The film, which recorded the liberation of Nazi concentration camps but which also documented Nazi atrocities, remained unreleased until 1985, when it was completed by PBS Frontline and distributed under the title *Memory of the Camps* (USA). Arguably, this documentary indelibly informed several key elements of *Psycho*, which, in turn, became the template for the psychological horror/slasher film on which both *Rosemary's Baby* and *The Shining* subsequently drew. See Nathan Abrams "The 'sub-epidermic' Shoah: *Barton Fink*, the Migration of the Holocaust, and Contemporary Cinema," *POST SCRIPT: Essays in Film and the Humanities*, 32:2 (Winter/Spring 2013), 6–19. Furthermore, Ed Bloch, author of the novel on which *Psycho* was based, wrote that serial murderer Ed Gein was "given to perversions in the time-honored tradition of the Nazi death camps." Quoted in Rebello, *Alfred Hitchcock*, 13. Gein, it was noted, was particularly obsessed with Nazi medical experimentation.
67. Margaret Tarratt, "*Rosemary's Baby*," *Screen* 10 (1969), 95.
68. David A. Cook, "American Horror: *The Shining*," *Literature/Film Quarterly*, 12:1 (1984), 2.
69. Jack Kroll, "Stanley Kubrick's Horror Show," *Newsweek Magazine*, June 2, 1980.
70. The mobile SS and Police units initially tasked with extermination in the Nazi-occupied territories.
71. Hilberg, *Destruction*, 189.
72. Zvi Aharoni and William Dietl, *Operation Eichmann: The Truth about the Pursuit, Capture, and Trial* (New York: Wiley, 1996), 171.
73. Hartouni, *Visualizing*, 36 n. 134.

164 Nathan Abrams

74. Ewa Kolasińska, quoted in Ewa Mazierska, *Roman Polanski: The Cinema of a Cultural Traveller* (London: IB Tauris, 2007), 122.
75. Joe McElhaney, "Urban Irrational: *Rosemary's Baby,* Polanski, New York," in *The City that Never Sleeps: New York and the Filmic Imagination,* ed. Murray Pomerance (New Brunswick, NJ: Rutgers University Press, 2007), 212; William H. Whyte, *The Organization Man* (New York: Simon & Schuster, 1956).
76. Alexander Walker, Sybil Taylor, and Ulrich Ruchti, *Stanley Kubrick, Director: A Visual Analysis* (revised and expanded edn., London: Weidenfeld & Nicholson, 1999), 297; David Riesman, Reuel Denney, and Nathan Glazer, *The Lonely Crowd: A Study of the Changing American Culture* (New Haven, CT: Yale University Press, 1950).
77. Zinoman, *Shock,* 209.
78. Arendt, *Eichmann,* 54.
79. Julia Ain-Krupa, *Roman Polanski: A Life in Exile* (Santa Barbara, CA: Praeger, 2010), 65.
80. Barbara Leaming, *Polanski, the Filmmaker as Voyeur: A Biography* (New York: Simon and Schuster, 1981), 85.
81. Kroll, "Stanley."
82. Marsha Kinder and Berverle Houston, "Seeing is Believing: *The Exorcist* and *Don't Look Now,*" in *American Horrors: Essays on the Modern American Horror Film,* ed. Gregory A. Waller (Urbana, IL: University of Illinois Press, 1987), 45.
83. Nathan Abrams, "'A double set of glasses': Stanley Kubrick and the Midrashic Mode of Interpretation," in *De-Westernizing Film Studies,* eds. Saer Maty Ba and Will Higbee (New York: Routledge, 2012), 141–51.
84. The coincidence in his and the director's first names being the same seems too heavy to pass mention.
85. Gordon later played a fun-loving free-spirited elderly Jewish Holocaust survivor in *Harold and Maude* (1971, dir. Hal Ashby).
86. Norman Podhoretz, *Making It* (New York: Random House, 1967), 161.
87. Virginia Wright Wexman, "The Trauma of Infancy in Roman Polanski's *Rosemary's Baby,*" in *American Horrors,* ed. Waller, 40.
88. See Abrams, "Double." Significantly, when Rosemary seeks refuge, it is to Dr. Hill in the Mount Sinai hospital that she runs and where she is betrayed. During Rosemary's dream, we see Michelangelo's paintings on the ceiling of the Sistine Chapel, including a ram's head, suggesting the sacrifice of Isaac.
89. Levin, *Rosemary's,* 109, 110.
90. Mazierska, *Roman,* 183.
91. Morrison, *Roman,* 67.
92. Ibid., 61.
93. Kinder and Houston, "Seeing," 46.
94. Neitzel and Welzer observe how if the murder of human beings is categorized as "work," then it is not interpreted as a crime and hence is normalized. See their *Soldaten,* 19.
95. Aaron Kerner, *Film and the Holocaust: New Perspectives on Dramas, Documentaries, and Experimental Films* (New York: Continuum, 2011), 157.
96. Levin, *The Boys,* 43. In the 1978 film version, directed by Franklin J. Schaffner, Ezra Lieberman (Laurence Olivier) explains: "He was the chief doctor of Auschwitz, who killed 2.5 million people, experimented with children—Jewish and non-Jewish—using twins mostly, injecting blue dyes into their eyes to make them acceptable Aryans." *The Boys from Brazil* was one in a spate of Nazi-themed books and films released contemporaneously with New Horror in the late 1960s and 1970s.
97. McElhaney, "Urban," 204, 212.

98. Levin, *Rosemary's*, 154.
99. However, he did retain a, perhaps revealing, reference to a book, *All of Them Witches:* "This was published in 1933. There were covens in Europe."
100. McElhaney, "Urban," 212.
101. Ibid., 204, 212.
102. Le Caen, "Into," 124–25.
103. McElhaney, "Urban," 212.
104. Zinoman, *Shock*, 80.
105. Ibid.
106. In this sense it is insightful, then, that Michael Herr recalled when he told Kubrick that he didn't feel like reading *The Destruction of the European Jews*, he replied: "'No, Michael [. . .] The book you don't want to read right now is *The Destruction of the European Jews, Part Two.*'" Michael Herr, "Kubrick," *Vanity Fair* (August 1999). Available at www.vanityfair.com/hollywood/classic/features/kubrick-199908. Last accessed April 2013.
107. Zinoman, *Shock*, 209.

10 Postsecular Ethics
The Case of Iñárritu's *Biutiful*

Robert Sinnerbrink

> "Those people, I always call them the invisibles. I think that European society in the last 15 years has been impacted in a way that they haven't even realized yet. And the way these people live is just amazing. I mean, there are one million Chinese immigrants in the UK now, but nobody wants to really accept or even to see it. And the conditions of these people who are looking for a couple of bucks more, unfortunately sometimes leads to exploitation. So I did a lot of journalistic exploration while I was making the movie, so the people and the places are real, and newspapers are full of those stories every day, so this is real."
>
> Alejandro González Iñárittu[1]

A man dying of cancer assists his brother in brokering a deal with a Spanish construction company who want to hire illegal Chinese workers. Disturbed at the exploitative conditions they have to endure, the man purchases some cheap gas heaters to keep them warm at night as they sleep, under lock and key, in a warehouse basement. One morning the warehouse owner unlocks the door, as he does every morning, and finds all of the workers, including a number of children, dead from asphyxiation. The warehouse owners panic, wondering what to do with the bodies. Later, one of the owners kills his partner and lover and escapes, seemingly without punishment. The dying man who purchased the heaters is distraught, feels guilty for their deaths, though he does not go to the police. He experiences guilt, remorse, and remains haunted by the spirits of the dead, turning to his spiritual confidante for advice. He tries to ask those who have died for their forgiveness, as he prepares himself and his broken family—his unstable, bipolar wife, his daughter and young son—for his own looming death from cancer. In death he is reunited with his own father, who died as a much younger man, fleeing from Franco's Spain to Mexico.

This scenario is taken from *Biutiful* (2010), a film by Mexican director Alejandro González Iñárritu, renowned for his cinematic engagement with the moral uncertainties and political complexities of everyday life in multicultural societies. His most recent features, *Babel* (2006) and *Biutiful*, present contrasting narratives that make explicit the challenges confronting marginalized subjects in a globalized world marked by pervasive social, religious, economic, and political conflicts. His films appear, moreover, in a cultural-historical moment of reflection, notably in Europe, on the question of *postsecularism:* the recognition of a resurgence of religion in public and political spheres, an acknowledgment of the overlapping boundaries of religion and culture. This postsecular awareness challenges the idea of a "secular modernity" and questions the viability of secular humanism as a framework for settling cultural conflicts and political disputes.[2] Indeed, the question of postsecularism has become pressing in a European context marked by divisions between cultural and ethnic minorities, economic recession and social instability, resurgent nationalism, and contentious debates over religion and politics. What can films such as *Biutiful,* with its culturally hybrid perspective on contemporary Europe, contribute to these debates? How might cinema "do ethics" in a postsecularist and pluralist cultural context?

In what follows, I address these questions by exploring Iñárritu's *Biutiful* as a case of postsecular cinematic ethics: a film aiming to evoke a transformative ethical experience that resonates with the postsecular turn in contemporary cultural practice.[3] To explore this, I contrast the network narrative structure of *Babel* with the more conventional narrative structure of *Biutiful,* which condenses the forces of globalization in the story of a dying man's attempts to reconcile faith, family, and survival in the impoverished underclass of Barcelona. I also contrast *Biutiful* with the Dardenne brothers' *La promesse* (1996), a film that explores similar themes within a European context (Belgium rather than Spain) but which deals with them in an aesthetically distinctive manner, one which highlights significant differences in the relationship between secularist and postsecularist approaches to ethical experience. Inárritu's thoughtful attention to contingency, mortality, bodily vulnerability, and moral ambiguity—not to mention the existential significance of religiosity—are striking examples, I claim, of a postsecular "cinematic ethics." By this term I mean films that use the aesthetic power of cinema to elicit an ethical experience of otherness; films that stage dramatic situations that complicate our ethical responsiveness while challenging reductive moral judgment that abstracts away from the social, economic, and political forces shaping the characters' situation. Cinematic ethics, from this point of view, expresses cinema's potential to affect and transform how we think and feel: the power to evoke an ethical experience that can prompt moral, psychological, even spiritual transformation and the "conversion" of our beliefs, attitudes, and ways of apprehending and responding to the world.

This question of ethical experience has become increasingly significant in light of recent interest in spiritual-religious questions within contemporary cinema. Many recent films, for example, explore the porous boundaries between ethical and religious experience.[4] Inárritu's *Biutiful* is one such film, striving to elicit an ethical experience that is transformative rather than illustrative, performative rather than abstract, experiential rather than didactic. My approach will thus focus on cinema's power to evoke ethical experience: to challenge and question through affective and emotional engagement—questioning and transforming our attitudes in ways that have cultural, political, even spiritual-religious significance.

CINEMA AND/AS ETHICS

Cinema has long been theorized as a medium with a power to enlighten and to manipulate. It can manipulate audiences through the seductive imposition of ideology; or it can emancipate them by interrupting the illusory transparency of the image. Despite the traditional focus on ideology in film theory, far less attention has been given to cinema's capacity for "aesthetic" persuasion: its capacity to evoke an ethical experience that is not reducible to explicit normative principles, propositional content, or fixed moral judgments; its power to elicit emotional engagement that might shift viewers' perspectives, sympathies and understanding. This aspect of ethical experience has not been theorized much in relation to contemporary cinema.[5] This is curious since one can hardly have ideology without affect or emotion, political manipulation without seduction or incitement, and emancipatory effects without persuasion or conversion. Yet, until recently, little theoretical work has been done to explain the ethical power of film to not only question or challenge but to engage, persuade, or convert via aesthetic means. With the "philosophical turn" in film theory, however, this "experiential" aspect of ethics in cinema has also begun to be addressed.[6]

To be sure, philosophical film theorists have long been concerned with moral questions in the cinema. Indeed, one of the most popular ways of articulating the relationship between film and philosophy is to analyze how intelligent films thematize moral issues or ethical problems in narrative form.[7] The "film as thought experiment" approach has proven very fruitful: *Eternal Sunshine of the Spotless Mind* (Gondry, 2004) as a Nietzschean counter-example to the utilitarian ethic of maximizing utility and minimizing pain; *The Third Man* (Reed, 1949) as a critical exploration of the Aristotelian account of friendship; *The Philadelphia Story* (Cukor, 1940) as an exercise in Emersonian moral perfectionism; Bergman's *The Seventh Seal* (1957) as a study in existential doubt and religious faith; and von Trier's *Dogville* (2005) as a perverse staging of the social contract scenario meets Old Testament divine retribution.[8] Such philosophically inflected readings of movies articulate their moral-ethical significance as works that are at once aesthetic and philosophical. At the same time, they leave open the question whether there is more to cinematic ethics than approaching films through an assumed philosophical *problématique* or reading them as ethico-moral thought experiments. What does it mean when Bazin describes Rossellini's way of presenting character and situation as an expression of love or when Godard remarks that "tracking shots are a question of morality"?[9] Why choose a non-European director to discuss postsecular cinema within a European context? One response would be that this stresses the importance of marginality and the figure of the "foreigner" precisely within a European context. At a time when the very meaning of "Europe" as a cultural, economic, and political project is being challenged, the question of the marginal, the foreign, and the multicultural assumes renewed importance. Sometimes "outsiders" can discern elements that "locals" might otherwise overlook. As a prelude to addressing such questions, which go to the heart of what film-philosophy can do, I turn to Iñárritu's *Biutiful* as an instance of postsecular cinematic ethics.

BIUTIFUL AS ETHICAL CINEMA

Mexican-born Iñárritu came to prominence with his debut feature, *Amores Perros* (2000), a network narrative set in contemporary Mexico City that combines kinetic action, melodrama, and moral ambiguity to depict a global city in social, economic, and cultural crisis. This was followed by his breakthrough feature, *21 Grams* (2003), another network narrative starring Naomi Watts, Sean Penn, and Benicio del Toro. The latter deals with the interconnected fates of three characters whose interwoven lives are shattered by a fatal hit-and-run accident—an event that forces intense moral and spiritual reckoning against a background of ethical and spiritual nihilism endemic to secular consumerist culture.

Amores Perros and *21 Grams* are examples of what we might call the "moral melodrama": films that use melodrama to elicit forms of emotional engagement that open up a space for moral questioning and critical reflection.[10] Moral melodramas combine intensely affecting performances, dramatic presentation of character, and the evocative disclosure of social situations within a melodramatic narrative framework that invites ethical engagement from the viewer (think, for example, of Almodóvar's work). Indeed, the very form of the melodrama, as Peter Brooks has argued, is a genre that has inherited some of the elements of tragedy in a historical and cultural context that has lost the tragic vision of the world and is no longer marked by an unequivocal faith in God.[11] From this point of view, *Babel* and *Biutiful* are moral melodramas that differ in narrative style, the former being a complex network narrative and the latter a more conventional character drama. Both narrative forms open up distinctive kinds of ethical experience, albeit with different rhythms, emotional dynamics, and aesthetic intensities. The network narrative's dispersed engagement, coalescing events, and clashing storylines contrast aesthetically with the moral melodrama's narrative development, affective intensity, and dramatic continuity. Yet both films use melodrama as a way of engaging viewers emotionally as a mode of ethical experience—not in the sense of offering a didactic moral lesson or rationally articulated critique but in the aesthetic sense of disclosing the alterity of a character's experience of the world. Both *Babel* and *Biutiful* disclose, via cinematic means, the complexity of that world in ways that elicit sympathy and understanding while inviting a critical questioning of their alienating conditions of social existence.

Babel and *Biutiful*, moreover, are films that explore many of the assumptions at play in debates on postsecularism: the idea that religious belief and experience must be acknowledged as contributing to, rather than mystifying, moral, social, and political discourse. *Biutiful* invites an ethical engagement with the characters' subjective experiences in order to disclose the complex social, economic, and political forces shaping their situation. Indeed, Iñárritu's work raises more generally the question of cinema as ethics: how to provoke an experience of ethical engagement—an ethics of contingency and finitude—without didacticism, abstraction, or moralism? This exploration is especially pertinent in a European social and political context marked by "deep diversity" where the intersection of religion and politics has become a defining feature of moral and cultural discourse.

Iñárritu's films are apt for exploring the idea of cinema as a medium of ethical experience for they generate the kind of affective and emotional engagement that often conflicts with our more "rationalist" impulses towards moralizing judgment. Such films "educate" the viewer's senses and heighten our sensibilities, thus offering a veritable "aesthetic education" towards developing a more receptive and perceptive form of moral imagination.[12] At the same time, they disclose fictional worlds in which the actions of ethically imperfect characters serve to reveal the social, cultural, and economic forces that undermine their moral agency. Such films do not assert moral claims or judge characters' actions; rather, they show cinematic worlds in which marginalized characters make difficult moral choices. In doing so, our own moral sympathies are elicited in ways that might conflict with our ethical attitudes or ideological prejudices. Cinematic ethics, in short, means showing, rather than telling, what ethical experience means, exploring what such experience reveals about the complexity of a character's world where this fictional world is disclosed through cinematic composition and dramatic action. It examines how cinema can attune our aesthetic and moral sensibilities to this complexity, fragility, and vulnerability and how it can thereby bring us to a deeper understanding of the social and cultural background that shapes these characters' possibilities and constrains their individual choices.

One way to articulate the ethico-political dimensions of films like *Biutiful*, I suggest, is through the idea of *aesthetic disclosure:* the critical disclosure of intolerable aspects of modern culture and the revealing of new or forgotten aspects of modern experience via the construction of virtual cinematic worlds.[13] For it is in the affective engagement and reflective responsiveness elicited by cinematic worlds that the ethico-political possibilities of cinema come to life. Here again it is not necessary to have a fully fledged theory of ideology, ethics, or of politics that could be handily applied to a film in order to unmask its ideological dimensions. It is enough, rather, to draw upon the ways in which certain films disclose what is intolerable in our world today or experiment with the disclosure of alternative ways of thinking, acting, and being. It is enough for a film to evoke an ethical experience that prompts us to question our beliefs, alter our perspective, transforming our way of approaching a problem or acknowledging that there is a problem demanding our attention. As Stephen Mulhall has suggested (following Nathan Andersen), this is one way in which films can "do philosophy": revealing new "paths of thinking" that reframe a problem or even redefine the horizons of our thinking.[14] An ethical problem presupposes a shared space of understanding in which we might exchange reasons for or against a position, principle, or argument. But what if we lack such a shared space? What if the very existence of something as a problem is invisible or unintelligible to us? Or if we simply do not care about it or have failed to give it proper consideration? This is where film can illuminate different aspects of our experience of the world and open up new paths for thinking. Cinema can evoke an ethical experience of questioning or thinking that prompts us to revise our horizons of meaning or acknowledge phenomena that previously remained opaque or obscure. This is especially important in the case of films that deal with spiritual-religious issues for it is in the fluid space between ethical questioning and religious reflection that cinema can evoke a transformative ethical experience. It is this conception of cinema as a medium of ethical experience that I am concerned to explore in *Biutiful*.

In many ways, *Biutiful* is a retelling of Kurosawa's classic *Ikiru* (*To Live*) (1952), the moving story of an unremarkable civil servant dying of cancer who finds renewed existential meaning in life as he approaches death. Iñárittu transposes Kurosawa's story of redemption through accepting mortality to the gritty underworld of social marginals struggling for survival in contemporary Barcelona.[15] Kurosawa's civil servant is transformed into a lone father and street hustler; Kanji Watanabe's (Takashi Shimura's) redemptive task of securing a children's playground is replaced by the dying Uxbal's (Javier Bardem's) provisions to ensure his children have a chance at a meaningful future. Both characters, Watanabe and Uxbal, are forced to reckon with mortality and with their personal failures and disappointments and both undergo an experience of despair culminating in a sleazy nightclub with only alcohol or drugs to dull the pain of their dwindling existence. *Biutiful*, however, does not confine this existential drama to a lifeless bourgeois existence but transfers it to the socially marginalized underworld of a major European city.

Given its realism and poeticism, it is tempting to approach *Biutiful* as allegorical, as reflecting a Spain or Europe in moral-spiritual distress, as suffering from a pervasive nihilism. From this perspective, *Biutiful* is a postsecular fable with moral-religious overtones responding to the aporias of globalization, a film that acts out the "post-traumatic" effects of historical and political oppression (consider, for example, the references to Uxbal's father fleeing Franco's Spain for Mexico). Far from an ideological regression to mystificatory religiosity, the film can be understood as exploring, in cinematic and poetic terms, both the moral-spiritual and economic-social underworld of European multiculturalism.

An alternative, more critical reading would emphasize the film's competing impulses towards social realism and metaphysical spiritualism. Indeed, one could imagine an alternative version of the film rendered in a more "realist" manner, exposing the hidden underclass of an affluent Western European city, the interconnection between economic exploitation, social marginalization, and the need for religion as a source of hope. From this more "secular' view, the character's religiosity would doubtless be portrayed as an expression of alienated self-consciousness, a mystification of the implacable social and economic forces deciding his fate. The tragedy of Uxbal's precarious social existence and that of the other characters in the film would serve as an allegory of the injustice pervading the larger social order. Such a realist-secularist approach to the film would treat it as belonging to the tradition of social realist exposés of class exploitation, bourgeois hypocrisy, or social contradictions. The latter would become manifest in the various forms of social suffering, alienation, despair, or violence afflicting characters all but crushed by their oppressive circumstances.

Yet this kind of reading cannot be sustained in the case of *Biutiful*. It refuses to present a harsh or disenchanted view of Uxbal's world; it refuses to depict him and his family as no more than alienated or passive victims of an unjust social and economic order.[16] It confounds the demand for social realism, however stylized (think of the Dardenne brothers' films) with a spiritualist dimension that coexists within the harsh world of social marginalization and economic struggle. Instead, *Biutiful* insists on humanizing Uxbal and his experience of social reality, however contradictory this may appear: it provokes moral sympathy for a character who participates in exploitative practices that lead to the deaths of innocent people; it puts Uxbal's spiritual-religious experience as a psychic medium or "seer" on the same level as his social role as a participant in exploitative work practices. In doing so, the film thus brings together all these domains of his experience as part of the same social struggle for survival.

At the same time, the film insists on the need to entertain a transcendent dimension if we are to acknowledge the reality of Uxbal's world, which is profoundly shaped by his spiritual experience. Uxbal is a psychic medium who communicates with the spirits of the dead, hearing their pleas, communicating their messages, and acknowledging their pain and suffering. He is a go-between who mediates between the living and dead, a liminal figure communicating with troubled spirits who cannot yet leave this world. The ambiguity of his role is underscored by his acceptance of payment for his services, a practice that underlines his precarious social and spiritual existence (he is, as Iñárittu notes, a contradictory character, a loving father and street hustler blessed with supernatural insight).[17] Indeed, the film's narrative is focalized by Uxbal's journey in preparing for death, chronicling the diminution of his vitality, the deterioration of his body, contrasted with the increasing clarity of his vision and purpose with the approach of death.[18] It even dares to find beauty in squalor, morality among the asocial, epiphany among the exploited. Tales of existential struggle, spiritual-religious crises, and moral conversion are usually reserved for characters of middle-class provenance.[19] *Biutiful*, however, finds its subject in the social underclass, whose own struggles, Iñárittu suggests, can be as tragic, moving, and imbued with dignity as those of anyone else. Critics might take this as ideological mystification—a reversion to religiosity that covers over the brutal reality of exploitation and degradation. Yet it is better taken as an argument to reconsider a purely secular understanding of globalization and the everyday struggles it engenders, for these remain abstract, lacking particularity, unless we can acknowledge the experiential perspective of the socially marginalized, which is precisely what *Biutiful*, as an ethically engaged moral fiction, attempts to do.

It is in this sense that I take *Biutiful* to be a postsecular film—a moral-existential melodrama that reveals the dignity of a character undergoing spiritual and social struggles in confronting death. It integrates a personalist-humanist perspective, acknowledging the spiritualist dimension of Uxbal's world while maintaining a critical perspective on the experience of social suffering generated by global capitalism.[20] More specifically, by highlighting the existence of poverty and social marginalization in contemporary Barcelona, *Biutiful* sheds light on what Iñárritu calls "the invisibles": socially marginalized individuals—including immigrants both legal and illegal—whose communal coexistence is one of the most significant features of globalization in European cities today.[21] A purely "moral" interpretation of the film misses the background of social and economic forces that converge in Uxbal's tragic story; a purely "political" reading misses the transcendent dimension of his religiosity and spiritual belief. It is the combination of these perspectives that makes *Biutiful* an existentialist, postsecularist film. It offers a poetic exploration of existential crisis and moral redemption compromised by the everyday struggles of a family caught within the social and economic underclass. It dramatizes how the social "invisibles" struggle to survive with dignity and faith, rendering their story poetically and realistically in order to evoke an ethical experience of sympathy and engagement.[22]

MAGIC SOCIAL REALISM

We might call this striking combination of poetry and politics a "magic social realism." The underworld of Barcelona, with its impoverished immigrants, black market economy, criminality, and corruption, is rendered in sharp and gritty detail, often using hand-held camera, natural light, and a grim urban color palette (predominantly grays, blues, dull greens, and browns). At the same time, Uxbal's personal perspective on this world, colored by his spiritual beliefs and the knowledge that he is dying of cancer, is expressed lyrically and poetically from a subjective point of view. The film's opening scenes, for example, which return at the end of the film, are shot from Uxbal's perspective, with objects, spaces, and hands rendered in loving close-up under muted light.

The film opens with a sequence of images accompanying what turns out to be Uxbal's final conversation with his daughter, telling her the story of the ring given to him by his mother, which in turn was given to her by his father before he fled from Spain as a young man. He reminisces about the radio program he used to hear as a child, with its soothing sounds of wind and waves. As he slips peacefully into death, he finds himself in a winter forest deep in snow where he sees a dead owl and meets a guarded young man, sharing with him a cigarette. The light is bright, the images sharp and crisp, the soundtrack now clear and spare. Snatches of conversation appear, which we will hear later in the film, the soundtrack of the radio program he heard as a child, phrases from his childhood, and a comforting silence, broken only by the muffled sound of boots in snow. All is illuminated; the images lucid and luminous. The sequence concludes with the young man moving out of frame, Uxbal looking off-screen, asking "what's over there?"—cut to black. This opening sequence or "prelude" sets a mood of intimacy, melancholy, and existential reverie, slipping imperceptibly between the final moments of Uxbal's life and his death, between this world and another, as though these two worlds were mutually communicating yet separated by an indiscernible border. It frames the movie as a study in mortality, opening and ending with death, an eternal recurrence of the same.

The entire film is an expression of Uxbal's life and death, animated by his mortality as immanent limit and unfathomable ground. The perspective on the film's world is that of a dying man who does not yet fully accept, or exists authentically within, the temporal certainty of his own death. His vision encompasses both the living and the dead, yet he finds this vision hard to turn upon his own finite existence. It is only towards the end of his life that he achieves this recognition and belatedly accepts his mortality. The temporal horizon of the film is that limit between life and death ordinarily covered over by what Heidegger calls our everyday "being-in-the-world"; the absorbed busy-ness that propels us along the inexorable temporal track of our own being-towards-death.[23] Expressed differently, Uxbal's story takes place between two deaths: the death that was always within him as the finite ground of his existence and the death that is only his own, his bodily and existential demise. This is the death no one else can take over for him and which gives the remainder of his life meaning and purpose. The entire film circles or cycles, radiates and returns from this moment—the moment that gives substance and significance to every moment he has lived. It is a meaning and purpose—of death in life and life in death—that had always been there, half-hidden, but which he had ignored, or recoiled from, as we all do.

Unlike an atheist work of art, however, *Biutiful* acknowledges the infinitude at the heart of our finitude. It does not shy away from the question of faith, whether in God, existence, or the soul. It acknowledges Uxbal's spiritual experiences as pointing to a transcendent dimension that remains immanent to his mundane existence. When Uxbal has visions of the dead, we bear witness to them as well. This is not simply a matter of subjective alignment with his point of view. In one sequence, for example, we glimpse a dead man in a mirror, a figure that Uxbal does not notice, thus underlining that the presence of the dead is a feature of this world rather than of Uxbal's perception, though it is clear that his vision is not one shared by others in the film. One could call it a form of religious experience or being existentially aware of mortality yet desirous of transcendence. Whatever we call it, the film develops its portrayal of Uxbal from the perspective of a radical finitude (his imminent death and palpable mortality) that is mediated by a transcendent dimension (his communication with the dead) that coexists on the same plane as his mundane life. This is one of the film's most daring psychological and moral propositions: to show everyday reality, with its social deprivation, its corruption and brutality, yet as enchanted by faith, limned by beauty, animated by belief.[24]

FROM MORAL FAILURE TO POLITICAL REFLECTION

For all the film's lyricism and supernaturalism, *Biutiful* also retains an air of social realism. Uxbal and his family—his bipolar wife Marambra (Maricel Álvarez), their children Ana and Mateo, and his brother, Tito—are embedded within the socioeconomic underworld of Barcelona. Everyday life, however, for all its difficulty and struggle, is also beautiful and luminous. Uxbal's world is portrayed as a complex social and spiritual reality that retains its share of pathos, tragedy, and dignity. It is social realism with a Levinasian face, moral melodrama in a humanistic key.[25] Much like what Deleuze and Guattari called "minor literature,"[26] Iñárritu's "minor cinema" takes an intimate and personal story of everyday suffering in a disenfranchised social milieu and uses these elements to disclose indirectly the dynamic whole (the "social totality") in which this story is embedded. These interconnecting forces are reflected in the microcosmic melodrama of the dying man, his Stoic struggle to ensure a future for his children with the help of Ige (Diarytou Daff), the wife of a Senegalese worker whose husband has been deported.

How, then, to capture the social and spiritual, immanent and transcendent dimensions of this story? In all of Iñárritu's films there is a layer of religiosity interwoven with the melodrama that gives his films a distinctively "postsecularist" sensibility. From this point of view, a postsecular film acknowledges the significance of religious and spiritual experience as part of a multicultural milieu marked by "deep diversity."[27] In consonance with recent theoretical and philosophical debates, the film explores the idea that the ethical and political aporias of globalization demand engagement with, rather than rejection of, spiritual and religious discourse. Instead of dismissing religiosity as an anachronistic vestige of an irrational past, postsecularist theorists—including rationalists like Jürgen Habermas—maintain that multicultural democracies need to recognize the contribution that religious belief and practice can make to the democratic cultural and public spheres.[28] It is clear that the contemporary intersection of religion and politics has profoundly challenged secularism as a way of defining modern societies and hence that we need to acknowledge different kinds of religious experience and belief in ways that move beyond the futile dichotomy of uncritical immersion versus dogmatic dismissal. A film like *Biutiful* makes a modest but significant cultural contribution to this difficult moral and social task.

A contrast here with the Dardenne brothers' celebrated film *La promesse* (*The Promise*) (1996) might be instructive. The latter is a realist social drama that also portrays the social underworld of a contemporary European city (the Seraing/Liège region of French-speaking Wallonia in Belgium) but without the postsecularist dimension of religious-spiritual experience that one finds in *Biutiful*. *La promesse* likewise focuses on the struggles of socially marginalized characters and the morally compromising decisions they are forced to make given their difficult social, economic, and legal circumstances (as illegal immigrants, for example). The film centers on the relationship between a father, Roger (Olivier Gourmet), and teenage son, Igor (Jérémie Renier), and also involves a tragic death for which the father bears some responsibility. Both also involve keeping a promise to a dying parent to look after their children: Igor promising Amidou in the case of *La promesse* and Ige promising Uxbal in the case of *Biutiful*. Like Uxbal, Roger is also involved in placing illegal immigrant workers in local building projects. Assisted by Igor, he organizes their travel, accommodation, and serves as their work supervisor and deceitful landlord. When immigration officials arrive on the building site for an inspection, the workers all scatter except for one, Amidou (Rasmane Ouedrago), who falls off his scaffold and is seriously injured. Igor rushes to his aid, promising that he will look after Amidou's wife and child. When his father arrives, Igor insists that Amidou must go to hospital, but his father decides this is too risky and refuses to help. The father's decision to let Amidou die, burying him in the building's concrete footings, and lying to Amidou's wife Assita (Assita Ouedrago) about his whereabouts, triggers a profound questioning in Igor, who until this point has reluctantly obeyed his father and participated in his dubious work activities. Faced with a moral choice between helping his father lure Assita into what appears to be sexual slavery, Igor decides, impulsively, to escape with Assita and help her find safety with relatives in Italy. In a final confrontation with his father, Igor literally chains him up, fleeing again with

Assita, a definitive break with his father's authority as well as with a life of exploitation in which he has been mired. In a profound moment of reckoning, he finally confesses the truth to Assita that her husband has died, a revelation that prompts her to abandon her plans for escape, and return, crushed, to her life in the city. Again on an impulse, Igor rushes to her side, again confirming his fidelity, honoring his promise to Amidou to stay with Assita and her child.

A number of commentators have noted the moral-ethical dimensions of this film, citing co-director Luc Dardennes' comment that the film is an attempt to stage Levinas's "face-to-face" encounter through cinema.[29] Yet both the realist visual style of the film and its naturalistic aesthetic suggest that it remains "secular" in orientation in the sense that it does not venture any speculative observations on, or offer subjective access to, the characters' personal beliefs or spiritual experience. Assita's animistic religious rituals, for example, and child-idol statue (smashed by racist hooligans, and later repaired by Igor) present these elements as part of her everyday social-cultural life rather than as offering intimate access to her subjective experience. Much like Bresson, the moral emotions and ethical responses of characters are depicted through gesture, expression, and action; there is no transcendent dimension rendered directly within the film's diegetic world or indeed its characters' perspectives on that world. Even the "Levinasian" interpretation that the film reveals this transcendent dimension through the "face-to-face" encounter must contend with the everyday, matter-of-fact, realist manner in which this encounter is presented. The film leaves it up to the spectator to decide on the moral-ethical, or indeed spiritual-religious dimensions of Igor's fidelity and honoring of his promise.[30]

As many commentators have noted, the Dardenne brothers' background in documentary informs their carefully composed and stylized version of social realism.[31] The brilliance of their work is to articulate the moral ambiguity of character actions against the oppressive social-economic background of a regional European urban city in decay. Like *Biutiful*, the characters in *La promesse* exist as social marginals within a difficult social and cultural milieu, and the narrative drama is structured around the question of moral responsibility for the deaths of illegal immigrants; but this is not a narrative or cinematic world in which religious faith or spiritual experience play a significant role in the characters' daily struggle for survival. *Biutiful*, by contrast, foregrounds this element against the background of social and economic marginalization, suggesting that, in order to makes sense of the characters' social struggles and existential choices, we must take their religious beliefs and spiritual experience into account. Although *La promesse* and *Biutiful* both depict socially marginalized characters against a background of economic exploitation, *Biutiful* provides an "interiorized" perspective on their everyday experience, imbuing it with beauty and pathos. In this respect, *La promesse* and *Biutiful* offer complementary presentations of social experience within contemporary European multicultural societies facing the social, cultural, and economic challenges of rampant globalization. The secular realism of the Dardenne brothers' presentation of moral experience contrasts with *Biutiful*'s postsecular depiction of personal-spiritual experience within a contradictory social-cultural milieu.

BIUTIFUL AS POSTSECULARIST WORK

Like a number of recent films that treat religious and spiritual themes, *Biutiful* has received a mixed response from critics, in some cases bordering on the hostile.[32] What causes critical offence, I suggest, is less the film's melodramatic or morally ambivalent elements than its undertone of spiritual transcendence: the metaphysical or supernaturalist dimensions that are rendered as realistically as the social drama with its global resonances.[33] *Biutiful* presents a world that shows morally ambiguous characters in a sympathetic light, along with religious or "metaphysical" motifs—Uxbal's psychic ability to communicate with the dead, his afterlife encounter with a version of his own father—presented on the same level as the more realist depiction of everyday social life in the Barcelona underclass.

This transgression of aesthetic and moral expectations has incurred the wrath of various critics.[34] A common reaction to the film, for example, was to praise its cinematic accomplishments, notably Bardem's performance as Uxbal, while criticizing Iñárittu's direction for failing in its moral mission. Consider Peter Bradshaw's criticisms:

> Uxbal's life reaches a crisis with a shocking and horrifying event, for which he is at least partly responsible, although it arises from his well-intentioned effort to do some good. He cries to his spiritual confidante: "I don't know if I should turn myself in!" My own response to this leniently conceived dilemma is: erm, yes, Uxbal, you should turn yourself in, and all your accomplices, too. But Uxbal does not do this, and is told merely to make some kind of spiritual amends to the dead, which is frankly getting off pretty lightly. No one in the movie is apprehended by the law, and the only cops visible are corrupt ones. Only a kind of ambiguous poetic justice appears to be visited on those responsible.[35]

Bradshaw is referring to Uxbal's role in the events leading to the shocking death of the Chinese workers. The "spiritual confidante" refers to Bea (Ana Wagener), a fellow psychic cum maternal figure to whom Uxbal goes, in a state of despair. She reminds him that he knows what he must do; seek forgiveness from the dead, and get his own affairs in order before he dies. Against Bradshaw's faulty recollection, the police do in fact intervene and arrest the Chinese relatives of the factory owners—clandestine gay lovers who have gone into hiding, an appalling situation made even worse when one of them murders the other and goes into hiding.

Bradshaw's criticism, however, is not aesthetic so much as moral: that the film does not insist on a secular or legal remedy, but allows a "metaphysical" notion of justice to take the place of police and the courts, representatives of the very institutions of power that the characters try to evade in their daily struggles. The critic here adopts the perspective of the law, morality, and the state; passing judgment on the moral culpability of the protagonist, criticizing the film for failing to hold these marginal characters to account. It also discounts the possibility of transcendent sources of meaning and value that remain irreducible to secular morality and legal remedies. Precisely this reductive, "moralizing" perspective, however, is what the film challenges, questioning its blindness to the social and economic forces that constrain Uxbal's moral agency and acknowledging the importance of spiritual-religious experience in his existential struggle with mortality.

It is clear that for Bradshaw, as for other critics, the film fails to create what Murray Smith calls moral "allegiance" for Uxbal's compromised character, not to mention that of "his accomplices."[36] What this approach misses, however, is that morally approving or disapproving of the characters and their actions may not be the point. The question of morality is situated, rather, within the compromised forms of responsibility that obtain under conditions of duress. *Biutiful* prompts us to question the limits of morality in a state of scarcity, pointing to the social, economic, and cultural conditions that must be in place for moral autonomy (or secular legal justice) to flourish. "Never trust a hungry man," warns one of the characters in the film, which could be taken as a motto for what *Biutiful* sets out to dramatize and to expose. The disjunction between Bradshaw's aesthetic admiration for the film and his criticism of its moral relativism reveals a common assumption: that in evaluating a work of art, aesthetic and moral judgment should align or cohere in a mutually supporting whole.

This is precisely what a moral melodrama like *Biutiful* attempts to undermine. Instead of judging morally flawed characters (depicting them unsympathetically), their flaws in character and failures of judgment are presented, rather, as reflective of a more complex social, economic, and political situation that motivates their "immoral" actions. To paraphrase Kant, politics without ethics is blind; ethics without politics is empty. The point is to show the interplay between the two—between the characters' moral choices and the social, cultural, and economic conditions that condition their exercise of moral agency. This is the cinematic ethics at play in *Biutiful*: evoking an ethical experience by aesthetic means in order to suspend moralizing judgment and thus foster a deeper understanding of the character's conduct in light of his or her social situation.[37]

This is an ethical experience of the suspension of moralizing (rather than moral) judgment in the search for deeper ethical understanding. The tragic deaths of the Chinese workers no doubt elicit a condemnatory response on the part of some viewers, but directed against whom or what? Bradshaw's critique reveals another common assumption: namely that such films should restore a sense of natural or social justice—movies as *mythos*. Thus, for moralizing critics, *Biutiful* reneges on its moral responsibility by allowing Uxbal to survive without acknowledging (in secular or legal terms) his responsibility for the workers' deaths, thereby abandoning the moral responsibility of the filmmaker to demonstrate (and thereby edify the audience) that secular justice has been served.

The tragic deaths of the Chinese workers, however, and Uxbal's moral-spiritual crisis in response, can only be properly understood in relation to the larger social and economic forces of globalization that shape this world. These forces appear as "irrational" fates capturing individual characters in situations they can neither fully grasp nor effectively control. To condemn Uxbal for failing in his moral duty, or dismissing the film for failing in its moral mission to fulfill secular legal justice, misunderstands the complex dialectical relationship between the characters' (limited) moral agency and the (complex) social forces constraining their exercise of moral autonomy.

The deeper ambiguity at the heart of the film, however, is that it both invites and undermines just this kind of moralizing judgment. Who, or what, is responsible for the deaths of the Chinese workers? Uxbal, who helped broker the deal—under pressure from his unscrupulous brother—to bring the Chinese onto a building site as illegal workers? Uxbal, who bought the cheap gas heaters, the only ones he could afford, because he was disturbed by how the workers were being exploited? What about the exploitative Chinese factory owner Hai and his partner, who insisted that the workers be locked in the factory basement every night?[38] Or the Spanish construction company manager Mendoza, who employed the cheaper illegal workers in order to circumvent the wages and conditions required for unionized Spanish workers? And let us not forget the well-heeled citizens and tourists who will buy and rent the apartments built using such exploitative labor. Ultimately, we are meant to see that it is the neoliberal global economic system that in fact brought the Chinese workers to be imprisoned within the factory in the first place. The intersecting lines of moral responsibility, economic exploitation, and social dependency, generated by the global economic system itself, profoundly constrain Uxbal's fitful attempts at moral redemption.

Condemning Uxbal (or indeed the film) for moral blindness obscures the social, economic, and political forces that generated this situation of exploitation and suffering. Insisting that Uxbal is to blame and should have confessed to the police betrays the central moral argument of the film: that we cannot understand, let alone judge, the lives and actions of those existing within the social underclass in our midst unless we are capable of understanding their situation by being emotionally engaged by their plight. In depicting these harrowing deaths so vividly, as well as Uxbal's tragic role in what happened, *Biutiful* prompts us to reflect on the deeper systemic forces, economic and social, that shaped his fateful decision. This is an ethical experience inviting the viewer to reflect upon and reframe their emotional response so as to encompass the broader social, economic, and political realities in which the characters vie for survival.

This emotional engagement and moral sympathy reveals the complexities of Uxbal's lifeworld with its economic scarcity, social struggle, and religious hope. Such ethical engagement thwarts the moralizing judgment that would condemn him as immoral while sparing the global system in which he and his family are embedded. It is only in acknowledging the invisible ghosts of the "spirit of capitalism," the restless victims with whom Uxbal communicates, that the viewer (or critic), might experience a degree of moral understanding through ethical acknowledgment—a postsecular affirmation of this "other world" in both its beauty and its dignity, an underworld of the socially dead that survives by resisting, however it can, global violence and senseless suffering.

Biutiful's mission is thus to evoke a postsecularist sense of ethical acknowledgement: acknowledging social suffering and the injustices faced by the exploited while affirming the dignity of those who struggle to find hope and meaning in the margins of urban society. It does so by aesthetic means, combining poetic lyricism and social realism, sympathetic insight into Uxbal's spiritual quest for redemption, and disclosure of the immigrant underworld of poverty and exclusion within our European cities. It depicts a complex cinematic world within which a character's moral choices throw into relief the ordinarily concealed background of social marginalization and economic exploitation. At the same time, it acknowledges the significance of spiritual-religious experience within contemporary social reality. As a work of postsecular ethics, Uxbal's story expresses both a meditation on mortality and a critique of European multiculturalism. *Biutiful* not only evokes an ethical experience that might transform our moral understanding, it is also an aesthetic reminder that modern life, despite its struggles and squalor, can be beautiful.

NOTES

1. Anne Brodie, "Interview with Alejandro González Iñárittu," *AskMen Magazine* (2011). Available at http://au.askmen.com/celebs/interview_400/495_alejandro-gonzalez-inarritu-interview.html.
2. See, for example, Peter L. Berger, "The Desecularization of the World: A Global Overview," in *The Desecularization of the World,* ed. P. L. Berger (Grand Rapids: William B. Eerdmans Publishing, 2005), 1–18. Alessandro Ferrara, "The Separation of Religion and Politics in a Post-Secular Society," *Philosophy and Social Criticism* 35:1–2 (2009), 77–91. Jürgen Habermas, "Secularism's Crisis of Faith: Notes on Post-Secular Society," *New Perspectives Quarterly,* 25 (2008), 17–29.
3. See the essays in *Post-Secular Philosophy: Between Philosophy and Theology,* ed. Phillip Blond (London: Routledge, 1998).
4. Here we could mention a number of recent examples, such as Bruno Dumont's *Hadewijch* (2009) and *Hors Satan* (2011), Bela Tarr's *The Turin Horse* (2011),

Lars von Trier's *Antichrist* (2009), and Terrence Malick's *The Tree of Life* (2011) and *To the Wonder* (2013).
5. For a welcome exception, see the Special Issue "The Occluded Relation: Levinas and Cinema," edited by Sarah Cooper. *Film-Philosophy* 11:2 (2007). Available at www.film-philosophy.com/index.php/f-p/issue/view/13.
6. See, for example, Lisa Downing and Libby Saxton, *Film and Ethics* (Abingdon: Routledge, 2010) and Jane Stadler, *Pulling Focus: Intersubjective Experience, Narrative Film, and Ethics* (New York and London: Continuum, 2008).
7. See Christopher Falzon, *Philosophy Goes to the Movies* (London and New York: Routledge, 2002), Thomas E. Wartenberg, *Thinking on Screen: Film as Philosophy* (Abingdon: Routledge, 2007), and Daniel Shaw, *Morality and the Movies: Reading Ethics through Film* (London and New York: Continuum, 2012).
8. See Wartenberg (2007) for discussions of *Eternal Sunshine of the Spotless Mind* and *The Third Man* as philosophical films. See Stanley Cavell, *Cities of Words: Pedagogical Letters on a Register of the Moral Life* (Cambridge MA and London: Belknap/Harvard University Press, 2004) for a discussion of Emersonian perfectionism. See Paisley Livingston's *Cinema, Philosophy, Bergman: On Film as Philosophy* (Oxford: Oxford University Press, 2009). On *Dogville*, see Andrea Brighenti, "Dogville, or, the Dirty Birth of Law," *Thesis Eleven*, no. 87, (November 2006), 96–111 and Costica Bradatan, " 'I was a stranger, and ye took me not in': *Deus ludens* and the Theology of Hospitality in Lars von Trier's *Dogville*," *Journal of European Studies* 39:1 (March 2009), 58–78.
9. See André Bazin, *What is Cinema? Volume I*, trans. Hugh Gray (Berkeley: University of California Press, 1967), 62. Jean-Luc Godard's quip was made during a roundtable discussion of Resnais' *Hiroshima mon amour* (1959), reversing a remark by Luc Moulet defending Samuel Fuller's films. See Libby Saxton, " 'Tracking Shots are a Question of Morality': Ethics, Aesthetics, Documentary" in Downing and Saxton's *Film and Ethics*, 1–18.
10. This is another way of approaching what Cavell called the "melodramas of the unknown woman" as ways in which cinema can "do ethics" (in his case, Emersonian moral perfectionism). See Stanley Cavell, *Contesting Tears: The Melodrama of the Unknown Woman* (Chicago: Chicago University Press, 1996).
11. Cf.

> Melodrama does not simply represent a 'fall' from tragedy, but a response to the loss of the tragic vision. It comes into being in a world where the traditional imperatives of truth and ethics have been violently thrown into question, yet where the promulgation of truth and ethics, their instauration as a way of life, is of immediate, daily, political concern. (Peter Brooks, *The Melodramatic Imagination: Balzac, Henry James, Melodrama, and the Mode of Excess* [New Haven and London: Yale University Press, 1976], 11)

12. Friedrich Schiller, *Letters on the Aesthetic Education of Mankind*, trans. Reginald Snell (Dover Publications, 2004). See also Martha C. Nussbaum, *Love's Knowledge: Essays on Philosophy and Literature* (Oxford: Oxford University Press, 1990), especially Chapter 5, " 'Finely Aware and Richly Responsible': Literature and the Moral Imagination," 148–67.
13. See Robert Sinnerbrink, "Re-enfranchising Film: Towards a Romantic Film-Philosophy" in *New Takes in Film-Philosophy*, eds. Havi Carel and Greg Tuck (London: Palgrave Macmillan, 2011), 25–47.
14. Stephen Mulhall, *On Film*, 2nd edition (New York: Routledge, 2008), 136 ff.

Postsecular Ethics 183

15. Iñárritu pays tribute to Kurosawa's *Ikiru*, which he acknowledges as a direct influence on *Biutiful*, by "borrowing" elements and even specific scenes (the nightclub scene where Uxbal confesses to a stranger that he has cancer). "What I like, too, [. . .] is that Kurosawa has put this personal, existential tragedy in the context of political criticism," something Iñárritu himself has accomplished with films like *Amores Perros, 21 Grams,* and *Babel*. "He's going from the individual, interior experience to a greater problem encompassing the spectrum of society." See Alejandro González Iñárritu, *Simple Beauty*, by Rob Feld, Directors Guild of America. Available at www.dga.org/Craft/DGAQ/All-Articles/1003-Fall-2010/Screening-Room-Inarritu.aspx.

16. See, for example, Iñárittu's comments in a recent interview:

    I don't want to subordinate my films to a political view. If I wanted to do that, I'd make speeches or write for the newspapers. I will never subordinate or sacrifice the drama or the truth I want in order to make a propaganda film. I think that no matter what you do, a film is political. Always, a film contains a statement. With every decision you make, you are proposing something, you are saying something. But something I didn't want it to end up being was preaching to people, or victimising these guys and blaming the government. I think the human drama is much more complex than that. (Russ Slater, "Interview with Alejandro González Iñárittu," *Sounds and Colours*, July 11, 2011. Available at www.soundsandcolours.com/subjects/film/art-should-provoke-an-interview-with-alejandro-gonzalez-inarritu/)

17. Cf.

    I saw Uxbal full of contradictions: a guy whose life is so busy and complicated that he can't even die in peace, a guy who protects immigrants from the law while he himself exploits their labor. A street man who has a spiritual gift and can speak with the dead and guide them to the light . . . but he charges money for it; a family man with a broken heart and two kids who he loves yet can't help but lose his temper with them; a man who everybody depends on but who also depends on everyone; a primitive, simple, humble man with a deep supernatural insight. (Iñárittu, "Biutiful," *Cannes Film Festival Notes*, 5)

18. Iñárittu comments on the shift from handheld realist camera earlier in the film to the use of more composed shots, different lenses, and slower pacing, which brings objects and places into more focused relief as Uxbal's illness worsens and his insight deepens:

    The handheld camera becomes much more stable—the movement of the camera—and there's a moment when I thought that he would be seeing everything in much more of an expanded way. He would be much wiser, in a way. So I changed the format from 1:85 to 2:40. And then I changed it even to anamorphic. After that, everything became more relaxed. And every time there's a point-of-view shot, every time Uxbal looks at an object, I change the speed. Instead of shooting 24 frames per second, I shoot 27, so everything in the moment becomes a little bit slower. He observes things more clearly. It's very subtle. But I think it helps to navigate the emotional journey. (Russ Slater, "Interview with Alejandro González Iñárittu," *Sounds and Colours*, July11, 2011. Available at www.soundsandcolours.com/subjects/film/art-should-provoke-an-interview-with-alejandro-gonzalez-inarritu/)

19. Tolstoy's *The Death of Ivan Ilych*, for example, or Kurosawa's *Ikiru*.

20. Cf.

> This is the worst era of dictatorship in my opinion. I am not exaggerating. Humans are living in the worst dictatorship ever, and this is the dictatorship of corporations, the dictatorship of the capitalists. These capitalists live by market rules and thus they do not have any God, any idealism, no intellectual purpose, nothing. . . . All they care about is income. There are no rules, there are no ethics, just income. Humanism and intellectualism and spiritualism are being killed by capitalism. All the values we once had are constantly being killed. And here is the most important thing to recognize: Ideas will be globalized, problems will be globalized, money will be globalized, services will be globalized but human beings are not being allowed to globalize. That is the most stupid thing and that is what will create systemic terrorism all over the world and our situation will be worse than it is now. . . . I believe that there is nothing inherently wrong with money or with owning property, it's just that the way it is currently being executed is completely irresponsible.

See Sergio C. Munoz, "Alejandro González Iñárittu explains new film *Biutiful*," *Poder360* Magazine interview, Dec. 2010. Available at www.poder360.com/article_detail.php?id_article=5050.
21. See the quotation that opens this chapter.
22. Alluding to Dreyer's religious masterpiece, Iñárittu remarks of *Biutiful* that

> The film could be titled 'The Passion of Uxbal'. It's a scrutinizing journey to find light, to explore human beings, to understand human nature in the worst conditions. And that's what existentialist writers do; they put an ordinary man into extraordinary conditions and observe what happens.

Iñárittu also acknowledges that *Biutiful* takes seriously Uxbal's spiritual experiences, endorses the reality of his psychic gift, and remains animated by the question of faith in God. See Eugen Rabkin, "Alejandro González Iñárittu, the Redeemer," *Planet Magazine* interview, Dec 29, 2010. Available at www.planet-mag.com/2010/features/eugene-rabkin/alejandro-gonzalez-inarritu/.
23. See Heidegger, *Being and Time,* trans. Joan Stambaugh (Albany: State University of New York Press, 2010).
24. During the press conference for *Biutiful* at the 2010 Cannes Film Festival, Iñárittu remarked:

> I think the film is full of splashes of hope. Even in all those circumstances that are against the character in the Greek tradition of tragedy—against a character who is trying to survive, trying to do things better. . . . [Like] the Book of Job, he's just trying to navigate against the will of God. . . . I think the guy is full of light, I think the guy gives himself. . . . I think that everything he inspires is very lovely, and I think there's a lot of forgiveness, which I think is a key word and what we are missing in this world. . . . This is the most hopeful of my films, by far. ("Director: *Biutiful* My Most Hopeful Film," *Digital Spy,* May 22, 2010. Available at www.digitalspy.com.au/news/a221023/director-biutiful-my-most-hopeful-film.html#ixzz2aPE0ksga)

25. The revelatory power of the face—above all Javier Bardem's/Uxbal's, but also those of his wife Marambra, his children Ana and Mateo, of those who have died, of Ige, the Senegalese woman, and of his dead father as a young man—is perhaps the most important aesthetic and ethical element of the film.
26. Gilles Deleuze and Felix Guattari, *Kafka: Towards a Minor Literature,* trans. Dana Polan (Minneapolis: University of Minnesota Press, 1986). See Gilles

Deleuze, *Cinema 2: The Time-Image*, trans. Hugh Tomlinson and Robert Galatea (Minneapolis: University of Minnesota Press, 1989), 215–24.
27. See Mark Redhead, *Charles Taylor: Thinking and Living Deep Diversity* (Lanham: Rowman & Littlefield, 2002).
28. See, for example, Jürgen Habermas, "A Post-Secular World Society? An Interview with Jürgen Habermas." Translated by Matthias Fritsch. Available at http://blogs.ssrc.org/tif/wp-content/uploads/2010/02/A-Postsecular-World-Society-TIF.pdf.
29. See Philip Mosley, *The Cinema of the Dardenne Brothers: Responsible Realism* (London/New York Wallflower Press, 2012), 78.
30. As Philip Mosley observes, one should be wary of taking the Levinasian reading too literally. Indeed, he cautions against taking the "positive confrontation" between Assita and Igor at the end of the film (after Igor confesses that Amidou is dead) as "an attempt to illustrate the face to face encounter, for it remains a transcendent experience and is empirically unverifiable." *The Cinema of the Dardenne Brothers*, 78.
31. See Mosley, *The Dardenne Brothers*, 39–62.
32. See Bradshaw's ambivalent but derisory comments on *Biutiful* as oscillating between brilliant and bogus: "Its attempt at a globalist, humanist aesthetic of compassion looks from certain angles thrillingly ambitious—and from others dreamy and self-congratulatory, like a Benetton ad from the 1990s, and verging on misery porn-chic." Peter Bradshaw, *Biutiful*—review, *The Guardian*, Jan. 27, 2011. Available at www.guardian.co.uk/film/2011/jan/27/biutiful-review.
33. Cf. Malick's *The Tree of Life*, which also garnered polarized responses, arguably also because of its religiosity. For a discussion of this point, see Robert Sinnerbrink, "Cinematic Belief: Bazinian Cinephilia and Malick's *The Tree of Life*," *Angelaki* 17:4 (2012), 95–117.
34. See Peter Bradshaw's scathing review of *Babel*, for example, which he claims is "exasperatingly conceited" because it extorts moral sympathy by illegitimate narrative means in its presentation of character: "They look up at the sceptical observer with the saucer-eyed saintliness of a baby seal in culling season, or a charity mugger smilingly wishing a nice day on the retreating back of a passer-by." Available at www.guardian.co.uk/film/2007/jan/19/drama.thriller.
35. Peter Bradshaw, *Biutiful*—review, *The Guardian*.
36. See Murray Smith, *Engaging Characters: Fiction, Emotion, and the Cinema* (Cambridge: Cambridge University Press, 1995).
37. Ashgar Farhadi's *A Separation* (2011) and *Le passé* (2013) are brilliant examples of this kind of cinematic ethics.
38. In an earlier scene between Hai and his lover/business partner, Hai remarks that Uxbal asked for money again to buy heaters for the Chinese workers and his partner replies that he will see to it. Hai agrees that they should give up making fake designer handbags and move instead into construction; there is more money in it, less risk of being caught, and it will ensure that they keep the "Mendoza contract," which is in danger of being lost. The point is that all of these interlocking social and economic relations are involved in the complex situation that Uxbal finds himself within when he makes the fateful decision to buy the faulty heaters. As he later laments, he knew that buying these heaters was risky but did so because he needed the money for his children. Money is clearly at the root of this particular "evil."

11 Understanding Religion and Film in "Postsecular" Russia

Jolyon Mitchell

INTRODUCTION

How is religion portrayed in Russian films? How have these portrayals evolved over the last century? To what extent is it possible to trace a return to a more positive representation of religion in Russian moviemaking? In order to understand the place of religion in contemporary Russian films, it is useful to consider how cinema has evolved in Russia over the last century by considering the answers to these questions. While another chapter in this volume explores the place of the holy fool in Russian cinema,[1] in this more broadly focused essay I chart the complex and changing relations between film and religion in Russia since the earliest days of cinema.[2] To understand the relation between religion and film in Russia, it is also useful to take into account the changing political context in which the films have been produced since the dominant themes and the content have often been heavily influenced by the political mood. I will therefore consider the interactions between religion and film in Czarist Russia, then in Soviet Russia and, more briefly, in post-Soviet Russia.[3]

While it may be possible and tempting to think about these periods in terms of religious, secular and postsecular ages, a more nuanced reading of Russian history reveals the ambiguous and changing place of religion over the last one hundred and twenty years in one of the world's geographically largest nation states.[4] The simple categorization of religious, secular and postsecular ages overlooks the ambiguity inherent within these categories, in particular with regard to the different understanding of secularization in the Soviet Union compared to Europe and the US. Such an approach can also fail to take account of the significant political influence on film production in Russia during this time. These are some of the reasons why the structure of this chapter underlines the political context in its consideration of the development of religion in Russian film.

Nevertheless, it is possible to describe many cultural elements within post-Soviet Russia as postsecular. Given this assumption behind my discussion, what exactly is understood by postsecular in this essay? With the lifting of restrictions on religious activities in post-Soviet Russia, religion became at once both private (where it had previously been explicitly forbidden it now offered a free choice) and public (with forbidden religion now establishing a public presence in numerous ways).[5] In spite of the state's renewed support for Russian Orthodoxy, there is now once again freedom to practice religion and an increasing plurality of religious and non-religious beliefs to be found around Russia.[6] The significant influence which this had on religious themes in films, particularly in contrast to the portrayal of religion during the Soviet era, is explored through discussion of a few carefully selected films. These are intended to be emblematic of the evolving presence of religion in Russian film.

RELIGION AND FILM IN CZARIST RUSSIA

Although most films during the early period of cinema were not overtly religious, it is important to understand how they were influenced by the political climate since the influence of those in power on what is depicted on screen is both far-reaching and prevailing. The first films to be screened in Russia were shown in May 1896 at the Aquarium, a summer theater in St. Petersburg. This coincided with the coronation of Nicolai II, which had attracted large crowds from around the world to St. Petersburg and Moscow. Included in the visitors were pioneers of cinema from France, England and the US, who saw an opportunity to expand into the new and as yet untested market of Russia. This first screening was shown before the third act of *Alfred-Pasha in Petersburg* and featured Lumière films such as *L'Arrivée du train en gare* and *Partie d'Ecarté*. Although received with mixed reviews, as the early films often were, it was obvious that the Russian film market would soon become a lucrative one for investors.

The first film actually made in Russia was shot a couple of weeks before the first screenings and captured scenes connected with a civil religious ritual: the Coronation of Czar Nicholas II on May 26 [O.S. May 14], 1896. This short sequence contains shots of the Imperial couple entering and leaving the Cathedral of the Assumption in the Kremlin, as well as a line of extravagantly dressed foreign dignitaries. The religious rituals at the center of the coronation are not recorded, as are neither the numerous Orthodox priests robed in gold nor the golden icons which covered the walls of the cathedral. However, a camera did record the moment a few days later when the Czar was presented to the Russian people, when a stand collapsed, leading to a stampede where hundreds were crushed to death. The film was confiscated and has never been seen since that time, although the film of the coronation became a popular one that was often shown in the newly built Russian film theaters and even to the Czar himself at his palace in Livadia.

For the first years, the film industry was controlled exclusively by the French, who did not hesitate to make use of the Russian and French political and economic alliances. This began to change after the Revolution of 1905 with other foreigners entering the scene for the first time. It was a difficult market however; the social and political realities that affected daily life left little time or inclination for indulging in the illusions of the screen, and the middle-class, laborers and peasants rarely patronized the theaters. It was only the more sophisticated among the city dwellers that showed interest in what was referred to as "The Latest Miracle of the Twentieth Century." This limited the audience, thereby also diminishing the influence of what was shown on screen, which, however, did not prevent a strong reaction from the Church.

From the beginning, the leaders of the Orthodox Church had an ambivalent and often suspicious attitude towards the cinema, and clergy were strictly forbidden to attend. The wary view of the Church was shared and supported by the Czar, particularly in the period leading up to the War. Initially, the cinematic depiction of Jesus was a complete taboo. The Orthodox Church responded almost immediately to one portrayal of Jesus with a letter issued by the office of the Holy Synod in 1898: "On the inadmissibility of holy subjects being shown by means of the so-called 'Living photography'." This was Russia's first film censorship document. Other early Jesus films provoked further controversy. *La Vie et La Passion du Christ* (Pathé; production began in 1902), the world's earliest color Jesus movie, was initially censored by the Orthodox Church's Holy Synod when it first arrived in Russia as a "violation of the Gospels," though it was permitted more widespread circulation in 1907. There were some supporters of such ventures who saw similarities between, on the one hand, cinematic communication, and on the other, religious iconography and painting. When it was finally screened, the police were present to ensure that everyone in attendance took off their hats as a sign of reverence. It still provoked controversy.

It was not only to onscreen religious depictions that the church and government responded. In 1913 the Czar famously wrote in the margin of a police report on cinema suggesting films could be divisive: "I consider cinematography to be an empty, useless and even pernicious diversion. Only an abnormal person could put this fairground business on the same level as art. It is all nonsense and no importance should be attributed to it." Nonetheless, he did make use of a court filmmaker to record significant events, and this established a precedent in Russian film, ensuring that other Russian filmmakers followed suit. Between 1907 and the Great War, over 1,800 newsreels were produced. The early days of Russian filmmaking concentrated upon grand state occasions and sometimes explicitly religious events such as the "solemn procession of Pilgrims at Kiev."

The wrath which a number of early films incurred on the part of the Church because of their content or their themes resulted in films being censored alongside other areas of suppression. Police would often visit the theater during the first showing of a film, confiscating those that were not within the official guidelines. Films on the French Revolution were banned from the earliest days, and from 1908 pornographic films were declared illegal. It was not long, however, before the Russian film industry was struggling to survive. The public loved the dramatic films from France, and Khanzhonkov's films of theater productions were equally popular. The solemn, pompous and political nature of Russian films could not compete, and towards the end of the first decade of the 1900s, Drankov pushed Russian film in a new direction, appealing in particular to sensual costumes and bawdy behavior.

Although the majority of popular films remained foreign imports, there was a steady, if not prolific, production in Russia. Alongside non-fiction news and documentary films there emerged a number of fiction films. Later, both religious themes and figures made appearances in Russian-made films. This cinematic trespassing into the world of the sacred contributed to recurring attempts by the Orthodox Church to control content far more rigorously than it had done up until this point in the early days of cinema.

Two examples suffice. First, the silent film entitled *Departure of a Grand Old Man* (*Ukhod velikovo startza*, 1912), directed and produced by Yakov Protazanov and Elizaveta Thiman, portrays peasants requesting land from Leo Tolstoy, his refusal to help on the grounds that his wife owns the land, his subsequent arguments with his wife, his increased depression and his final encounter in the clouds with Christ. In Russia at that time, the power of censorship lay with the Orthodox Church, who banned this film on the grounds that they found the depiction of Tolstoy, himself excommunicated in real life, being led into heaven as blasphemous. Others have suggested that the film was censored due to the negative depiction of Tolstoy's wife.

The Second is *Father Sergius* (*Otets Sergiy*, 1917), co-directed by Yakov Protazanov and Alexandre Volkoff. This silent film, the last to be made before the October Revolution, is based on Leo Tolstoy's homonymous short story (published in 1898). The central figure discovers on the eve of his wedding that his fiancée has had an affair with Nicholas I. Deeply disillusioned, he turns to the Church, becoming first an Orthodox monk and then a hermit, beset by doubts and temptations. Over one hundred and twelve minutes it brings together religion, politics, lust and heartbreak, culminating in the protagonist's demise. This tragic tale cinematically reflects the tension between religious commitment and personal desire and has been described as both scandalous and ground-breaking. The filming of this story in 1917 in an unstable political climate was inviting trouble for the filmmakers, although it remains uncertain whether this was one of the reasons why the film was not screened until 1918. The lack of anti-religious overtones in the film could be an indication of the turmoil of the political climate in which uncertainty regarding both the regime and the Church were still being worked out. This, however, was set to change over the next decade when religion would often be portrayed as ludicrous, dishonest and tyrannical.

RELIGION AND FILM IN SOVIET RUSSIA

Films immediately following the 1917 February and October Revolutions and the ensuing civil war were undeniably linked to the political climate of the day, and the new communist leaders were swift to encourage the use of film for propaganda purposes. Censorship had a part to play in determining what the audience was encouraged to believe by controlling what was seen on screen. Scripts for film proposals were subject to approval, certain themes being encouraged while others were firmly rejected. Certainly throughout the 1920s, considered by some the Golden Age of cinema in Russia, the Party would make suggestions on how the arts in general and cinema in particular could, with the implied imperative, offer support of the socialist ideology. Consider Leon Trotsky's article in *Pravda* on "Vodka, the Church, and the Cinema" (July 12, 1923). In it he berates his comrades for not making better use of film to persuade the masses. "Here is an instrument which we must secure at all costs!" He portrays the cinema in competition "not only with the tavern but also with the church." He believes that "this rivalry may become fatal for the church" if the cinema is put to effective use. For Trotsky, the cinema provides "spectacular images of greater grip than are provided by the richest church" or "mosque or synagogue." Trotsky asserts that "the cinema amuses, educates, strikes the imagination by images, and liberates you from the need of crossing the church door" and that it is "the most important weapon" in propaganda. For some, like Trotsky, cinema had the potential to replace the need for visiting traditional places for worship; for others, it was perceived as a powerful tool of persuasion to be used to promote the new regime, particularly because it was accessible to everybody and had the power for educating the masses by pushing the audience in the direction deemed necessary by the Party.

During the 1920s and 1930s, filmmakers appropriated and inverted religious themes. Martyrs, not for the Church but for the Soviet cause, are commonly depicted and celebrated. Some filmmakers' personal experience of the Orthodox Church informed, perhaps even haunted, their filmmaking. The director Sergei Eisenstein never forgot the dramatic rituals he experienced in church as a boy and would sometimes refer to his Jewish heritage. According to one biographer, Marie Seton, Eisenstein once confessed that "he had spent sixteen years of his life striving to destroy the fascination that religion exerted over him." This disregard for the Church is explicitly depicted in many of his films through "typage" and "intellectual montages."

In *Battleship Potemkin* (1925), the officers, with their pince-nez, waxed moustaches and distinguished airs and graces are clearly representative of the upper classes. The sailors represent the proletariat, and it is in the midst of an on-board mutiny that harsh criticism of the Orthodox Church emerges. The Church is clearly aligned with the officers and therefore with those in authority. A seemingly crazy Orthodox Priest, with wild hair which reinforces his wild power, is the Church's representative in this film, and with Eisenstein's love of "typage," this is surely a reflection of his personal feelings toward the Church. In one scene, the priest taps his ornate cross while a sailor fiddles with his sword. The link between Church and armed forces as protectors of the autocracy is impossible to miss. This relationship between religion and authority is reinforced later with a montage of Captain and Priest. Shortly thereafter, in the midst of the rebellion, the priest rebukes the sailors, declaring that they are fighting God. Making use of another effective montage, Eisenstein inter-cuts shots of the priest waving his cross with a shot of a sailor and an officer engaged in hand-to-hand combat. The cross is eventually pried from the priest's hands and it falls onto the deck, where it gouges into the wood like an axe: a symbol of grace is aligned with a deadly weapon. The message here is clear; not only the upper classes and those with authority but the Church, too, is oppressive and tyrannical.

Similarly, Eisenstein's depictions of priests and other members of the Orthodox Church are far from flattering in *October* (1927/8), with the image of a worshipping priest juxtaposed with pictures of the supposedly corrupt leaders of the 1917 provisional government. *October,* produced to commemorate the Bolshevik revolution ten years before, begins with the destruction of the statue of Alexander III holding the symbols of "God" and "country": an orb and a scepter. Towards the end of the film, the Czar and Czarina's private apartments in The Winter Palace are overrun by the Bolsheviks who "find a host of sentimental icons portraying the allegiance of religion and the state, including Christ blessing the imperial family."[7] Through the use of an "intellectual montage," which brings together a baroque image of Jesus, Hindu and Aztec Gods, the Buddha and a collection of primitive idols, Eisenstein appears to portray all religions as the same. The juxtaposition of this with military paraphernalia reflects the perceived parallels between patriotism and delusional belief. This disdain for religion is also representative of the almost ignored role of the Orthodox Church's protests against the Socialist government found not only in Eisenstein's films but in films in general during this period.

Eisenstein's unfinished *Bezhin Meadow* (1936/7), mostly destroyed by fire during a bombing raid in the Second World War, includes shots of a church being transformed into a club for workers. The overturning of the old order is symbolically represented by an inverted reflection of a church in water. The icons are carried without ceremony and deference, the workers become part of the icons themselves and a life-size crucifix is removed under the arm of a bearded laborer. Through the "sanctification of the peasant," here is the "triumph of the people's vital energy over lifeless deities."[8] In his anti-German historical epic *Alexander Nevsky* (1938), the monk associated with the Teutonic crusading knights appears to look on approvingly as baby after baby is dropped into a fire.

In the midst of the negative portrayal of religion in early Soviet films, Eisenstein's *Strike* (1924) should be added to the films discussed above as well as Pudovkin's *Storm Over Asia* (1928), which celebrates the deaths of martyrs for the Soviet anti-religious cause, and Dovzhenko's *Earth* (*Zemlya*, 1930). In this film, a vigorous young man, Vasil, is murdered and then portrayed as a martyr for the new Soviet way of life. Dovzhenko's revised script (completed in 1956) promotes a fervent anti-religious message, with Vasil's father declaring to the priest: "There is no God . . . Because if there had been a God, even if he weren't altogether almighty or all-merciful, even if he'd been a miserable little God, turned a bit senile by age and all that worship, even one like that wouldn't have let my son die that way." Later, at the collective farm board, Vasil's father "begs" his listeners: "If my Vasil has died for a new life . . . he should be buried in a new way. I don't want priests and deacons seeing him out for a fee, but our own boys and girls with new songs about the new life." While an old priest calls down God to smite the people, they sing a new song in a "godless" world. Through this film Dovzhenko belittles the old elites: landowners and church leaders.

There are many other explicit anti-religious cinematic statements to be found during the 1930s. *The Feast of St Jorgen* (1930; dir. Protazanov Prazdnik), sometimes described as "an exposé" of religious faith, shows how two thieves escape from prison, hide in a Church and while there they observe the riches accumulated by the priests. The result is that they aim to relinquish the Church of its ill-gotten gains. In other films, such as the different animated versions of *The Tale of the Priest and of His Worker Balda* (1934, dir. Michael Tsekhanovsky; 1940, dir. Panteleimon Sazanov; 1956, dir. Anatoly Karanovich; 1973, dir. Inessa Kovlevskaya), based on an 1830 poem by Alexander Pushkin, priests were represented as lazy, dishonest or exploitative scoundrels. Nuns also became the focus of satire or parody. Alexander Medvedkin's 1934 irreverent comedy, *Happiness,* includes the sight of nuns wearing transparent tops and a priest fighting for money.

Filmmakers perceived cinematic dramas or fairy-tales as the "opiate of the people," with realist documentaries celebrated as a more true form of communication. Dziga Vertov, for example, was a vociferous proponent and practitioner of such a view, with the first reel of his 1931 film *Enthusiasm* including actual footage from 1929 of steeples being pulled down, icons or relics being removed and churches converted into workers' clubs. This complex film received much hostile criticism in Russia, not for its obvious atheistic tendencies, but rather for its failure to show the followers of religion involved in a fight against socialism. Religion, like subservience to the Czar and addiction to alcohol, is relegated to a historical shadow rather than a dynamic force countering the Soviet state.

Not all Soviet filmmakers were entirely negative towards established religion, particularly from the 1940s. Certainly in Eisenstein's later films, there is a departure from the Marxist-Leninist interpretation of history present in his earlier films. He now offers an individual and truthful depiction of history rather than perpetuating Stalinist myths. Alongside this, there is greater ambiguity towards religious figures and spaces in both *Ivan the Terrible Part 1* (1944) and *Part 2* (1946; released in 1958). The religious leaders both conspire against and stand up to Ivan's tyrannical rule, reminiscent of Stalin's paranoid leadership, while the cathedral becomes a place of failed assassination and murder. Some film historians argue that a similar ambivalence towards religion is to be seen even more clearly among other filmmakers during "the Thaw" following the death of Stalin in 1953. For example, Tony Shaw suggests that even during the religious persecutions initiated by Nikita Khrushchev, several films were more sympathetic portrayals of priests. This is a persuasive argument when considered in the light of films such as *The Miracle Worker* (1960; dir. Vladimir Skuibin), where a young pioneer is "designated a saint after finding a 'miracle-working' icon," or *Clouds over Borsk* (1960; dir. Vasilii Ordyskii,), which sympathetically depicts "religious sects that believed in speaking in tongues," or the compassionate priest in *Everything Remains for the People* (1964; dir. Georgii Natanson). Shaw concludes that such "relatively sympathetic portrayals of clerics were a far cry from those seen on Soviet cinema screens in the 1920s and 1930s when priests were characterized as criminal deviants, or in the late 1940s and early 1950s when their role as agents of Western influence was accentuated."[9]

Ambivalence toward religion almost becomes celebration in the seven films directed by Andrei Tarkovsky. Tarkovsky himself described his films as being "about one thing: the extreme manifestation of faith." His films have of course received considerable attention from those concerned with the relation between film and religion, which is not surprising given the explicit religious themes and common use of religious art and symbols. For instance, *Andre Rublov* (1966) goes behind the apparently peaceful world of religious iconography to reveal a sixteenth-century Russia torn by conflict and an artist wracked by guilt and the inability to create. The film is an exploration of testing religious beliefs in the face of reality. Andre Rublov learns about love, community and brotherhood as a monk in the Holy Trinity Monastery of St Sergius. Outside the monastery, however, he is confronted with suffering, and it is only after losing his faith through an inability to reconcile his idea of good with the harsh reality that he once again arrives at the starting point of love, good and brotherhood. This black and white world is only transformed into color in the last few minutes of this over three-hour film, where Tarkovsky slowly reveals to the viewer some of Rublov's most famous icons, and especially the Holy Trinity. Unlike the rapid montage movements of Eisenstein, Tarkovsky is not afraid to hold a shot on a face or a landscape or an interior and allow the viewer to savor what they are seeing. This focus on the Trinity reinforces the triumph of good over evil; the seemingly empty suffering of the world is redeemed through faith and love. Not only does this message have positive religious connotations, but it is also a message that is critical of the regime.

Stalker (1979) makes explicit use of religion, with quotations from the Gospel of Luke and Revelation and a crown of thorns introduced in the midst of a discussion on forgiveness. *Stalker* is based on the novel *Roadside Picnic,* a science-fiction story by Arkadi and Boris Strugatsky. Aliens leave behind a dangerous Zone after visiting earth, and it is only with the help of a Stalker, a guide in the Zone, that visitors are allowed into this area. Visitors enter the Zone in search of a room where their innermost desires can be realized, offering an opportunity for philosophical views to be explored in the film through the journey of two people, the Writer, who approaches life in a pragmatic way, and the Scientist, with a more rational approach. The Stalker offers a morally superior alternative, seemingly incorruptible and committed to his own spirituality. The loyalty and devotion of the Stalker's wife offer a different philosophy to the cynicism and moral decay of the world in which the Writer and Scientist are living. It is not known how far this is intentional critique of the context in which Tarkovsky found himself, but the alternative morality depicted in the film is hard to ignore.

Lingering shots are also effectively used in Tarkovsky's last film, *The Sacrifice* (1986), a Swedish production which he made knowing he was dying of lung cancer. The film famously depicts the self-sacrifice of Alexander, a journalist, theater and literary critic and former actor, who offers his life, his home and even his son to God in order to try to avert a nuclear war which would destroy everything. Like several of his earlier Russian films, it is hard to avoid the recurring religious motifs, though this provokes diverse responses, with some critics claiming God is absent while others celebrate his presence through Tarkovsky's works. This argument aside, it is acknowledged that Tarkovsky's largely sympathetic treatment of religious themes provides a marked contrast to the early *agit* films, part of the anti-religious propaganda of the 1920s and 1930s. Each of his films, especially those already discussed as well as *Mirror* (1972) and *Nostalghia* (1983) are worthy of careful study by those concerned about religion and film.

Tarkovsky's work is a comparative rarity, especially among the films produced during the seven decades of communist rule, and his films anticipate many of the themes to be found in films produced following *glasnost* and the end of the Soviet regime. The censorship which continued until the mid-1980s, and so frustrated Tarkovsky, prevented any serious outworking of religious themes. This was also perpetuated by the lack of widely available theology, which meant that while some people were exposed to and influenced by an Orthodox way of thinking, their belief lacked any systematic understanding of the doctrine of the Russian Orthodox Church, resulting instead in a syncretic system which combined Orthodox Theology with ideas from other religions and philosophies.[10]

RELIGION AND FILM IN POST-SOVIET RUSSIA

From the mid-1980s, Russia underwent a number of dramatic political and cultural transformations. With the accelerated economic restructuring of *perestroika* and the increased freedom of expression through *glasnost*, the Russian people experienced radical political, social and economic changes. These transformations, which began under Mikhail Gorbachev's leadership, had a significant impact upon the depiction of religion in Russian film. *Repentance* (1986/7; dir. Tengiz Abuladze) lauded as a significant example of the relaxation of censorship, represents the first notable work from the *glasnost* era that is permeated with religious themes. Set in a small Georgian village, it tells the haunting story of a woman who is on trial for repeatedly exhuming the body of a former town leader. This is a powerful Georgian parable about digging up the past, in particular the painful Stalinist past, and atoning for buried wrongs. It was an extremely important political film, being anti-Stalinist and an excellent artistic production, raising questions about evil, death, Satan and the Last Judgment alongside beauty and hope for the future. At one point, an old woman asks a rhetorical question; "What good is a road if it doesn't lead to a temple?" A reminder, perhaps, of freedom that was lost but a future that can be redeemed.

While many of the films from this era are deeply critical of past evils, some are equally critical through their narratives of religious intolerance or anti-Semitic tendencies. Pavel Lounguine's *Luna Park* (1991) is one example which questions anti-Semitism. Protagonist Andrei has lived a life in which competition between Russian heroes like his deceased father and the enemy, including Jews and foreigners, is a part of life. His mother is particularly intolerant and incites anger and violence in Andrei and his gang. One day in a drunken state she reveals that his father is in fact a Jew and not the dead man who raised him. Andrei's initial anti-Semitic rage in confronting his father is eventually won over by his father's charm and civility. This film opposes anti-Semitic and xenophobic views by exposing a human side to those perceived to be a threat.

More recently, films have depicted protagonists seeking to escape their violent pasts and searching for peace. There is often a religious resonance to this quest. In *The Hero* (2006; dir. Veledinski), Kir, a soldier returning from the Chechen Wars, first encounters the ghosts of his two fallen comrades and then an Orthodox priest, Father Sergei. In real life, the two actors who play Kir and Father Sergei are twins. There is one memorable scene in the film where they wrestle like Jacob and the angel in the Biblical story (Gen. 32), but this violence aside, the priest appears to be trying to help Kir come to terms with his past. He later helps him find the graves of his fallen comrades. Unlike the anti-clerical depictions of the 1920s and 30s, the Orthodox priest is now regularly depicted in a more favorable light.[11]

One of Russia's most popular films of 2006 was *The Island* (dir. Pavel Lungin), which is primarily set on an isolated island monastery somewhere in Northern Russia in 1976 and depicts a small group of Orthodox monks in endearing detail. The central figure, Father Anatoly (played by Pavel Mamonov) is portrayed as an uneasy figure, searching for personal forgiveness for being forced to shoot his captain during the Second World War. While this inner war rages on, he attracts other people to his boiler room come sooty cell, in search of advice, healing or holiness. Before his death, he is reconciled on several different levels, and for all his idiosyncrasies, he is depicted highly sympathetically. The film attracted considerable support from the Orthodox Church, with some advertising the film and others buying out entire cinemas. In ways reminiscent of how certain churches in North America made use of *The Passion of the Christ* (2003; dir. Mel Gibson), so some Orthodox Christians made use of *The Island*. At one cinema, viewers were even encouraged to take off their hats and pray before it began.

Rather than rejecting religious belief, some figures are now depicted as embracing religious faith. Two contrasting examples will suffice. First, in Vladimir Khotinenko's *The Moslem* (1995), a young man, Kolya, is captured while fighting in Afghanistan and converts to Islam. His return to his home village is far from peaceful as, in the light of his new-found faith, he refuses to conform. Second, towards the end of *Cargo 200*, one of the most talked about films of 2007, one of the central characters, Artem Kazakov, a professor of Scientific Atheism at Leningrad University, goes to church and asks to be baptized. This represents a clear shift from a place where religion was forbidden in favor of the state. There is a willingness to explore not only Orthodox religion but also an acknowledgement of religious pluralism and the place religion may have in public life.

CONCLUSION

Following the downfall of the Soviet Regime, cinematic depictions of religion are changing. In sharp contrast to the 1920s and 1930s where Russian Orthodoxy was largely reviled, its priests and beliefs are now often portrayed far more sympathetically. These depictions are going beyond some of the more ambiguous and occasionally favorable depictions from the 1970s. Orthodox priests and monks act as guides or become models of those searching for peace and the transcendent. Other religious traditions are also sometimes depicted in more favorable terms. In these recent Russian cinematic contexts, religion is portrayed as not an entirely divisive force, and more commonly as an agent for different kinds of spiritual searching. One way of describing this religious landscape is as the postsecular, or least as partly postsecular, or even beyond the postsecular. These cinematic worlds provide insights into how the place of religion in Russia has evolved over the last three decades. There is evidence of fragmentation as well as sporadic religious freedom and expression.

The different examples from the post-Soviet period, discussed earlier, reflect how film in Russia has become increasingly sympathetic towards religious themes, characters and controversies. While it is tempting to interpret this as a return to pre-revolutionary depictions, such a circular description does not do justice to the varied ways in which film has evolved in Russia over the last century. Religion remains a complex and powerful force which is emerging with greater confidence into the public sphere. The Russian films of the last two decades reflect not only greater openness to Russian Orthodoxy, but they are also beginning to reveal some of the religious fault-lines within post-Soviet Russia.

NOTES

1. See in this volume Alina Birzache, "'Casting Fire onto the Earth': The Holy Fool in Russian Cinema."
2. I am grateful to Professor Julian Graffy (Professor of Russian Literature and Cinema at University College London) for his extremely helpful advice during the early stages of my research for this chapter. I am also indebted to Dr. Jenny Wright for her assistance in the later stages of work on this chapter.
3. This essay is an updated, expanded and adapted version of "Portraying Religion and Peace in Russian Film" in *Studies in World Christianity* 13:3 (Summer 2008), 142–52 and "Religion and Film in Russia" in *The Encyclopedia of Religion and Film,* ed. Eric Mazur. (Santa Barbara, California and Oxford: ABC-CLIO, 2011), 373–80.
4. See, Robert Service, *The Penguin History of Modern Russia: From Tsarism to the Twenty-First Century,* 3rd ed. (London: Penguin, 2009). See also Martin Sixsmith, *Russia: A Thousand Year Chronicle of the Wild East* (London: Random House, 2011). This book accompanied the entitled BBC radio series *Russia,* first broadcast on BBC Radio 4 in 2011.
5. An interesting discussion of the public and private nature of religion in Russia has been explored by Orthodox scholar Alexander Kyrlezhev. See, for example, his conference paper "Postsecularism in Post-Atheist Russia." Available at www.pecob.eu/politics-culture-religion-postsecular-world. Last accessed June 20, 2013.
6. For a detailed discussion of the changing shape of religious life in Russia and the complex relationship this has on culture and identity, see Alexander Agadjanian, "Revising Pandora's Gifts: Religious and National Identity in the Post-Soviet Societal Fabric," *Europe-Asia Studies* 53:3 (2001), 473–88. For a more detailed discussion on the relationship between Orthodoxy and Islam, see Juliet Johnson, Marietta Stepaniants and Benjamin Frost (eds.). *Religion and Identity in Modern Russia: The Revival of Orthodoxy and Islam* (Aldershot: Ashgate, 2005).
7. David Bordwell, *The Cinema of Eisenstein* (London: Routledge, 2005), 94.
8. Ibid., 181–2.
9. See Tony Shaw, "Martyrs, Miracles, and Martians: Religion and Cold War Cinematic Propaganda in the 1950s," *Journal of Cold War Studies* 4:2 (Spring 2002), 3–22.
10. See John B. Dunlop, "Religious Themes in Recent Soviet Cinema," *Religion, State and Society: The Keston Journal* 16:3 (1988), 210–26.
11. This can also be seen in television depictions such as the hugely popular eleven part series about a *Punishment Battalion* (2004) during the Second World War. The local priest not only fights with extraordinary bravery, but he also blesses his comrades before the final battle.

FURTHER READING

Agadjanian, Alexander. "Revising Pandora's Gifts: Religious and National Identity in the Post-Soviet Societal Fabric." *Europe-Asia Studies* 53 no. 3 (2001): 473–88.
Adam Bingham, "Poetry in Motion: Alexander Dovzhenko's Earth." *Senses of Cinema* website. Available at: www.sensesofcinema.com/contents/cteq/04/earth.html.
Birkos, Alexander S. *Soviet Cinema: Directors and Films.* Hamden, CT: Archon, 1976.
Bryher. *Film Problems of Soviet Russia.* Territet, Switzerland: (no publisher), 1929.

Cohen, Louis. *The Cultural-Political Traditions and Developments of the Soviet Cinema, 1917–1972*. NY: Arno Press, 1974.

Dickinson, Thorold, and Catherine De la Roche. *Soviet Cinema*. London: Falcon Press, 1948.

Dovzhenko, Alexander. *Two Russian Film Classics*. New York: Simon and Schuster, 1973.

Dunlop, John B. "Religious Themes in Recent Soviet Cinema." *Religion, State and Society: The Keston Journal* 16, no. 3 91988): 210–26.

Eisenschitz, Bernard, ed. *Lignes d'ombre: Une autre histoire du cinéma soviétique (1926–1968)*. Milan: Edizioni Gabriele Mazzotta, 2000.

Eisenstein, Sergei. *The Eisenstein Reader*. Edited by Richard Taylor. Translated by Richard Taylor and William Powell. London: BFI, 1998.

Gillespie, David. *Russian Cinema*. Inside Film Series. NY: Longman, 2003.

Johnson, Juliet, Marietta Stepaniants and Benjamin Frost. (eds.). *Religion and Identity in Modern Russia: The Revival of Orthodoxy and Islam*. Aldershot: Ashgate, 2005.

Leyda, Jay. *Kino: A History of Russian and Soviet Film*, 3rd ed. Princeton: Princeton UP, 1983.

Liehm, Mira, and Antonin J. *The Most Important Art: Soviet and East European Film After 1945*. Berkeley: University of California Press, 1977.

Mitchell, Jolyon, and S. Brent Plate. 2007. *The Religion and Film Reader*. London and New York, Routledge.

Padunov, Vladimir (ed.). *Russian and Soviet Cinema Bibliography* (University of Pittsburgh) Available at: www.pitt.edu/~slavic/video/cinema_biblio.html.

Plakhov, Andreï. *Soviet Cinema*. Moscow: Novosti, 1988.

Rimberg, John. *The Motion Picture in the Soviet Union, 1918–1952: A Sociological Analysis*. NY: Arno, 1973.

Rimberg, John, and Paul Babitsky. *The Soviet Film Industry*. NY: Praeger, 1955.

Roberts, Graham. *Forward Soviet: History and Non-fiction Film in the USSR*. London: I.B. Tauris, 1999.

Service, Robert. *The Penguin History of Modern Russia: From Tsarism to the Twenty-First Century*, 3rd ed. London: Penguin, 2009.

Shaw, Tony. "Martyrs, Miracles, and Martians: Religion and Cold War Cinematic Propaganda in the 1950s." *Journal of Cold War Studies* 4, no. 2 (Spring 2002): 3–22.

Shlapentokh, Dmitry, and Vladimir Shlapentokh. *Soviet Cinematography, 1917–1991: Ideological Conflict and Social Reality*. NY: Aldine de Gruyter, 1993.

Sixsmith, Martin. *Russia: A Thousand Year Chronicle of the Wild East*. London: Random House, 2011.

Taylor, Richard, and Ian Christie (eds.). *The Film Factory: Russian and Soviet Cinema in Documents, 1896–1939*. London: Routledge, 1988.

Tsivian, Yuri. *Early Cinema in Russia and Its Cultural Reception*. Edited by Richard Taylor. Translated by Alan Bodger. University of Chicago, 1998.

Vlasov, M.P. (ed.). *Istoriia otechestvennogo kinematografa: Programma kursa*, Moskva: VGIK, 1997.

Youngblood, Denise J. *Movies for the Masses: Popular Cinema and Soviet Society in the 1920s*. Cambridge, UK: Cambridge University Press, 1992.

Youngblood, Denise J. *The Magic Mirror: Moviemaking in Russia, 1908–1918*. Madison: University of Wisconsin Press, 1999.

Zorkaia, Neia. *Istoriia sovetskogo kino*. St. Petersburg: Aleteia, 2005.

Zorkaya, Neya. *The Illustrated History of Soviet Cinema*. London: Hippocrene Books, 1989.

Final Remarks
What is the Use of Postsecularism?
Conceptual Clarifications and Two Illustrations

Camil Ungureanu

Motto:
> "Wittgenstein influenced me a great deal, but not in the sense that one tries to appropriate the world, but rather that, as he said himself, it is better to be silent than to try to express the inexpressible. It's the mystical aspect of Wittgenstein's thinking that especially attracted me."
>
> (M. Haneke)[1]

> ". . . one must recover words like 'grace,' holiness,' for the profane world, we should not simply grant organized religion a monopoly over this language."
>
> (Bruno Dumont)[2]

Various chapters of this book support the view that there is a current wave of outstanding European directors who, from their position as self-declared atheists (Bruno Dumont, Michael Haneke, Nanni Moretti) or unconventional believers (Vladimir Sokurov, Semih Kaplanoğlu), make innovative films dealing with religious experience without celebrating the self-sufficiency of a secularist reason or an official-institutional discourse. Differences between these directors notwithstanding, they believe that religion cannot be dismissed as obsolete and irrelevant. Instead, these directors express by cinematographic means the conviction that it can be a powerful source of values and experiences (of faith, forgiveness, responsibility, guilt, solidarity, gift-giving, sacrifice, transcendence, mystical insight and conversion) that a secularism focused exclusively on a immanent reason is unable to account for. These cinematographic developments are at loggerheads with an influential secularist narrative that pits reason against religious tradition and prophesizes the "death of God" and the disappearance of religion in modernity. Indeed, in spite of the decline of church-going, especially in Europe, this secularism hostile to religion per se has become implausible. As Costica Bradatan points out in the "Introduction" to this volume, religious and quasi-religious experiences remain, often in heterodox, transformed and disguised forms, salient for a good part of Europeans. In several European countries, the authority of institutional religion has weakened, while the interest in (individualized) spiritual-religious experiences has grown. Even atheists have become more and more concerned with spiritual-religious experiences. As a reaction to the persistent existence of a plurality of spiritual-religious practices in the "secular age" (Charles Taylor), in the past decade, a new wave of philosophers, social theorists and sociologists have questioned the secularist opposition religion vs. modernity and faith vs. reason. Jürgen Habermas, Charles Taylor, John Caputo, Jacques Derrida, Ronald Dworkin, Thomas Nagel, Jean-Luc Nancy, Gianni Vattimo, José Casanova, Peter Berger—to name but a few—form a complex constellation of contemporary thinkers who reject, on account of philosophical and sociological arguments, the black-and-white vision of the "new atheists" (Christopher Hitchins, Richard Dawkins). By building on empirical studies and taking inspiration from (post-)Enlightenment philosophical debates around Kant, Hegel, Nietzsche and Kierkegaard, these contemporary thinkers and scientists posit a more complex and interactive role of religion in modernity—a role that some of them call "postsecular."

But what exactly is postsecularism? And does this philosophical and socio-theoretical concept have any use in cinema studies? Authors included in this volume understand "postsecularism" differently, and some of them are explicitly suspicious concerning its usage (e.g., Paul Coates).[3] Such critical reactions to this concept should not come as a surprise: like other "post" terms—postmodern, poststructural, postnational, postsovereign, postcinematic, posthuman—the use of "postsecular" invites *prima facie* skepticism. While the term "postsecular" has acquired prominence in philosophy, social theory and sociology in the last decade, its meaning and use has been vague and debatable, leading to potential confusion. Does "postsecular" refer to a new era following the secular one, as Habermas, Caputo and Hent de Vries suggest? Or does postsecularism refer to a new type of society (Habermas)? Furthermore, does postsecularism entail the overcoming if not the rejection of secularism? Or is the postsecular talk simply a passing fashion in social theory and philosophy (Veit Bader)?

In these "Final Remarks," I argue that, once properly circumscribed and severed from inflationary definitions, "postsecularism" can usefully designate a relevant trend in philosophy, social theory and cinema.[4] I will illustrate the fruitfulness of the postsecular perspective in analyzing film as part of a broader philosophical turn in cinema studies. In the following, I shall tackle the questions: what is the precise meaning and usefulness of speaking of a postsecular constellation? What is the relation between postsecular, secular and secularist? How productively can the term "postsecular" be applied to the study of film? I will start from characterizing the notion of "postsecular" and clearing away common misunderstandings of it (Section I). To illustrate the argument about the interaction between cinema and philosophy from a postsecular perspective, I shall analyze more in-depth two cases—Haneke's *Caché* (Section II) and Dumont's *The Life of Jesus* (Section III). I shall argue that *Caché* (2007) and *The Life of Jesus* (1997) display deep affinities with Derrida's postsecular rethinking of faith, transcendence and the mystical after the "death of God."

SECTION I POSTSECULAR, SECULAR, SECULARIST

"Postsecularism" has been interpreted as referring either to a novel age or to a new type of society coming after the secular one. According to this view advanced by philosophers as different as Habermas, Caputo or Vattimo, in a postsecular age/society, religion plays a fundamental role in the social-political sphere, and individuals are able to overcome divisions between reason and faith. Habermas, for one, speaks of a new "postsecular society" in which religious and non-religious citizens engage, predominantly in the social-public sphere, in a process of mutual learning and reconciliation through dialogue and reason-exchanges. For Habermas, (non)religious citizens are able to attain agreements and enrich "public reason" by means of rational dialogue understood, in large part, as leading to translations from the sacred language into the secular one.[5]

In turn, Caputo's version of postsecularism distances itself from Habermas' rationalist view of the role of religion in society. By developing Derrida's deconstructive reading of religion, Caputo interprets the end of the secular age as the abandonment of the belief in the death of God and religion proclaimed by Feuerbach, Marx and their likes ever since. For Caputo, we have entered a new postsecular age characterized by the "the death of the death of God," namely, by a shift in focus away from God as Reality and Truth to God as Love.[6] Like Derrida and Vattimo, Caputo argues that deconstruction of the question of the existence of God, namely, the onto-theological critique of religion has a liberating political-religious impact: bracketing the question of the Reality of God opens up the possibility of God as passionate and, at once, impossible love beyond Church dogma.[7]

These divergent understandings of postsecularism are, from a socio-theoretical perspective, unconvincing. First, Western societies have never become secular, just as Western states have never become neutral with respect to religion. In Europe, religion played an important role in private life, society and politics even when the gigantomachia between capitalism and communism eclipsed it in-between World War II and the fall of the Berlin Wall. Moreover, in European societies nowadays, Habermas' rational agents are, at worst, fictional and, at best, a minority; and, in any case, persons willing to learn from religious or secular traditions do not represent a novelty.[8] The existence of such a minority group cannot justify the diagnosis of a passage to a new age and/or kind of society. Likewise, religious people willing and able to bracket the question of the (non)existence of God so as to cultivate a post-Kierkegaardian impossible love for Him are far from representing the common religious believer. Instead, they constitute a group of philosopher-believers—be they post-Heideggerian deconstructivists influenced by Derrida and Caputo, or hermeneuts influenced by Vattimo—rather than the *differentia specifica* of a new epoch or society.

The "postsecular" does not describe the coming of a new age or society after the secular one, i.e., a rational one incorporating dialogically religious contributions (Habermas) or a deconstructive one based on overcoming false dichotomies and the cultivation of an impossible love for God (Caputo).[9] More convincingly, "postsecular" refers to a trend whose roots can be traced back to one (post-) Enlightenment reaction to modern secularism and its radical challenge to the dominance of religion in society and arts as well as to the rejection of reactionary anti-modernism.[10] "Postsecular" has, in this sense, a chronological connotation designating a modern development but does not work as a chronological criterion announcing the advent of a new epoch or society. More persuasively, we find ourselves, in particular in the West, in an age of accelerated pluralization in all societal fields. Together with forms of militant atheism and religious conservatism, postsecularism represents only one trend of such pluralizing dynamic—Habermas, Derrida, Vattimo and Caputo being part of it. This agonistic pluralization characterizing Western societies will not, most likely, wane any time soon.

The term "postsecularism" raises further suspicion given that, it entails the rejection of the secular. But this is not necessarily so. It is true that conservative and anti-modern forces can instrumentalize postsecular rhetoric, yet postsecularism is opposed not to the secular, but to secularism. "Secular" is a broad category referring to discourses and practices that are premised on the modern process of separation and differentiation of various spheres of society (state, arts, law, etc.) from both theology and religion. Secularism, in turn, is a normative view that takes simple and violent ideological and practical forms (Stalinism) or subtle philosophical ones (Feuerbach, Marx). Secularism is a fighting creed. It is a militant set of ideas and practices aiming not only at separation and differentiation between religion and other societal spheres (i.e., politics, law), but regards the dismantling of religion as a premise of a free, emancipated society. For secularists, the relation between religion and modernity is a zero-sum game and one of mutual exclusion; the proclamation of God's death means that religion is irrelevant for understanding current ethical, value and socio-political issues, and it should gradually wane with the advent of a modernity. Such issues are to be made sense of by means of what Charles Taylor calls, in his influential *A Secular Age,* "exclusive humanism" and "immanent frame."[11] "Immanent frame" is another name for secularism and militant atheism, and it refers to a family of views (Marxism, utilitarianism, scientism, psychoanalysis, etc.) that rely on the image of a self-sufficient immanent reason.

The postsecular trend pertains to the very development of modernity; it emerges as a reaction of dissatisfaction with the influential tradition of militant atheism and rationalist secularism built on the Manichean opposition between reason and faith, emancipation and religion. In contrast to secularism, postsecularism regards the relation between religion and modernity as one of tension *and,* at once, as a positive-sum game of mutual interaction and transformation; from this perspective, experiences of transcendence, conversion, faith, transfiguration and sacrifice are not seen as the monopoly of Church or other religious institutions, but can be vital for heterodox believers and even atheists as well.

Here "postsecular" designates a series of discourses and practices that cannot be circumscribed and defined in essentialist terms; instead, a more fruitful strategy is to characterize it in terms of "family-resemblances" (Ludwig Wittgenstein)[12] and "constellation" (Richard Bernstein).[13] In *Philosophical Investigations* (§66), Wittgenstein famously considers the case of games, and asks whether we call "games" . . . [to] look and see whether there is anything common to all . . . the result of this examination is: we see a complicated network of similarities overlapping and criss-crossing: sometimes overall similarities"; he characterizes them as "family resemblances" (§67). At §67, Wittgenstein introduces the metaphor of a thread made of an overlapping of different fibers:

> we extend our concept . . . as in spinning a thread we twist fibre on fibre. And the strength of the thread does not reside in the fact that some one fibre runs through its whole length, but in the overlapping of many fibres.[14]

Applied to "post-secularism," the Wittgensteinian conceptual strategy has the merit of better accommodating the ever growing variety of spiritual-religious experiences and their continuous transformations; it has also the advantage of admitting the relevance of borderline cases whose appurtenance to a category or another (secular/post-secular/conventional religious) can be elusive and controversial.[15] From this viewpoint, "postsecular" designates a family or a set of families of discourses and practices (philosophical, socio-theoretical, cinematic, political, etc.) that are premised on the search for a complex, open and interactive relation between modern reason and religion, as well as for retrieving in non-dogmatic, non-authoritarian, creative and heterodox ways the salience of faith, sacrifice, transcendence, mystical insight, transfiguration, conversion and sacrifice, beyond the self-complacencies of both conventional religion and militant atheism.

"Postsecular" describes, therefore, a complex center between, on the one hand, secularism and militant atheism and conventional religion and a renewed religious conservatism, on the other.[16] The "postsecular constellation" is constituted of "families" organized around emblematic figures, that is, around "star figures." To illustrate: Habermas, Derrida, and Vattimo are school-makers and founders of different families of conceptions of religion in modernity—the families of deliberativists, hermeneuts and deconstructivists. Notwithstanding differences and even oppositions between them, they are all members of a broader postsecular constellation in virtue of their rejection of secularism and of the search for an open, positive and interactive relation between reason and religion in modern societies.

SECTION II BACK TO CINEMA: FIRST ILLUSTRATION (*CACHÉ*)

This volume supports the view that there is a significant trend made of European directors who express by cinematographic means the belief that religious practice and tradition can be a wellspring of values and experiences. These artists contribute to what I've called the postsecular constellation. Moreover, different chapters in the book contribute to the recent philosophical turn in cinema studies by making use of postsecular theorizations (see, for instance, Richard Sinnerbrink's, Catherine Wheatley's, Paul Coates's, Camil Ungureanu's and John Caruana's chapters in this volume).[17] Drawing on debates around postsecularism as part of the broader philosophical turn in cinema studies is still incipient, and it remains implicit in some of the chapters of this book. To make more explicit the claim about the merits of the interaction between cinema and philosophy from a postsecular viewpoint, I turn now to analyzing two films—*Caché* and *The Life of Jesus*. By means of an analogy with Derrida's postsecular project, I shall search into why two self-declared atheist directors are still interested in retrieving religious experiences.

Haneke's generally bleak cinematic visions are far from Dumont's positive concern with articulating a "sacred humanism" and from the latter's keen interest in the power of Jesus's example of sacrifice and redemption (see especially Caruana's chapter in this volume). Yet I argue that *Caché* retrieves Christian motives beyond the belief in God and Church dogma as it articulates a "mystical" and "transcendent" dimension of guilt, sin and collective responsibility that cannot be reduced to an immanent moral reason. Haneke's movie revolves around the transcending quality of these experiences, that is, around a question that he purposefully does not fully answer: what is the nature of guilt and responsibility of community members towards its victims without transparently and directly identifiable perpetrators and victims?

Caché is the story of a family—Georges Laurent (Daniel Auteuil) and Anne (Juliette Binoche), his wife—that begins to receive surveillance videotapes of their house accompanied by grotesque drawings of faces covered with blood. Nothing particularly happens in the videotapes, yet Georges and Anne become ever more disturbed: why are they being watched and who is their author? The search for Haneke's "double" in the movie leads Georges to an apartment at the Parisian periphery. Trusting "he knows who it is" but not sharing his thoughts with Anne, Georges finds the apartment where an Arab, called Majid (Maurice Bénichou), lives. It quickly turns out that Georges had known Majid as a child. Adopted by Georges's family, Majid had been his Arab-Tunisian "brother" for a while. Majid is now a middle-age man, not particularly happy, and living rather modestly in Romainville with his teenage son. Majid freely concedes that he has seen Georges on his TV talk show but, quite persuasively, manifests perplexity at his allegation concerning the videotapes. Oddly enough, this visit turns up on videotape that is mailed to both Georges's wife and to his boss at the television station. When Anne confronts Georges with evidence that he was telling lies, Georges confesses that Majid's parents worked on the Laurent farm when he was a child, that his father liked them as they were good workers, and that Majid was adopted after his parents had disappeared during a political manifestion in Paris. When, subsequently, Pierrot, the Laurents' eleven-year-old son, fails to come home one night, Georges and Anne go to the police; without any evidence whatsoever, Georges has Majid and his son arrested and taken to spend a night in jail. A short while after that, Georges responds to Majid's request to visit. Majid is again persuasive in denying any involvement whatsoever. At this point we witness the most shocking scene of Haneke's movie. In front of the accusatory Georges, Majid calmly takes a razor blade from his pocket and slits his own throat. After this dramatic episode, Pierrot is found and, in a disconcerting final scene, he is shown from a distance talking with Majid's son in front of a school.

Now, who is the ghost-director in Haneke's movie?[18] According to a first hypothesis, the enigmatic director is one of the characters of the film. This is the most natural hypothesis. It is in conformity with the traditional and recurrent narrative conventions in filmmaking: according to a basic narrative principle of a crime or mystery film, the author of a misdeed or bizarre occurrence is one of its characters. Yet *Caché* is far from providing any clues concerning the actual involvement of the characters; quite to the contrary, Haneke goes to great lengths to convince the audience that none of the characters is guilty. The most likely candidate, Majid, is insistently presented as innocent. In turn, each and every one of the movie's character is ruled out.[19]

According to a second interpretation, the anonymous "director" symbolizes an impartial or objective moral judge.[20] The impartiality-hypothesis is, however, equally unpersuasive. Haneke's film does not advance the perspective of a detached, moral *j'accuse;* the image of a self-sufficient moral reason is not consistent with his purposeful and methodical intent to preserve an enigmatic and "mystical" dimension of responsibility and guilt. This hypothesis does not square either with Haneke's explicit concern with the inexpressible and mystical[21] as well as with retrieving elements of the Christian tradition. As Haneke affirms, "(t)he theme of guilt is present in all my films. . . . It's inherent in our Judeo-Christian tradition, and especially in Central Europe. Actually, in all the West."[22] A more convincing hypothesis, I argue, takes seriously into consideration the significance of the enigma of guilt and responsibility, i.e., the significance of leaving *unanswered* the central question of the movie.[23] To begin with, the movie intimates that guilt and responsibility have a trans-individual, historical dimension. Haneke's declared intention was to build the relation between Georges and Majid by taking into account its historical-political background, namely the responsibility of the French community towards the victims of the *Nuit Noire*[24]—the night when the French police staged an unprovoked massacre.[25] Still, it remains unclear why Haneke's enigma would be really needed if what is at stake is expressing the transindividual dimension of guilt and responsibility. After all, agreeing nowadays on the collective character of specific forms of guilt and responsibility—e.g., of the French community towards the victims of the *Nuit Noire*—strikes a familiar chord. Shouldn't the main contribution of the movie be seen as refreshing public memory about the forgotten victims of the *Nuit Noire*? And, if the movie is a "whistle-blower," why keep the secrecy over the film's central question? Is this an artificial narrative device?

Not necessarily so. At this juncture, it is clarifying to introduce an analogy between Haneke's *Caché* and Derrida's postsecular interpretation of the "mystical" foundation of authority and community. In "Force of Law: 'The Mystical Foundation of Authority'," Derrida argues that the foundation and perpetuation of a political democratic community has a "mystical" dimension. For Derrida, the term "mystical" does not refer either to a direct and non-verbalizable experience of God or, from the positivistic perspective of Wittgenstein's *Tractatus*, to what goes beyond the "proper" use of language, namely the representation of external Reality. By the "mystical" foundation of authority, Derrida designates the condition of the absence of a transparent *Grund* of political activity and the consequences of it. The very foundation of a bounded community—that is tracing its borders, defining who-is-in-and-out, the members of the demos and adopting specific laws of regulating human relations—always involves a "mystical" moment of undecidability between illegitimacy and legitimacy, violence and justice; this "mystical" dimension haunts any democratic practice.[26] Benjamin underscores this idea with the phrase "rechtsetzende Gewalt"; Derrida translates it into French as *violence fondatrice* (violence that founds). All law and authority is in part based on violence inasmuch as there is no original law/authority, but rather they are instituted and re-instituted through acts of exclusion. As the law presupposes the legitimacy of its own origin, it ultimately refers to an extra-legal/illegitimate act, to an act that also involves violence; and this violence that is *not fully nameable, knowable* or even *representable* constitutes the groundwork of the authority of law whenever the law and authority explicitly appeals to the "legitimacy" of its own institution and reinstitution.

For Derrida, this paradoxical condition of establishing law and authority is an obscure foundational enigma which "inhabits" the performative character of democratic practice: "Here a silence is walled up in the violent structure of the founding act" ("Il y a là un silence muré dans la structure violente de l'acte fondateur").[27] The "mystical," says Derrida, is an abyss in the heart of what is supposedly well founded: "vanished cruelties at the moment of constituting a state, forgotten terror when new law comes into force, events which remain historically "uninterpretable or indecipherable (ininterpretables ou indéchiffrables)."[28] In other words, the democratic dynamic—foundational and post-foundational—is inextricably linked to forms of exclusions; these can be violent or not, explicit or hidden, well-known or merely secret. In Derrida's striking reading of S. Kierkegaard's

Fear and Trembling,[29] he goes as far as to argue that nowadays Abraham's sacrifice of Isaac has become a common occurrence as we often are indirect and secretive accomplices of death. Whether or not we accept Derrida's hyperbolic language,[30] we can agree that such exclusionary processes are inevitable; they are a structural feature of any legal-political community from its very constitution. Community-building creates victims to be mourned, and they haunt it continuously. Certain acts of violence and exclusion are covered or forgotten and, sometimes, are brought to light (e.g., at least some of the acts against victims of the *Nuit Noire*). Other such acts are hidden and covered in a "mystical" silence as they can remain "unthematized" and unverbalized, beyond even the current (dominant) moral imagination. These acts are not named and not even nameable; they are anonymous, just like the "director" in Haneke's movie, a dead-and-alive ghost haunting Georges and his family.

The point of this interpretation is not that we can never identify victims and their perpetrators. We can often do that with reasonable assurance. However, in any community, no matter how just, there are significant blind spots; there are silences (what Haneke calls the "inexpressible") over processes of exclusion and discrimination. Hence, while we can and need to reason about guilt and responsibility, these also have a transcending, ghostlike and "anonymous" dimension. From this perspective, it becomes less surprising that Haneke, a staunch atheist, resorts to a language anchored in the Judeo-Christian religious heritage. We are, from Haneke's perspective, the "children" of the sinful injustices committed by our ancestors: "(w)e are all the inheritors of sins committed by our parents, and of their . . . non-sins! . . . It's unavoidable." Here Haneke's interest is, in my view, not the dogma of sin as "absolute certitude," but as mystery.[31] Guilt and responsibility have a "secret" or "mystical" dimension (which is not to say irrational or opposed to reason); this can explain the significance of preserving the enigma of an anonymous "director," a ghost implacably haunting our most cherished practices and unsettling our most comfortable beliefs. It can also explain why an unfaltering atheist such as Haneke reclaims the idiom and mystery of inevitable sin by means of a quasi-religious language situated between two opposite legitimizing discourses: first, that of a self-sufficient moral reason able to shed a fully transparent light on the issue of guilt and collective responsibility; second, that of conventional religion regarding the mystery of fallenness of humanity as a result of one couple's sin.

SECTION III   A SECOND ILLUSTRATION
(THE LIFE OF JESUS)

Not unlike Haneke's *Caché*, Dumont's first feature movie is centered on an enigma of visibility/invisibility: what are we to make of a movie entitled

The Life of Jesus which does not contain a single clear reference to Jesus and his life?

The filmic narrative of *The Life of Jesus* is relatively simple (see Caruana's chapter in this volume for a more detailed analysis). The film, based on Dumont's script, is set in the 1990s and portrays the slow-paced life in a small village in Northern France. We become acquainted with Freddy (David Douche): he is around twenty, unemployed, and in love with Marie (Marjorie Cottreel), a cashier at a local store. We also come to know Freddy's buddies, a gang of aimless youngsters. Freddy is their leader. They kill time by going around on their motorcycles and by directing their aggressiveness and frustration at Arabic immigrants. Amongst them, there is Kader, an equally aimless and defiant young male. Tension mounts when Marie, Freddy's girlfriend, takes an interest in Kader. As affection and complicity grow between them, Marie becomes estranged from Freddy. Freddy and his friends decide to punish Kader for what they consider to be "such a provocation." On a sunny day when everything appears to be routine, they catch Kader on an empty country road, and beat him to death. At the end of the movie, we see Freddy fleeing the law and seemingly regretting his misdeed.

How to interpret Dumont's performative contradiction of *The Life of Jesus* without Jesus? I argue that the movie develops a double-bind logic towards Christianity that has deep affinities with elements of Derrida's postsecular project that do not have an echo in Haneke's cinema. *The Life of Jesus* deconstructs the foundational event of Christianity, Jesus's sacrifice, by unraveling the close relationship between sacrifice, transcendence and sacredness. Dumont substitutes the lynching of a common Arab immigrant for Jesus's sacrifice, the God-made-man. (As Caruana argues, Freddy echoes Jesus's figure as well—see below). By severing the sacrifice from God and theodicy, the innocent lamb becomes a mere victim: there is nothing sacral about Kader's murder; Freddy's killing is a moral mistake, a tragic misjudgment and not a sacrifice (*sacer* + *facere*). The murder is something to be appalled at, not to be sublimated and inscribed in a higher scheme of divine justice. The victim is an irremediable loss to be mourned.

Still, Dumont's deconstruction is not a one-way street: he does not reduce the Christian narrative of redemption through sacrifice to a secular tale of immanent moral injustice.[32] *The Life of Jesus* can neither be reduced to a moralizing tale condemning the maltreatment of Arab immigrants in France, nor captured by an ideological catchphrase. In contrast, Dumont advances a cinematographic vision of a "Christianity without Christ" which displays deep affinities with Derrida's/Caputo's development, at the philosophical level, of a "religion without religion." Dumont and Derrida's visions emerge under the double impact of the death of God and the decline of Church attendance. Both position themselves against the onto-theological faith in the existence of God as Reality or Presence. They also take a stand against the institutionalization, through rigid power hierarchies, of absolute certainties. However, for neither of them the loss of Transcendence and the decline of the power of the Church are accompanied by a loss of interest in religion. Conventional religion and the Church cannot monopolize and confiscate fundamental experiences such as that of faith, redemption, transfiguration, sacred and (self-) transcendence. Both Derrida and Dumont break with the strict opposition between *ratio* and *fides,* and look for a "minimal religion," a "religion without God" centered on such fundamental experiences.[33] Consider, first, Derrida. In his most systematic treatment of religion, "Faith and Knowledge: the Two Sources of 'Religion' at the Limits of Reason Alone,"[34] Derrida retrieves fundamental religious or quasi-religious experiences and challenges a specific narrative of Enlightenment hostile to religion.[35] Reinterpreting Kant's project,[36] Derrida distinguishes between two strata of religion or faith. One stratum of religion is the holy, the sacrosanct, the pure or the safe. Religion is characterized, for Derrida, by a drive or desire towards the immunization or sacralization of beliefs, images, places, objects, etc. This drive results in "absolute" certitudes and "infallible" dogmas enforced through rituals and protected by religious-political establishments, often through physical and symbolic violence. The other stratum of religion is a "faith without dogma," a "mystical" experience of transcendence that "punctures" any existent moral-political or theological horizon. For Derrida, in communicative exchanges at the basis of human relationships there is implicitly involved a projection of faith transcending any current finite agreements, a mutual implicit pledge that points towards truth and justice.[37] While neither rational nor moral per se, this experience of faith and transcendence represents, in Derrida's view, what is universalizable about religion. Just as Kant wanted to "salvage" rational faith out of Christian tradition, and criticized positive religions for being dogmatic and authoritarian, Derrida aims to retrieve the experience of faith and transcendence in the promise of non-violent truth and justice from the self-aggrandizing belief in an ultimate foundation of community.[38] He projects a political and religious community that abandons the claim of having access to absolute certitudes and their institutionalization. Such community is fundamentally hospitable to the other, even if community border-drawing leads, unavoidably, to exclusion. The excluded are not, from Derrida's perspective, sacrificed victims to be inscribed into a sacral history of redemption; they are victims to be mourned.

Dumont attempts, not unlike Derrida, to retrieve basic "religious" experience from the monopoly of Church discourse and beyond the rigid dichotomy *ratio* vs. *fides.* The French director is unambiguous about this task: "one must recover words like 'grace,' holiness,' for the profane world, we should not simply grant organized religion a monopoly over this language. I desire a sacred humanism, indeed a spiritual life, transcendence, but without God or the Church."[39] Dumont's "sacred humanism" breaks with the bond between sacred and violence, and connects the former with experiences of (self-)transcendence, forgiveness, redemption, love and hospitality. However, his humanism does not discard God-talk as irrelevant.

Just like for Derrida and his follower, J. Caputo, the death of God as ultimate Reality opens up new possibilities of experiencing the divine; Dumont does not necessarily abandon speaking about God. While for Derrida and, more emphatically, for Caputo, there is still place for an impossible love of God, and for God as love;[40] Dumont carries on the Romantic tradition of the belief in the God of poets. He characterizes himself as a non-believer, yet he also asserts: "God interests me only in a poetic manner."[41] Likewise, Dumont believes in Jesus's story not because it is *strict sensu* historically real, but because it sheds light on the poetic-mystical dimension of existence. Echoing Pasolini's statement from the beginning of *Riccotta*, Dumont says: "I believe that the story of Christ is one of the most beautiful poetic expressions of the human tragedy. *I believe in it like I believe in a poem.* I believe in the frescoes of Giotto, the Passion of Bach."[42]

In *The Life of Jesus*, the killing of Kader is a limit-situation that occasions an experience of transfiguration and self-transcendence. After murdering Kader, Freddy flees the law: in a long scene, the fugitive is shown lying in a field, in hiding. In a moment of suspended temporality, Freddy agonizes in silence over his terrible mistake. Yet Freddy's inner transformation and self-transcendence occur precisely in this instant of hitting rock bottom of his desolate humanity. In this stirring scene, the camera registers Freddy's fixed look towards the sky. We are not sure what his transformation consists of—the experience of verticality is not entirely verbalizable—words can only approximate it. Dumont invites the audience to feel and intuit it by minimalist cinematographic and acting means. Freddy seems to transcend his state of mindless drifter: he realizes his wretchedness and abysmal misstep, as well as an unspoken desire to redeem himself, to look beyond his current life. This long scene focusing on Freddy's inner transformation is not a straightforward religious scene; it does not expresses the certitude of a Divinity ready to bestow grace and redemption on him despite his mortal sin, but a transfiguration and an innermost yearning for self-overcoming.

The experience of verticality represents a central topos of Dumont's film. It imperceptibly binds its main characters (see also Caruana's chapter, this volume). The yearning for overcoming and transcendence brings together the two main characters, the perpetrator and victim, Freddy and Kader. In one scene, as Marie and Kader walk along a deserted street, we perceive the subtle growth of a mutual complicity and affection between Marie and Kader. As they walk, Marie and Kader notice a big hole in a fence and go through it. One expects an enchanted garden symbolizing the promise of Romantic love. Instead they enter a derelict building, all in unpleasant shambles. "It reeks like urine," says Kader, in disgust. Both remain silent, lost in their thoughts, and the camera hardly moves, as if time is standing still. And yet, it is in this improbable place that a revelatory bonding between them occurs: they embrace silently, without any seeming sensual connotation. She enigmatically tells him, "forgive me," without giving him any reason or explanation. Their connection has an enigmatic dimension: does she ask for forgiveness for something *she* has personally been involved in, even if indirectly, or for her community? Or is her asking for forgiveness a premonition of what is going to happen in the future? These questions remained unanswered. Marie's asking for forgiveness echoes the enigma of unconditional forgiving (consider Jesus's advice that Peter forgive "seventy times seven" or Derrida's late works on unconditional forgiveness, gift and hospitality).[43] Marie does not offer unconditional forgiveness like Jesus; she asks to be forgiven—hers appears to be an unconditional act since she has not wronged him in a clearly identifiable way. Her act is a free gift, enigmatic in its content and motivations. The enigma of Marie's words is enhanced by the continuation of the scene. As if guided by Kader's look, the camera moves slowly upwards from their entranced embrace towards the light blue sky. We realize that the ruined building is a church, and we look at the sky through the remains of the ceiling. The flow of time has come to a halt; the sky is motionless and empty. There is no trace of God. And yet the vertical movement of the camera gestures towards transcendence: the event of forgiveness occurring between Kader and Marie elevates them, against expectation, beyond the determinants of their different communities and condition. In the instant of their embraced transfiguration, the two seem to build a bond of forgiving complicity transgressing the existing frontiers between community and strangers: her enigmatic "forgive me" is an unconditional gift of love and gratuitous hospitality beyond past and present wrongs. *The Life of Jesus* intimates that, after the death of God and decline of the Church, experiences of transcendence and transfiguration can emerge from within the horizontality of human encounters, in forgiving, gift-giving, hospitality and love.[44]

* * *

As Bradatan points out in the "Introduction" this present book remains pluralistic—it contains analyses of secular and conventional-religious movies as well. It would therefore be artificial to classify every movie analyzed herein as pertaining to the "postsecular constellation." In addition, speaking of "postsecular" in relation to cinema refers to a broad constellation of movies that can be placed on a continuum between the categories of missionary and conventional religious ones,[45] on the one hand, and secular ones,[46] on the other. At one pole, there are religious movies that explore religion in subjective, personal and polemic ways (e.g., Trier's *Breaking the Waves*; see Ungureanu's chapter in this volume) or non-polemic ways (S. Kaplanoğlu's film *Honey*; see Suner's chapter in this volume). In the middle of the continuum, there are movies and directors that, while not strictly speaking religious, aim in a systematic way to retrieve spiritual-religious experiences even for non-believers and atheists (e.g., Dumont, Kieślowski; see Caruana's, Coates's and Bradatan's chapters in this volume). In turn, Haneke and Iñárritu are closer to the secular pole since they do not have such as systematic project focused on a religious model (for instance, Jesus for Dumont). Still, such movies aim at showing the relevance of a "spiritual," "mystical" or "transcending" dimension of experience that cannot be accounted for by a self-sufficient reason (see Sinnerbrink's chapter in this volume).

To sum up, these "Final Remarks" have aimed, first, to characterize "postsecularism" more persuasively and reject some objections concerning its usage. Second, they have aimed to make more plausible and explicit the usefulness of this concept in relation to the intersection between cinema studies and philosophy. I have argued that Haneke shares with Dumont an ambivalent attitude towards religion, and an attempt at a retrieval of the "mystical" and "transcendent." While for Dumont there is an affirmation of the positive "desire" for redemption and self-transcendence (in Freddy's case), for Haneke transcendence is only understood in relation to the guilt and responsibility transmitted (secretly, in part) from one generation to another. Dumont's and Haneke's movies are characteristic of the process of subjectivization and secularization of religion in Europe, and part of a postsecular trend that steers its course between self-sufficiency of secular reason and conventional religion. This postsecular logic of overcoming and retrieving, of departing from *and* reflecting on religious tradition, undermines—much like Derrida's "religion without religion"—the rigidness of the opposition of religion vs. secular reason, immanence vs. transcendence.

NOTES

1. Michel Cieutat, "Interview with Michael Haneke: The Fragmentation of the Look," in Peter Brunette, *Michael Haneke*, (Urbana and Chicago: University of Illinois, 2010), 146.
2. In Damon Smith, "Bruno Dumont, 'Hadewijch'," *Filmmaker* (Dec. 22, 2010). Available at www.filmmakermagazine.com/news/2010/12/bruno-dumont-hadewijch/. Last accessed May 9, 2013.
3. With reference to Eric Santner's postsecular political theology of the neighbor, Paul Coates comments the following:

    (w)hereas Santner designates the possibility of miracle in terms that simultaneously all-but withdraw the word, preferring to describe it not as "a form of religious thinking" but as '*postsecular*,' the inherent vagueness of the content of a notion of 'the postsecular' is problematic, as both the reference to miracle and the assertion of secularity's obsolescence suggest religiosity. Santner might be accused of frustrating, through dogmatic attachment to the vocabulary of materialism, the logic both of his argument and his terminology, as the opposition to the 'secular' within the reference to the 'postsecular' implies a somewhat substantial divergence from its predecessor. The 'postsecular' seems to be either secularity sublated in an incomplete dialectic, or even 'the secular' itself by another, obscurely denied name—with the invisible supports superadded amenable to non-mention just because unseen.

4. Somebody may prefer another word to designate the trend we have in mind. The term is, from my perspective, a tool (see below).
5. For the mushrooming literature on Habermas' postsecularism, see www.habermasforum.dk/.
6. From John Caputo's numerous writings on religion, see *On religion* (London: Routledge, 2001). This book is interesting because it applies "postsecularism" to cinema studies as well (with reference to *Star Wars*). Here I cannot enter

What is the Use of Postsecularism? 213

a detailed analysis of Caputo's interpretation of *Star Wars*. Still, it seems to me that his interpretation is questionable in that it mistakenly takes Derrida's argument from deconstructing dichotomies (religious/scientific; spiritual/material) as a way of problematically rejecting them *de plano*.

7. The light "atmosphere" of Vattimo's hermeneutic approach rooted in the notion of *pensiero debole* (weak thought) is quite different from Derrida's and Caputo's Kierkegaardian pathos.
8. Learning is not reduced to Habermas' abstract reason-exchanges, but it involves emotions, passions, imagination, etc.
9. For a polemic rejection of postsecularism, especially in Habermas' version of it, see Bader's recent writings, e.g., "Post-secularism or liberal-democratic constitutionalism?" in *Erasmus Law Review*, 5:1 (2012), 5–26.
10. James Schmidt, *What is Enlightenment?: Eighteenth-Century Answers and Twentieth-Century Questions* (University of California Press, 1996); Mark Lilla, *The Stillborn God: Religion, Politics and the Modern West* (NewYork: Knopf, 2007).
11. For a detailed analysis of "immanent frame" and "exclusive humanism," see Charles Taylor, *A Secular Age* (Harvard: Harvard University Press, 2007).
12. Ludwig Wittgenstein, *Philosophical Investigations*, 4th ed. (London: Blackwell, 2009).
13. I borrow the term "constellation" from Richard Bernstein, *The New Constellation: Ethical-Political Horizons of Modernity/Postmodernity* (The MIT Press, Cambridge, MA, 1992). A "constellation" has a certain degree of cohesiveness, yet it does not exclude inner tension and even opposition (e.g., between Habermas and Derrida). It is noteworthy that there has been a rapprochement between the continental and analytical branch of philosophy with respect to religion. An interest in religious issues has been a traditional concern of continental philosophy in its German or French versions from Walter Benjamin to Emmanuel Levinas, in addition to the new wave of thinkers such as Derrida and Vattimo. In analytical philosophy, a postsecular turn has occurred only recently—in particular in the works of Thomas Nagel and Richard Dworkin.
14. Wittgenstein, *Philosophical Investigations*.
15. Here we follow Wittgenstein. At §68, he states:

    > I can give the concept 'number' rigid limits . . . that is, use the word 'number' for a rigidly limited concept, but I can also use it so that the extension of the concept is not closed by a frontier. And this is how we do use the word 'game.' For how is the concept of a game bounded? What still counts as a game and what no longer does? Can you give the boundary? No. You can draw one; for none has so far been drawn. (But that never troubled you before when you used the word 'game'). (Wittgenstein, *Philosophical Investigations*)

    From this perspective, the role of the theorist is not that of policing conceptual borders on account of providing supposedly ultimate definitional criteria. To pursue Wittgenstein's image, in some cases, given that the thread is thicker, applying a term such as secular or postsecular holds water; in other borderline case, the thread is thinner, and it can be a matter of dispute whether a phenomenon (a movie, a book) is secularist or postsecular, conventional-religious or postsecular.
16. The mutual borrowing, exchange and interaction between modernity and religion does not automatically result in postsecular phenomena (consider contemporary religious-political fundamentalism). For the emphasis on non-authoritarianism in understanding the postsecular, see Maeve Cooke's recent

articles, e.g., Maeve Cooke, "A Secular State for a Postsecular Society? Postmetaphysical Political Theory and the Place of Religion" in *Constellations* 14:2 (2007), 224–38.
17. My approach draws on the recent methodological debate surrounding Stephen Mulhall, *On Film,* 2nd ed. (London: Routledge, 2008). Mulhall rightly aims to overcome the artificiality of the rigid separation between philosophy and cinema. One needs to steer away from the intellectualist fallacy to reduce film to a mere representation of abstract ideas, and philosophy and cinema as complex and multi-layered experiences to be found in a dialectical relation of mutual learning.
18. For some important literature on Haneke's cinematography, see Peter Brunette, *Michael Haneke;* Thomas Y. Levin, "Five Tapes, Four Halls, Two Dreams: Vicissitudes of Surveillant Narration in Michael Haneke's Caché," in *A Companion to Michael Haneke,* ed. Roy Grundmann (London: Wiley-Blackwell, 2010), 75–90; Kevin L. Stoehr, "Haneke's Secession: Perspectivism and Anti-Nihilism in Code Unknown and Caché", in Roy Grundmann (ed.), *A Companion to Michael Haneke,* 477–94; Jefferson Kline, The Intertextual and Discursive Origins of Terror in Michael Haneke's Caché," in Roy Grundmann (ed.), *A Companion to Michael Haneke,* 551–62. In these short "Final Remarks" I cannot do justice to the growing literature on Haneke's cinematography.
19. Majid's grown son may know, but denies it, and he is equally surprised and persuasive in his claims; similarly, Pierrot, Georges's son, does not appear to have anything to do with it.
20. Haneke's rejection of a traditional narrative convention should not come as a surprise: his cinema often turns upside down previous conventions (e.g. *The Seventh Continent, Funny Games,* etc.). But what is the meaning of it? Is Haneke's invisible "double" a reference to an all-knowing, accusatory God? The hypothesis of a God as a moral judge is *prima facie* plausible. The videotapes and drawings might be interpreted as symbols of a divine, all-seeing Eye, and of an omniscient Judge. This reading is not implausible but, in the last analysis, it is unconvincing. The God-hypothesis is at loggerheads with Haneke's unambiguous atheism, as well as with the patent absence, in *Caché,* of any reference whatsoever, not even implicit, to God.
21. See the motto to this text.
22. Michel Cieutat, "Interview with Michael Haneke: The Fragmentation of the Look," 146–47.
23. Ibid.
24. For more details on these events and the origin of Haneke's movie, see Kline, "The Intertextual and Discursive Origins of Terror in Michael Haneke's *Caché.*"
25. In the movie, Majid's parents disappeared in this massacre. In the movie, Georges is Haneke's mouthpiece; he explains the complex background of his relation to Majid as follows:

> (i)n October '61 the FLN called all Algerians to a demonstration in Paris. They went to Paris. On October 17th, Papon, the police massacre. They drowned about 200 Arabs in the Seine. Majid's parents were probably among them. In any case they never returned. When my father went to Paris to search for them, the police told him that he should be glad to be rid of these 'jigaboos.' My parents decided to adopt the boy, I don't know why. They must have felt responsible in some way.

26. Derrida, "Force of Law: 'The Mystical Foundation of Authority'," in *Cardozo Law Review* 11 (1990), 920–1045.

27. Ibid., 942–43.
28. Ibid., 990–91.
29. Søren Kierkeegard, *Fear and Trembling. Repetition.* (Princeton University Press, 1983).
30. Derrida argues persuasively that community building, including the legal-democratic one, is based on excluding others—that is, on making victims. However, I have doubts about his analysis of the concept of duty starting from Abraham's sacrifice. For a critique, see Camil Ungureanu, "Derrida's Tense Bow," *European Legac* (July 2013).
31. It is rather common to forget about this aspect of dogma. But see even the *Cathechism of the Catholic Church,* especially paragraphs 385–420. At 404, it is said: "Still, the transmission of original sin is a mystery that we cannot fully understand." Available at www.vatican.va/archive/ccc_css/archive/catechism/p1s2c1p7.htm. Last accessed April 3, 2013.
32. I have learned a great deal from Caruana's chapter in this volume. Apart from analyzing in detail Dumont's "sacred humanism," Caruana examines the analogies between his cinematic compositions and religious painting, as well as his affinities with Robert Bresson's and Fyodor Dostoevsky's technique of deformation. My argument concerning Dumont's *The Life of Jesus* is complementary to Caruana's approach to his cinematography.
33. For a similar "move," see Krzysztof Kieslowski's reflections in Paul Coates, " 'The Inner Life is the Only Thing That Interests Me': A Conversation with Krzysztof Kieslowski," in *Lucid Dreams. The Films of Krzysztof Kieslowski,* ed. Paul Coates (Trowbridge, UK: Flicks Books, 1999). Kieslowski's reflections on religion and mystery are discussed by Coates and Bradatan in their chapters in this volume.
34. Jacques Derrida, "Faith and Knowledge: the Two Sources of 'Religion' at the Limits of Reason Alone," in *Religion,* eds. Jacques Derrida and Gianni Vattimo, (London: Polity, 1998), 61. For an excellent albeit incomplete collection of Derrida's writings on religion, see Derrida, *Acts of Religion,* ed. Gil Anidjar (London: Routledge, 2002).
35. Here I will refer to Derrida's later work which deals with religion in a more systematic way. Let me briefly give three examples. 1. In "Comment ne pas parler" ("How to Avoid Speaking"), Derrida argues that praying can refer to "God, for example" ("Dieu par example"), in Derrida, *Psyche. Inventions de l'autre* (Paris: Galilée, 1987), 572. 2) In E. Roudinesco's interview with Derrida, the French philosopher reiterates that the other can be human or divine; see Elisabeth Roudinesco and Jacques Derrida, *De quoi demain . . . Dialogue* (Paris: Fayard, 2001), 40 and 80–81. 3) Finally, in "Epoché and Faith," Derrida emphatically rejects the label of "atheist" and speaks about the possibility of a secret faith in a personal God; see *Derrida and Religion. Other Testaments,* eds. Yvonne Sherwood and Kevin Hart (New York and London: Routledge, 2005), 28–30. For a comprehensive analysis, see Hent de Vries, *Philosophy and the Turn to Religion* (Baltimore: Johns Hopkins University Press, 1999).
36. For Kant's philosophy of religion, see Immanuel Kant, *Religion and Rational Theology, The Cambridge Edition of the Works of Immanuel Kant,* eds. Allen W. Wood and George di Giovanni (Cambridge: Cambridge University Press, 2005).
37. E.g., Derrida, "Remarks on Deconstruction and Pragmatism," in *Deconstruction and Pragmatism,* eds. Chantal Mouffe and Simon Critchley (London: Verso, 1996), 81. According to Derrida, "(t)he universalizable culture of this faith, and not of another before all others, alone permits a rational and universal discourse on the subject of 'religion'." Derrida, "Faith and Knowledge," 56–57.

38. Derrida, *The Gift of Death* (Chicago: University of Chicago Press, 1995), 49.
39. Ibid.
40. Derrida's stand with respect to the issue of God is different from Dumont's. Derrida points towards the possibility of a God without presence, a God without sovereignty who does not let "itself" be used and manipulated in order to establish one's absolute power and sovereignty over others. See, *inter alia*, Derrida's remarks in "Epoché and Faith," 41–42. By developing Derrida's notion of "religion without religion," Caputo advances a conception that is more explicit about understanding God as love. Amongst Caputo's writings on religion, see Caputo, "Without Sovereignty, Without Being: Unconditionally, the Coming God and Derrida's Democracy to Come," in *Religion and Violence in a Secular World*, ed. C. Crockett (Charlottesville: University of Virginia Press, 2006), 137–56.
41. See Jean-Marc Lalanne, "Bruno Dumont: Mystique or Profane?" November 25, 2009. Available at www.lesinrocks.com/actualite/actu-article/t/41633/date/2009-11-25/article/bruno-dumont-mystique-ou-profane/. Last accessed May 1, 2013. Cited in Caruana [Caruana's trans.; my italics]
42. Walsh, "Interview with Bruno Dumont." The commonality between Dumont and Pasolini does not stop here. Pasolini cultivated as well as an ambivalent attitude to religion, and also drew heavily on the tradition of Christian painting and music. Albeit a Marxist atheist, films such as *Accattone*, *Mamma Roma* and *Riccotta* contain crucial religious references. Therein, Pasolini substitutes Jesus with ordinary people drifting at the outskirts of the Italian society (See Geoffrey Nowell-Smith's chapter in this volume).
43. I cannot discuss here the intricacies of the theme of unconditional forgiveness in the Gospels and Derrida's philosophical approach (which is, in part, a deconstruction of the Christian view). With reference to the Gospels, I would just point out that there are also passages that suggests that Jesus had a conditional view of forgiveness. For a Christian-theological examination of forgiveness, see L. Gregory Jones, *Embodying Forgiveness: A Theological Analysis* (Grand Rapids: Eerdmans, 1995); for a philosophical examination, see also chapter five of Richard Swinburne, *Responsibility and Atonement* (Oxford: Clarendon, 1989).
44. In spite of changes in tone and atmosphere, there is a clear continuity between *The Life of Jesus* and *Humanité* (1999), *Hadewijch* (2009) and *Hors Satan* (2011). Here I cannot expand on this point.
45. In her chapter " 'Casting Fire Onto the Earth': The Holy Fool in Russian Cinema," Alina Birzache analyzes Pavel Lungin's *The Island* (2006) as conveying the post-9/11 desire to reconnect with the nation's Christian Orthodox heritage of the pre-Soviet era. Lungin's agenda is characteristic of a new assertiveness of the religious-national conservatism in Eastern Europe after the fall of communism.
46. Movies falling into the category of "secular" can be placed on a continuum. 1) At one extreme there are those movies that polemically reject and/or satirize religion as being obscurantist, corrupt, immoral and passé. These movies are the visual *analogon* of secularist discourses in philosophy and literature. Sergei Eisenstein's *Battleship Potemkin* (1925; see Jolyon Mitchell's chapter in this volume), Luis Buñuel's *L'Age d'or* (1930), *Viridiana* (1961) and Monty Python's *Life of Brian* (1979) are examples of anti-religious and anti-Christian movies. 2) At the other extreme, there are movies that echo and reflect religious tradition as a socio-political, historical or cultural fact. Issues like multiculturalism, Islam, immigration and terrorism have, unsurprisingly, acquired ever more importance in contemporary European cinema. Such movies deal with religion as an "objective fact" but do not explore the

positive existential signification of experiences normally confined to the "official" religious domain—faith, sacrifice, transfiguration and transcendence. To illustrate, Nathan Abrams analyzes, in this volume, Kubrick's *The Shining* by taking the influence of Judaism on it as a mere cultural matter. Abrams takes into consideration what Jon Stratton calls "Jewish moments" in movie analysis and decodes what is sometimes unconscious—historical-cultural references, behavior, profession, names, physiognomy, foods, verbal and body language, visual signs, speech patterns and accents, hairstyles, anxieties—in relation to the heritage of Judaism after the death of God and not of Judaism as an alive faith. 3) Finally, in the middle of the continuum, there is a subcategory of movies that register the fragmentation and break-up of religious faith and tradition. For instance, *East is East* (1999; dir. Damien O'Donnell) is an empathic exploration of how a Muslim Pakistani father living in the UK gradually loses all his authority given by religious tradition over his children. Likewise, the 2006 Turkish film "*A Man's Fear of God*" (*Takva;* dir. Özer Kiziltan) is an intimate and sympathetic exploration of the loss of faith of a simple man called Muharrem under the pressure of secular life.

List of Contributors

Nathan Abrams is Professor of Film Studies at Bangor University in Wales. He has published extensively on Jewish film and new media, including most recently *The New Jew in Film: Exploring Jewishness and Judaism in Contemporary Cinema* (Rutgers University Press, 2012). He is also the founding co-editor of *Jewish Film and New Media: An International Journal*. He is currently working on two book-length projects: the first explores the ethnicity in the films of Stanley Kubrick, while the second is titled *The Hidden Presence of Jews in British Film and Television* (contracted to Northwestern University Press).

Alina Birzache was an assistant lecturer at the Faculty of Orthodox Theology in Bucharest before she moved to United Kingdom where she obtained a PhD from the University of Edinburgh with a thesis on holy foolishness in European cinema. She has interests in religious representations in art, literature and film, and has taught and published on these topics

Costica Bradatan is Associate Professor in the Honors College at Texas Tech University. He is the author or editor (co-editor) of seven books, mostly recently *Philosophy, Society and The Cunning of History in Eastern Europe* (Routledge, 2012), and has written for such publications as *Dissent*, *The New Statesman*, *Times Literary Supplement*, *New York Times*, *CNN.com (CNN Opinion)*, *The Australian*, *Christian Science Monitor*, *The Globe & Mail* and others. Bradatan currently serves as Religion/Comparative Studies Editor for *Los Angeles Review of Books*.

John Caruana is Associate Professor of Philosophy at Ryerson University and the Graduate Program in Communication and Culture (Ryerson and York University). His research interests include European philosophy of religion, philosophy of film, and psychoanalysis. His publications include work on Adorno, Heidegger and Levinas, as well as the cinema of Kieslowski, Kiarostami and Rohmer.

Paul Coates is a Professor in the Film Studies Department of the University of Western Ontario. His publications include *The Story of the Lost*

Reflection (1985), *The Gorgon's Gaze* (1991), *Lucid Dreams: the Films of Krzysztof Kieślowski* (1999), *Cinema, Religion and the Romantic Legacy* (2003), *The Red and the White: The Cinema of People's Poland* (2005) and *Colour and Cinema* (2010). His *Screening the Face* was published by Palgrave Macmillan in 2012.

Jolyon Mitchell is Professor of Communications, Arts and Religion and Director of the Centre for Theology and Public Issues (CTPI) at the University of Edinburgh. He worked as a producer and journalist for BBC World Service and BBC Radio 4 before he was appointed to the University of Edinburgh. His recent publications reflect some of his research interests and include: *Promoting Peace, Inciting Violence: The Role of Religion and Media* (Routledge: 2012); *Religion and the News* (co-editor, Ashgate, 2012); *Martyrdom: A Very Short Introduction* (Oxford University Press, 2012); *Media Violence and Christian Ethics* (Cambridge University Press, 2007) and *The Religion and Film Reader* (co-editor, Routledge, 2007).

Geoffrey Nowell-Smith is Honorary Professorial Fellow at Queen Mary University of London. He has written extensively about Italian cinema and translated *The Prison Notebooks* of Antonio Gramsci. His most recent publication is a revised and expanded edition of his book *Making Waves: New Cinemas of the 1960s* (Bloomsbury, 2013)

Robert Sinnerbrink is Senior Lecturer in Philosophy at Macquarie University, Sydney. He is the author of *New Philosophies of Film: Thinking Images* (Continuum, 2011), *Understanding Hegelianism* (Acumen, 2007) and co-editor of *Critique Today* (Brill, 2006). He is a member of the editorial board of the journal *Film-Philosophy* and has published numerous articles on the film-philosophy relationship in journals such as *Angelaki, Film-Philosophy, Screening the Past* and *Screen*.

Asuman Suner is Professor of Media and Cultural Studies at the Department of Humanities and Social Sciences at Istanbul Technical University in Turkey. She is the author of *New Turkish Cinema: Belonging, Identity and Memory* (London: I.B. Tauris, 2009) and the co-editor of *Turkishness and its Discontents*, a special issue of *New Perspectives on Turkey* (Fall, 2011). Her articles have appeared in various edited volumes and journals, such as *Screen, Cinema Journal, Sight and Sound, Social Identities* and *Inter-Asia Cultural Studies*. She is currently working on the politics of social memory in recent cinema of Turkey.

Camil Ungureanu is Lecturer in Political Theory at the Universitat Pompeu Fabra, Department of Social and Political Sciences (Barcelona, Spain). He published in quarterlies such as the *Journal of Political Philosophy* and the

European Journal of Political Theory. He co-edited *Law, State and Religion in the New Europe: Conflicts and Dilemmas* (Cambridge University Press, 2012, with Lorenzo Zucca) and *From the Nation-State to the Postnational Constellation: Jürgen Habermas' Theory of Law and Democracy*, vols. I–II (Ashgate, 2011, with Klaus Günther and Christian Joerges).

Catherine Wheatley is Lecturer in Film Studies at King's College London. She is the author of *Michael Haneke's Cinema: The Ethic of the Image* (Berghahn Books, 2009) and a BFI guide to Haneke's *Hidden* (Palgrave MacMillan, 2012). She has also published work on the question of the animal; spectatorship and moral philosophy; and on Kant, Stanley Cavell and Jean-Luc Nancy. Catherine's current research is concerned with what happens to Christianity in postsecular film and philosophy.

Index

Abraham 129–33, 141
Accattone (1961) 70
accident 79, 93, 95, 96–7, 100
Adorno, T. W. 100–2, 105
Agamben, G. 105–6
Alexander Nevsky (1938) 191
Amore e rabbia (1969) 69
Amores Perros (2000) 169
Andersen, J. 92
Andrei Rublev (1966) 33–5, 193
Angelicchio, Luigi 69
Antichrist (2009) 8, 133–8
Arat, Y. 57
Arendt, Hannah 145, 148, 149, 154, 155, 156
atheism 14, 15, 18
Attali, J. 96–7
Aytaç, S. 50, 59

Babel (2006) 166, 169–70
Badiou, Alain 100
banality of evil 145–65
Battleship Potemkin (1925) 190
Bazin, André 2, 11, 24
Benjamin, W. 100, 106
Berger, Peter 12, 23, 25–6
Bergman, Ingmar 1–5, 49
Bezhin Meadow (1937) 191
Bini, Alfredo 64
Binoche, J. 95–6, 99
Biutiful (2010) 8, 166–81; comparison with *La promesse* (1996) 177–8
Blind Chance (1981) 8, 74–82, 85, 88, 107
Blanchot, Maurice 116
Blethyn, B. 102
Bouchareb, R. 91, 102
Bradshaw, Peter 178–9, 185
Braque, Georges 114

Breaking the Waves (1996) 8, 128–33
Bresson, Robert 11–12, 49, 120–3, 124n19

Caché (2005) 204–7
Camera Buff (1979) 108n13
Caputo, John 123n1, 201–2
Cargo 200 (2007) 196
Catholic Church, Catholicism 7, 61, 63, 67, 81, 152
Çayır, K. 57–8
Chaudhuri, S. 59
Christian/Christianity 205, 207, 208–10
Christian Democracy (Italy) 62, 65
Christian–Marxist dialogue 68
Cizre, Ü. 58
Clouds over Borsk (1960) 193
Coates, Paul 5–6, 79
Code inconnu (2000) 91, 96–7, 99, 101, 104–6
Communist Party of Italy 61, 62, 63
Concordat (Lateran Pact) 62, 66
crisis of religion 4–6
Critchley, Simon 3

Dardenne Brothers 8, 177
Davoli, Ninetto 69–70
Dekalog (1989) 102, 104
Deleuze, Gilles 59, 175
Departure of a Grand Old Man (1912) 189
Derrida, Jaques 20, 127, 206–7, 209–10, 215–16
Di Gennaro, Giuseppe 65–7
Diriklik, S. 47
disclosure, aesthetic 170–1
Dostoevsky, Fyodor 33, 120–3, 125n23
Double Life of Véronique, The (1991) 107

224 Index

Dr. Strangelove (1964) 147, 149
Dumont, Bruno 8, 111–25, 199, 207–11
Dyer, Richard 14, 16, 25

Earth/Zemlya (1930) 191
Eichmann, Adolf 145, 148, 149, 154, 155
Eisenstein, Sergei 2, 6, 191
Eliade, Mircea 86–8
Eligür, B. 57
Enthusiasm (1930) 192
ethical experience 170–1, 179
ethics 167–8; cinema as 168–9; cinematic 167, 179
Europeanness/Eurocentrism 7–8, 92, 94, 101, 104, 106, 108, 167, 169, 171–2
Evans, G. 61
Everything Remains for the People (1963) 193
evil (also radical evil) 134, 135–8, 144, 145–5
exploitation 180, 181

face 101–2
faith 2–5, 83; and film 2–4
Fall, the 18–19
Fascism 62, 66, 71
Father Sergius (1917) 189
Feast of St Jorgen, The (1930) 192
film and religion 1–9
film as philosophy 171
finitude 175
Finn, H. 59
Flandres (2006) 119
forgiveness 210–11
Freud, Sigmund 147, 153
Friedan, Betty 149

Generation, A (1955) 108n4
Giotto 114–16
global capitalism 173, 180, 181, 184
globalisation 171–2, 180
Gnostic/Gnosticism 128, 139, 140
God 1–2, 4–6, 8, 11–12, 14, 18–19, 21, 28–9, 32, 34–5, 37, 39–41, 69–71, 75–6, 79, 81, 83, 97, 104, 108, 110–13, 118, 129–32, 133, 136, 139, 209, 210, 211
Godard, Jean-Luc 64
Gospel according to Matthew 64, 67–8
Gospel according to Matthew, The (1964) 7, 67–9, 70–1
Gregoretti, Ugo 64

Habermas, Jürgen 176, 201, 202, 213
Habemus Papam (2011) 7, 11–25, esp. 15–19
Hadewijch (2009) 111, 119, 123
hagiographic 28–9; cinematic 27, 29–41; and criticism of modernity 33, 36, 37, 39; modernization of figure 33, 35; political function of 29–30; religious function of 28, 30–41
Haneke, Michael 8, 91, 96–7, 100–2, 104–6, 108, 199, 204–7
Happiness (1934) 192
Havel, Václav 81
Hawks and Sparrows (1966) 69, 71
Headless Woman, The (208) 91–4, 105, 107
Heidegger, Martin 174
Hilberg, Raul 145, 148, 149, 154, 155, 61n19, 165n106
Hitchcock, Alfred 146, 161n12, 163n66
Holbein, Hans 115–16
Holland, Agnieszka 81
Hollywood 6, 145, 146
Holocaust/Shoah, the 145–65
holy fools 27–41
Holy Girl, The (2004) 95
horror (genre) 145–65
Hors Satan (2011) 125n26
L'Humanité (1999) 119

Ikiru (1952) 171
Inárittu, Alejandro González 8, 166–7
inexpressible 199, 206–7, 210–11
interpretation 77–9
Islam and cinema 7, 15–16, 46–8
Islamic cultural field 44–6, 55
Island, The (2006) 30–2, 195
Israel 149–50
Ivan the Terrible I (1944) 29–30, 192
Ivan the Terrible II (1958) 192

James, William 107
Jankun-Dopartowa, M. 98
Jesus 35, 39, 65, 66–8, 100, 102, 114, 118, 121, 125, 133, 138, 143, 188, 191, 204, 208, 210
Jews, Judaism 68, 126, 145–65, 217
John XXIII (pope) 63, 67, 68
Johnson, Diane 151, 153
Justice and Development Party (AKP) 46

Kafka, Franz 147, 153
Kant, Immanuel 129, 132, 137, 144, 209

Index 225

Kaplanoğlu, S. 7, 44–50, 53–4, 56–7, 59–60
Kasaba, R. 45, 57
Kaufman, Philip 98
Kiarostami, A. 49, 59
Kickasola, Joseph 82–3
Kierkegaard, Soren/Kierkegaardian 100, 105, 127, 129–31, 137, 139, 140, 141
Kieślowski, K. 7–8, 60, 74–90, 91–5, 100, 104, 106–8; and Catholicism 81; on geographical determinism 83–5; as a religious thinker 81–3
Kouyaté, S. 103
Kracauer, S. 102
Kristeva, Julia 3, 8, 110, 115–19, 122
Kubrick, Stanley 8, 145–65
Kurosawa, Akira 171, 183

Lazarus 114, 121–2, 125n23
Levin, Ira 150, 151, 158, 159
Levinas, Emmanuel 91, 101–2, 116–17, 177
Linda, Boguslaw 74
Luna Park (1992) 195
Lungin, Pavel 7, 30–2
Lutheranism 68

Maktav, H. 46, 58
Malick, T. 60
Mamma Roma (1962) 65, 70
Mardin, Ş. 55, 57, 59
Martel, Lucretia 8, 91–5, 105–8
Marxism 61, 68, 85
Medea (1969, Pasolini) 71, 72
melodrama 169–70
Mengele, Josef 158–9, 164n96
messianic 105
Metz, Christian 2
miracle 95, 106
Miracle Worker, The (2000) 193
Mirror, The (1975) 194
moral autonomy 179
moral experience 178
morality 179; limits of 179
moral judgment 179–80
moral melodrama 169–70, 173
Moretti, Nanni 7, 11, 17–18, 21–5
mortality 174–5
Moslem, The (1995) 196
Mulhall, Stephen 171
multiculturalism 176
Mulvey, L. 49
Munch, Edward 80
music (in film) 96–9, 101

Mussolini, Benito 66
mystical 138–9, 199, 206–7, 209

Nancy, Jean-Luc 7, 11–26; *Dis-Enclosure: The Deconstruction of Christianity* 11–13, 19–20, 25–6; *The Inoperative Community* 13, 25; *The Sense of the World* 13, 25
neighbour 8, 93, 96, 99–106
Nietzsche, Friedrich 41, 110
No End (1985) 81
noise 93, 95–9
Nostalghia (1983) 37–9, 107, 194

October (1927) 191
Oedipus Rex (1967, Pasolini) 71
Orthodox Church / Russian Orthodoxy 1, 7, 28, 32, 187, 190, 194, 195, 196

Pareyson, Luigi 14
Pasolini, Pier Paolo 7, 61–72, 137, 138, 210, 216
Passion of the Christ, The (2004) 196
Pius XI (pope) 66
Pius XII (pope) 62, 63
Plate, S. Brent 3–4
Poland 76–8, 81, 83–84
Polanski, Roman 8, 145–65
Pope, the (also Supreme Pontiff) 7, 17–19, 21–2, 26
postsecular/postsecularism 6, 8, 81, 167, 170, 175–6, 202–3; in Caputo 201–2; and cinema 8, 81, 173–4, 178, 199, 204–11, 216–17; in Habermas 201–2
postsecular ethics 8, 167, 181
"priest's film" / "priest's story" 11, 12, 16, 24
Promesse, La (1996) 8, 176–8; comparison with *Biutiful* 8, 177–8
Protestantism 129–31, 133, 139
Psycho (1960) 146, 152, 153, 154, 163n66

Rabbia, La (1963) 63
Reik, T. 99
Renan, Ernest 111
Repentance (1984) 194
responsibility 205–7
Ricotta, La (1962) 64–7, 69, 70
RoGoPaG (1963) 64
Rosemary's Baby (novel, 1967) 150, 151, 158, 162n45

Index

Rosemary's Baby (film, 1968) 8, 145–65
Rossellini, Roberto 64
Russia 8, 186–98; Czarist Russia 8, 187–9; Soviet Russia 8, 189–94; post-Soviet Russia 8, 194–6
Russian/Soviet cinema 29–30, 36, 186–98

sacrifice 39–40, 70–2, 96, 98, 127, 128–33, 138, 206–10
Sacrifice, The (1986) 39–40, 194
Said, Edward 16
Saint Paul 2, 83
Saktanber, A. 47, 58
Salò, or the 120 Days of Sodom (1975) 71
Santner, E. 105–7
Satan 126, 133, 135, 137, 138
Scheherazade 80
secular/secularism 12, 14, 22–5, 126, 204
Shining, The (novel, 1977) 150, 151, 152
Shining, The (film, 1980) 8, 145–65
Short Film About Love, A (1988) 108n13
Smith, M. 179
Sobolewski, Tadeusz 76
Sopralluoghi in Palestina (1965) 64
spiritual experience 5–6, 172–3
Stalin, J. V. 30
Stalker (1979) 35–7, 107, 193
Stok, Danusia 83, 87
Storm Over Asia (1928) 191
Strike (1925) 191
Subini, Tomaso 64
sublime 128–33, 142
Suner, A. 59
Swamp, The (2002) 91–2, 94–5

Tale of the Priest and of His Worker Balda, The (1940) 192
Tarkovsky, Andrei 7, 32–41, 49, 107–8, 138, 143

"terror of history" 84, 86–8
theology of absence 79–81
Three Colours: Blue (1993) 91, 93, 95–8, 105
Three Colours: Red (1994) 91, 93, 95, 100, 104–5, 107–8
Three Colours: White (1994) 92–3
time-image 49–50, 59
Togliatti, Palmiro 62, 63
transcendence 80–1, 131, 138, 139, 144, 178, 207, 208, 209, 211
Trotsky, Leon 190
Twentynine Palms (2003) 119
21 Grams (2003) 169

Unbearable Lightness of Being, The (1988) 98

Vatican 17–19, 21–2
Vatican II (Second Vatican Council) 63, 68
Vertov, Dziga 192
Vie de Jésus, La (1990) 111, 114, 117, 119–20, 122, 207–11
Vie et La Passion du Christ, La (1903) 1, 188
violence 134–5, 136–8, 206–7
Virgin Mary 92, 94, 99, 104, 107–8
Von Trier, Lars 6, 8, 60, 126–39, 142, 140, 143–4

Wajda, A. 108n4
Welles, Orson 64, 65
Wittgenstein, Ludwig 199, 203, 213
world-making 3–4, 7

Yashin, Y. N. 45, 57
Yavuz, H. 57–8

Zigaina, Giuseppe 72
Žižek, S. 60, 74, 80, 91, 101–2